Italian for Comn

SECOND EDITION

Titles of Related Interest

HARVARD, J. and MILETTO, M. M.
Bilingual Guide to Business and Professional Correspondence
(Italian-English)

HARVARD, J. and ARIZA, I. F.
Bilingual Guide to Business and Professional Correspondence
(Spanish-English)

HARVARD, J.
Bilingual Guide to Business and Professional Correspondence
(German-English)

HARVARD, J. and ROSE, F.
Bilingual Guide to Business and Professional Correspondence
(French-English)

COVENEY, J.
International Organization Documents for Translation

REYES OROZCO, C.
Spanish/English: English/Spanish Commercial Dictionary

Italian for Commerce

SECOND EDITION

by

JULIAN POPESCU

PERGAMON PRESS

OXFORD · NEW YORK · BEIJING · FRANKFURT

U.K.	Pergamon Press, Headington Hill Hall, Oxford OX3 0BW, England
U.S.A.	Pergamon Press, Maxwell House, Fairview Park, Elmsford, New York 10523, U.S.A.
PEOPLE'S REPUBLIC OF CHINA	Pergamon Press, Room 4037, Qianmen Hotel, Beijing, People's Republic of China
FEDERAL REPUBLIC OF GERMANY	Pergamon Press, Hammerweg 6, D–6742 Kronberg, Federal Republic of Germany
BRAZIL	Pergamon Editora, Rua Eça de Queiros, 346, CEP 04011, Paraiso, São Paulo, Brazil
AUSTRALIA	Pergamon Press Australia, P.O. Box 544, Potts Point, N.S.W. 2011, Australia
JAPAN	Pergamon Press, 8th Floor, Matsuoka Central Building, 1-7-1 Nishishinjuku, Shinjuku-ku, Tokyo 160, Japan
CANADA	Pergamon Press Canada, Suite No. 271. 253 College Street, Toronto, Ontario, Canada M5T 1R5

Copyright © 1987 J. Popescu

First edition 1968

Second edition 1987

Library of Congress Cataloging in Publication Data
Popescu, Julian.
Italian for commerce.
Bibliography: p.
1. Italian language—Business Italian.
2. Italian language—Text-books for foreign speakers
English. I. Title.
PC1120.C6P67   1987   453'.21'08865   87–10275

British Library Cataloguing in Publication Data
Popescu, Julian
Italian for commerce.—2nd ed.
1. Commerce—Dictionaries   2. English
language—Dictionaries—Italian
3. Commerce—Dictionaries—Italian
4. Italian language—Dictionaries—
English. I. Title
380.1'03'51   HF1002

ISBN 0–08–033956–5 Hardcover
ISBN 0–08–033957–3 Flexicover

Printed in Great Britain by A. Wheaton & Co. Ltd., Exeter

Contents

PREFACE TO THE SECOND EDITION   viii
PREFACE   ix
INTRODUCTION   xi

1. Cardinal and Ordinal Numbers   1

    Cardinal numbers   1
    Ordinal numbers   3
    The calendar   4
    Public holidays in Italy   4
    Exercises   5
    Il contadino e l'asinello   7

2. Small Advertisements   9

    Correspondence   12
    Exercises   13
    L'aeroporto   14

3. Book-keeping   16

    Exercises   18
    Il cane, la mucca e l'oca   20

4. Insurance   21

    Exercises   23
    Correspondence   26
    La scommessa   27

5. Banking   29

    Bills of exchange   30
    Cheques   32

Exercises	36
Il dottore e il cappone	40

6. Carriage of Goods on Land   41
Exercises	45
Il terremoto di Messina	47

7. Merchant Shipping   49
Bills of lading	50
Exercises	54
Sulla spiaggia	56

8. The Sale of Goods   58
Exercises	63
L'agente di cambiavalute	65

9. Companies and the Stock Exchange   66
Companies	66
The Stock Exchange	67
Exercises	68
Pastore Italiano	70

10. Commercial Correspondence   72
Commercial letter writing	73
Some standard beginnings of letters	74
Standard endings of letters	75
Miscellaneous model letters	76

11. Translation Techniques   83
Model translations	83
Abbreviations of commercial terms and organizations	88
Italian weights, measures and sizes	90
Organizations	92
Trade unions	92
Political parties	93
Newspapers	93
Press agency	93

12. Computers: Hardware and Software 94
   Exercises 97

BIBLIOGRAPHY 99

COMMERCIAL VOCABULARY 101

INDEX 165

Preface to the Second Edition

THE Second Edition of *Italian for Commerce* aims at keeping abreast with the evolution of business and technical terminology in an age of rapid and constant change. It contains a new chapter on computer terminology and an entirely new English-Italian commercial vocabulary. Scores of new words have been incorporated in the Italian-English section and new meanings added to some of the old words. The student and technical translator should find the present edition an up-to-date and versatile instrument for grasping the finer distinctions of commercial Italian.

I wish to thank the expert linguist, Mr. Harry Fields, for his kind help with research work.

Suffolk   JULIAN POPESCU
November 1985

Preface

THIS book has been written to assist the student or business man who already knows some ordinary Italian. It covers all the aspects of Italian commerce with lists of terms and expressions as well as exercises and tests. There are anecdotes and selected prose to refresh the reader's memory of ordinary Italian on which commercial Italian is based. Chapters should be read before the exercises are begun, as many of the answers are to be found in different sections of each chapter.

Translation techniques have an entire chapter to themselves because of the growing importance of translations in commerce.

There is a list of abbreviations to be used as a key to the abbreviations in this book. There is also a list of various organizations in Italy and tables of Italian weights, measures and sizes.

The commercial vocabulary at the end of the book is brief and effective. It contains words which are often used in commercial correspondence, documents and literature, including the most up-to-date commercial expressions. The comma is used for decimals as in Italian practice, and the full stop for figures of one thousand or more.

I wish to thank the London representatives of the Credito Italiano and Banco di Roma for their valuable assistance with illustrations and a number of technical points.

Henley-on-Thames   JULIAN POPESCU
July 1966

Introduction

PEOPLE say Italy originally meant "land of cattle", but few people remember the old meaning of the name today, because the country has changed so much during its long history from the foundation of Rome on the shores of the Tiber. The name belonged at first to the centre and south of the peninsula but it spread gradually to the north.

Italy's present territory in rough outline came into being during the second half of the nineteenth century. The movement for Italy's unification, known as the Risorgimento, was successful in 1861. But even today Italy includes two small sovereign states. The Vatican State of about 110 acres in the heart of Rome is ruled by the Pope, head of the Roman Catholic Church, and the Republic of San Marino, perched on rocks about 35 kilometres from Rimini, is 54 square kilometres in size with a population of 15,000. This tiny republic thrives on the tourist trade, its wines and its craftsmen.

Italy herself is a peninsula, shaped like a boot jutting southwards into the Mediterranean Sea.

The Mediterranean is deep, but never cold. The shallow sill stretching from Gibraltar to Ceuta is a barrier against the cold currents of the Atlantic Ocean. This sill and the warmth coming from the homothermal layer of the sea keep the Mediterranean warm all the year round.

Italy is warm too. Her land covers 301,000 square kilometres. She is bordered by a variety of seas—on her east by the Adriatic; on her south by the Ionian Sea, which once carried Roman galleys to Africa; on her west side lies the Tyrrhenian Sea, and to the north-west is the Ligurian Sea and the Italian riviera. Her coast line is dotted with famous resorts and cities steeped in history. Venice and the beaches of Rimini,

Riccione and Cattolica are only a few of the famous on her Adriatic coast; Amalfi and Positano bask in sunshine in the Gulf of Salerno; Sorrento overlooks the wide Bay of Naples; Rapallo and Portofino are on the Riviera di Levante, and San Remo and Alassio on the Riviera di Ponente. Nowadays they are all haunted by the tourist.

There are a number of islands around Italy, some big, some small. In the south there is Sicily, separated from the mainland by the Messina Straits, which are 3 kilometres wide. In the west there is Sardinia, separated from Sicily by 260 kilometres of sea, yet only 160 kilometres from Tunisia. Among the smaller islands is Elba off the Tuscan coast, where Napoleon was in exile. Southwards lies Ponza with modern hotels and cafés, linked by steamer services to Anzio. Capri and Ischia are at the entrance to the Bay of Naples, Capri having been, according to legend, inhabited by mermaids in the days of Ulysses. In the south, in the Tyrrhenian Sea, lie the Lipari islands, including Vulcano and Stromboli, the legendary abode of Aeolus, which has a volcano that is still active.

Italy's northern land frontiers are guarded by the rugged arc of the Alps which separate her from France, Switzerland, Austria and Yugoslavia. The Alps are the highest range of mountains in Europe, with peaks rising about 4,600 metres, the most famous of which are Monte Bianco (Mont Blanc in French), Monte Rosa and the Cervino, better known to us as the Matterhorn. There are some large lakes among the mountains in the central Alps, such as Lake Maggiore, Lake Lugano, Lake Como and Lakes Iseo and Garda.

South of the lakes and the Alps is the Po valley. Thousands of years ago it was under water, a gulf of the Adriatic, but through the centuries the land was lifted by earth movements, and silt was deposited there by rivers and glaciers until it became the great northern plain of Italy. Now there are great cities and industry where once there was water. The river Po, known in ancient times as the Eridanus, flows across the plain from east to west, travelling 665 kilometres before it reaches the fourteen mouths of its delta and, at last, the Adriatic Sea.

The Po's drainage basin has four important regions. The first in the west is called the Piedmont which means simply "at the foot of the mountain", and is a country of mountains, hills and little farms in green valleys. The capital of Piedmont is Turin which stands on the banks of the Po. With more than one million inhabitants, it is the home of Italy's car industry. Electric locomotives, aircraft, machine-tools and rubber products are made there. Industry there is greatly helped by the tremendous force of electricity supplied by the hydro-electric power stations in the Alpine valleys.

East of Piedmont is the region of Lombardy, called after the Longobards, a sixth-century tribe of German invaders. Lombardy is the heart of the Northern Italian Plain with herds of cattle and flocks of sheep and maize, rice, wheat and barley often grown with the help of irrigation. Milan is the capital of Lombardy. It stands near the foothills of the Alps where rails and roads meet, linked to the rest of Europe by the Simplon and St. Gotthard tunnels. It has a population of nearly a million and a half who specialize in light engineering, textiles, machine-tools, rubber, glass and food processing. Milan has the leading stock exchange in Italy and is a centre for banking and insurance.

Piacenza is the middle of the Po valley near the bridge carrying the great Sun Motorway. This motorway links Milan to Piacenza and runs across the Apennines to Florence 245 kilometres further south en route to Rome and Naples. The old city of Piacenza is medieval, with its *duomo* and *campanile*; but it has a modern side too with a food-processing industry, tractor and cycle factories, cement, brick and tile works and an ultra-modern oil refinery.

Cremona is another ancient city standing further down the Po. There silk is woven, musical instruments made, flour milled for the great pasta industry, and agricultural products sold.

The region of Emilia is south of the Po, nearer the Adriatic. Famous for her orchards and brandy, her premier city is Bologna, which is astride the famous Via Emilia and has a population of almost 400,000. It is a centre for Italy's tobacco and leather industry and has machine-tool, electrical and food-processing factories.

The region of Veneto is north of the Po. Though mainly an agricultural region, it has some rapidly expanding light industries at Mantua and Verona. It also has Venice, famous and loved queen of the Adriatic, living on her charm and tourist industry, while nearby is Murano, famous for her glass.

The Italian peninsula proper is divided from the Po valley by the backbone of the Apennine mountains which curve to touch the western end of the Alps. Here between the mountains and the sea is the region of Liguria. The capital of the region, Genoa, is at the head of the gulf of Genoa. A steep mountain ridge surrounds the city on the north and north-west, giving it an appearance of terraces from the sea. Genoa is one of Italy's most important seaports capable of handling the biggest ships afloat, with a population of nearly three-quarters of a million. Its docks serve passenger and cargo traffic for most of northern Italy, including the twin industrial giants of Turin and Milan. Genoa has extensive shipyards and factories, specializing in heavy engineering, electrical machinery and aircraft, as well as flour and textile mills.

Stretching from Liguria down to the toe of Italy are the Apennine mountains. These mountains are mostly clay and sandstone in the north, while in the centre and south they are mostly limestone. Their average height is 2440 metres and their highest peak, the Gran Sasso (Big Stone), is 2911 metres high.

The Apennines are a serious and continuous barrier between the two sides of the peninsula restricting road and rail communication between the coasts. The roads across the Apennines run through deep gorges and go over passes such as the Abetone, Futa, Montereale and Rio Nero. The soil on the Apennines is mostly poor, and fir and pine trees grow on its upper reaches, thin scrub and pastures further down, while vines and olive, chestnut and almond trees all grow among the foothills.

Nearly all the rivers of the Italian peninsula are short. They start as mountain streams, rushing madly through limestone gorges, but they dwindle quickly, becoming little more than a trickle of water in hot weather, often losing themselves among sand and pebbles before ever reaching the sea. But there are exceptions: the Arno river, for instance, flows through Florence and Pisa and on into the Ligurian Sea north of Leghorn. And there is the Tiber, or Tevere, which rises in the Emilian Apennines, flows south through Rome and joins the Tyrrhenian Sea at Ostia.

The outstanding regions of central Italy are Tuscany in the north-west, with its capital Florence, and Latium further south, with Rome as its capital.

Florence, in the valley of the Arno, is reached by several routes across the Apennines from the Northern Plain. The city is of Etruscan origin and grew prosperous by trade and banking in the Middle Ages. With her monumental buildings and art galleries, Florence represents the greatness of Italian Renaissance more than any other town in Italy. She is still an artistic centre for the manufacture of luxury goods such as artistic furniture, porcelain, gold and silver trinkets, musical instruments and fancy leather and straw goods. Modern industries are represented by diesel engineering, optical instruments, and food and tobacco factories, employing a good proportion of her 400,000 inhabitants.

Tuscany's sea outlet is Leghorn, or Livorno, with its artificial harbour and good docks handling a busy traffic in industrial goods. Leghorn's population of 160,000 specializes in light engineering, oil refining, and chemicals and flour milling.

Italy's capital, Rome, dominates the centre of the Mediterranean. According to legend, Rome was built by Romulus in 753 B.C. on the Palatine Hill, where the crossing of the river Tiber was made easy by the Isola Tiberina. The first Roman city was known as the Roma Quadrata. Later on Rome became known as the "City of the Seven Hills" and over the centuries she expanded along the banks of the Tiber.

Rome's buildings and monuments are world famous which alone accounts for the outstanding importance of the tourist industry. The Vatican is within her walls but since becoming the capital of modern Italy, administrative buildings have increased and new suburbs have appeared, to house the growing population of nearly two million. The modern side of Rome is represented by commerce and industry and there are many banking houses, a stock exchange, printing works and film studios. Other important industries are light engineering, food processing, chemicals, textiles and shoes.

West of the Apennines is Vesuvius, the centre of a volcanic area and the only active volcano on the mainland of Europe. At the foot of Vesuvius and on the famous Bay of Naples, is the largest city of southern Italy and one of the most beautiful. This is Naples, which has a population of well over 1,000,000, specializing in heavy engineering, textiles and food processing.

The ruins of Pompeii and Herculanum are close by and there

you can see what remained after the eruption of Vesuvius in A.D. 79.

South of Naples the land is varied. Some is agricultural: chestnut and almond trees and vines grow in the hills, olive groves and peach orchards in the valleys, and some wheat and maize are grown also, for local consumption. Where the land is mountainous and arid, macchia or brushwood grows and there is still poverty.

Facing Calabria, Italy's most southern region, is the island of Sicily, 25,460 square kilometres in size. Along the northern side of Sicily there are mountains which drop steeply to the sea, leaving only a narrow coastal plain. On the east side there is the plain of Catania, the largest plain in Sicily, and here too there is Mount Etna which rises 3,263 metres into a volcanic cone which is snow-capped in winter. Southern and western Sicily have yellow-tinted limestone uplands cut by river gorges. Many of the hills are terraced and there the peasants grow vines and citrus fruits, olives and vegetables and the vineyards near Marsala produce the famous Marsala wine.

Sicily's capital city, Palermo, was founded by the Phoenicians. It has many magnificent medieval buildings, for example the church and cloisters of San Giovanni. The cathedral, which was built in 1174, is famous for its glass mosaics. The city has more than half a million inhabitants and a thriving food-processing industry.

Siracusa, on the south-east coast, was founded by the Greeks in 743 B.C. Cut out of solid rock, its threatre is still in a good state of preservation. Other important towns in Sicily are Agrigento, also of Greek origin, Ragusa, Catania and Messina overlooking the Messina Straits. An increasing number of tourists are visiting Sicily, attracted by her climate, her monuments and magnificent scenery, but there is still poverty to be found for those who care to look.

Italy's other large island, Sardinia, has much savage beauty. Her mountains are ranged against a blue sky which has always the same softness of hue and shade. There are many old churches and *nuraghi* or old stone towers. Farming is still simple, with little mechanization and irrigation is necessary on the plains. The farmers grow hard wheat, almonds and hazel nuts, and they sell olive oil and wine.

Sardinia's capital, Cagliari, has a population of over 150,000. It has a fine harbour and is a railway centre for the island.

The Italians, like other Europeans, are a mixed race with strong Latin roots. The Italic tribes who lived in the Apennine valleys at first resisted the power of Rome but in time they were overwhelmed and absorbed by the Eternal City. The great Latin family was born of Umbri, Brutii and Sabini, of Marsi and Lucani who were united with the people of Latium and Campania. To these were added Greeks and Siculi in the south, Venetians, Gauls and Goths in the north. These peoples spoke a vulgar Latin which in time gave way to imperial Latin. But this was not to last, for imperial Latin was in its turn influenced by dialects, which preceded the process of Romanization. The barbarian invasion and Byzantine influence caused the break-up of the linguistic unity of imperial Latin, leaving it in fragments. Regional dialects appeared and later found their first authoritative expression in the Italian of Dante's works.

Today Italians, like their ancestors, prefer to live in towns. Hamlets and isolated houses are rare, particularly in the south. Towns and villages are often strategically placed on hill tops, or on the lower reaches of mountains or dominating a valley. Italians are often outside or sitting on their doorsteps and they will even eat outside, taking their tables and chairs with them. On a summer evening they promenade up and down the main street or *corso*, drinking in the wine shops or cafés, or simply sitting under striped umbrellas watching the world go by. In the south the people are still essentially agricultural. Tradition, custom and superstition still have an almost feudal hold on them. The women are hardly emancipated and are not expected to work in factories. One has to be careful not to offend local customs.

In the north of Italy life is more modern. Here there is a great mercantile and industrial tradition. History tells us that the towns and cities of the Po valley and Mediterranean seaboard had great wealth and influence in the Middle Ages. The merchants of Genoa, Leghorn, Pisa, Florence, Milan and Venice were known all over Europe for the spices, silks and jewellery which they carried in their argosies. Double-entry book-keeping was first used by Venetian counting houses. Insurance, though first practised by Byzantium, was later taken over and improved by Italian firms. The word bank has come from the Italian *banco* which was the counter on which money-lenders and gold- and silver-smiths used to count money.

Today Italy exports a great many agricultural and manufactured goods such as citrus fruit, fresh fruit, vegetables, rice, dairy products, tinned food, woollens, motor vehicles, refined petroleum products, machine tools and steel products. She exports wines from Piedmont, Tuscany and Sicily while olive oil is handled by Genoa, Trieste, Lucca and Bari. Murano exports glass wares, Florence straw articles. There is marble from Carrara which is sent to many countries, and sulphur from Sicily. There are the things the tourists take home in thousands— leather goods, ceramics, lace and embroidery, silk and clothes, silver objects, and all kinds of souvenirs. They are all a silent, unsponsored advertisement for Italy, part of her increasingly important tourist trade.

Regions and their capital cities: Piedmont (Turin); Val d'Aosta (Aosta); Lombardy (Milan); Trentino-Alto Adige (Trento); Veneto (Venice); Friuli-Venezia Giulia (Trieste); Liguria (Genoa); Emilia-Romagna (Bologna); Marche (Ancona); Tuscany (Florence); Umbria (Perugia); Latium (Rome); Abruzzi (L'Aquila); Molise (Campobasso); Campania (Naples); Puglia (Bari); Basilicata (Potenza); Calabria (Reggio); Sicily (Palermo); Sardinia (Cagliari).

Main ports: Genoa, Savona, Imperia, La Spezia, Leghorn, Civitàvecchia, Naples, Trieste, Venice, Ancona, Pescara, Bari, Brindisi, Taranto, Reggio Calabria, Palermo, Messina, Catania, Augusta, Siracusa and Cagliari.

Cities in order of importance: Rome, Milan, Naples, Turin, Genoa, Palermo, Florence, Bologna, Catania, Venice, Bari, Messina, Trieste, Verona, Taranto, Padua, Cagliari, Leghorn, Brescia, Reggio Calabria.

CHAPTER 1

Cardinal and Ordinal Numbers

KNOWLEDGE of numbers is basically useful for commerce, and one of the easiest tasks in any language is to learn how to count. Numbers, whether cardinal or ordinal, follow each other with a certain rhythm of speech and their memorizing should present no difficulty.

Cardinal Numbers

The cardinal or simple numbers are:

1	uno, una	18	diciotto	101	centouno
2	due	19	diciannove	102	centodue,
3	tre	20	venti		etc.
4	quattro	21	ventuno	200	duecento
5	cinque	22	ventidue	300	trecento
6	sei	23	ventitre, etc.	400	quattro-
7	sette	30	trenta		cento,
8	otto	31	trentuno		etc.
9	nove	32	trentadue, etc.	1.000	mille
10	dieci	38	trentotto, etc.	1.100	mille-
11	undici	40	quaranta		cento,
12	dodici	50	cinquanta		etc.
13	tredici	60	sessanta	2.000	duemila
14	quattordici	70	settanta	3.000	tremila
15	quindici	80	ottanta	100.000	centomila
16	sedici	90	novanta	1.000.000	un milione
17	diciassette	100	cento		

As can be seen from the above table, the final vowel is omitted (before *uno* and *otto*) from *venti*, *trenta*, etc., and this continues up to *cento*, when it is retained.

The English way of saying "one hundred" and "one thousand" are translated into Italian simply as *cento* and *mille*, since they do not take

1

any article. Although "one thousand" is *mille*, two thousand is *duemila* because the plural of *mille* is *mila*.

Cardinal numbers are used for expressing the days of the month, with the exception of the first day. Thus "the tenth of March" is: *il dieci marzo*.

Age, dates and time of the day are also expressed in cardinal numbers.

Examples

> *Io ho vent' anni.* I am twenty years old.
>
> *Sono nato il quattro luglio.* I was born on July the fourth.
>
> *Il suo compleanno è l'otto ottobre.* His birthday is on October the eighth.

The question *Che ora è?* (What is the time?) is answered by: *È l'una.* It is one o'clock. *Sono le due.* It is two o'clock. *Sono le sette e un quarto.* It is a quarter past seven. *Sono le otto e mezzo.* It is half past eight. *Sono le nove meno un quarto.* It is a quarter to nine. *Sono le dieci e cinque.* It is five past ten. *Sono le undici meno venti.* It is twenty to eleven.

The question *A che ora?* (At what time?) is answered by: *All'una.* At one o'clock. *Alle tre.* At three o'clock. *A mezzogiorno.* At noon.

A few words derived from ordinal numbers have idiomatic meanings such as *decina, quindicina, trentina.*

Examples

> *Ci sono una decina di uomini sulla piazza.* There are about ten people in the square.
>
> *Ho trascorso a Roma una quindicina di giorni.* I spent a fortnight in Rome.
>
> *Ho visto una trentina di navi nel porto.* I saw about thirty ships in the harbour.

Un paio is used for a pair and *paia* for pairs:

Examples

Un paio di scarpe. A pair of shoes. *Due paia di guanti.* Two pairs of gloves.

Ordinal Numbers

The ordinal numbers which show position in a series of sequence are:

primo, first
secondo, second
terzo, third
quarto, fourth
quinto, fifth
sesto, sixth
settimo, seventh
ottavo, eighth
nono, ninth
decimo, tenth
undicesimo, eleventh
dodicesimo, twelfth

tredicesimo, thirteenth
quattordicesimo, fourteenth
quindicesimo, fifteenth
sedicesimo, sixteenth
diciassettesimo, seventeenth
diciottesimo, eighteenth
diciannovesimo, nineteenth
ventesimo, twentieth, etc.
trentesimo, thirtieth
quarantesimo, fortieth, etc.
centesimo, hundredth
millesimo, thousandth

Il primo is used for the first day of the month. Thus February the first is *il primo febbraio.*

From 11th upwards ordinal numbers are formed by omitting the final vowel and adding *-esimo.*

Ordinal numbers agree in gender and number.

Examples

Il primo carnevale, the first carnival; *la prima ragazza*, the first girl; *i primi cittadini*, the first citizens; *le prime carrozze*, the first carriages.

Ordinal numbers are used to show order of succession of kings and queens: *Giorgio Quarto*, George IV; *Elisabetta Seconda*, Elizabeth II.

Cardinal numbers are used to express the numerator of fractions while ordinal numbers are used for the denominator.

Examples

¼, un quarto; ¾, tre quarti; ⅝, cinque ottavi; ⅞, sette ottavi; ⁷⁄₁₀, sette decimi.

The Calendar

Italy, like most countries of the world, uses the *calendario gregoriano* established by Pope Gregory XIII in 1582.

The months of the year are: *gennaio*, January; *febbraio*, February; *marzo*, March; *aprile*, April; *maggio*, May; *giugno*, June; *luglio*, July; *agosto*, August; *settembre*, September; *ottobre*, October; *novembre*, November; *dicembre*, December.

The days of the week are: *lunedì*, Monday; *martedì*, Tuesday; *mercoledì*, Wednesday; *giovedì*, Thursday; *venerdì*, Friday; *sabato*, Saturday; *domenica*, Sunday.

Periods of the day are: *mattina*, morning; *mezzogiorno*, noon; *pomeriggio* or *dopopranzo*, afternoon; *sera*, evening; *notte*, night; *mezzanotte*, midnight.

Days are called: *l'altroieri*, the day before yesterday; *ieri*, yesterday; *oggi*, today; *domani*, tomorrow; *dopodomani*, the day after tomorrow.

Public Holidays in Italy

Most shops and public offices are closed on Sundays and on bank holidays. A bank holiday is called *festa nazionale*. The following *feste nazionali* are observed in Italy:

Il giorno di Capodanno—New Year's Day	1st January
Epifania—Epiphany	6th January
Il giorno di San Giuseppe—St. Joseph	19th March
Lunedì di Pasqua—Easter Monday	date variable
Festa della liberazione—Liberation Day	25th April
Primo Maggio or *Festa del Lavoro*—May Day	1st May

Il giorno dell' Ascensione—Ascension Day   date variable
Il giorno del Corpus Domini   date variable
Festa della Repubblica—Republic Day   2nd June
Santi Pietro e Paolo—St. Peter and Paul   29th June
La festa dell' Assunzione or *Ferragosto*—Feast
  of the Assumption   15th August
La Festa di Ogni Santi—All Saints Day   1st November
Anniversario della Vittoria—Victory Day   4th November
Festa dell' Immacolata Concezione—Feast of
  the Immaculate Conception   8th December
Il giorno di Natale—Christmas Day   25th December
Il giorno di Santo Stefano—Boxing Day   26th December

Vocabulary I

anno, year	*scendere*, to get down
stagione, season	*fermata*, bus stop
mese, month	*mi rincresce*, I regret
settimana, week	*avere un ritardo*, to be late
giorno, day	*tasca*, pocket
compiere, to complete	*occupato*, busy
compleanno, birthday	*ecco*, here is
parere, to appear	*ritornare*, to return
comprare, to buy	*previsione*, forecast
bottone, button	*ritardo*, delay
appuntamento, appointment	*maltempo*, bad weather
promesso, promised	*spettacolo*, show
filobus, trolley bus	*fa*, ago

Exercises

I. Read in Italian the following numbers:
4; 9; 11; 16; 23; 36; 45; 68; 101; 234; 768; 1532; 2560; $\frac{1}{8}$; $\frac{3}{8}$; $\frac{3}{4}$; 5th; 10th; 20th; 100th; 1000th.

II. Translate into English:

Un anno ha quattro stagioni, dodici mesi e cinquantadue settimane. Un mese ha poco più di quattro settimane. Una settimana ha sette giorni. Il giorno in cui si compiono gli anni si chiama compleanno. Il compleanno di mio fratello è il cinque aprile.

Mi pare che il treno per Roma parta alle tre meno venti. Da venti minuti sono qui, ed ancora non è arrivato il mio amico. Ho un appuntamento per le nove precise. Oggi le previsioni del tempo non sono buone. Perchè non siete venuti alle cinque come avete promesso? Mancano dieci minuti alle sei. Da quando mi aspetta Lei? Dalle due in punto. Mi rincresce che abbia dovuto aspettare tanto tempo ma il treno ha avuto un ritardo di un'ora circa a causa del maltempo. Abbiamo comprato due paia di scarpe e una decina di bottoni. Per andare al teatro prendete il filobus e scendete alla quarta fermata. Lo spettacolo è incominciato mezz'ora fa.

III. Translate into Italian:

Yesterday we started to learn Italian. Last year we went to Italy. What is the time now please? I wonder whether it is eight o'clock? I go to the office at half past eight. I have only 50 lire in my pocket. How many have you got? What is the rate of exchange? Here is a pair of shoes, a pair of gloves and a packet of 20 cigarettes. I returned home just before midnight. On Tuesday I am very busy. Come and see me on Wednesday. How much is a pair of socks *(calzini)*? Has Andrea arrived from Rome? No, he hasn't arrived yet. He will arrive tomorrow.

IV. Write brief answers in Italian to the following questions:

1. Le previsioni del tempo sono buone oggi?
2. Che ora è, per favore?
3. A che ora parte per l'ufficio?
4. Qual è il Suo numero di telefono?
5. Quando è il Suo compleanno?
6. Qual è il terzo mese dell' anno?
7. Quando si celebra la festa della Repubblica?
8. Cos' è il Ferragosto?
9. Quali feste nazionali si celebrano in Italia?
10. Come si chiamano i giorni della settimana?
11. Quanti abitanti ha Torino?
12. Qual è il cambio di 100 lire italiane?

13. Qual è il prezzo di un pacchetto di 20 sigarette?
14. Quanto costa un paio di scarpe?

Vocabulary II

contadino, peasant	*povero*, poor
figlio, son	*dare ascolto*, to heed
asinello, ass foal	*ugualmente*, equally
guarda!, look!	*groppone*, croup
sciocco, silly	*soddisfare*, to satisfy
allora, then	*spalla*, back
proseguire, to continue	*pazzo*, mad
a cavallo, mounted	*ridere*, to laugh
salire a cavallo, to mount	*piacere*, to like

Il Contadino e l'Asinello

Un contadino ed il suo figlio andavano al mercato e dietro a loro veniva l'asinello.

La gente che li vedeva, diceva, "Oh, guarda che sciocchi. Hanno l'asino e vanno a piedi!"

Il contadino pose allora il figlio sull'asino e così proseguirono il cammino.

Ma la gente che l'incontrava, diceva: "Oh, guarda! Il ragazzo a cavallo e il povero padre a piedi! Bell'amore di figlio!"

Il padre pose allora giù il ragazzo e salì a cavallo. Ma la gente: "Oh, guarda, guarda! Il padre che è un uomo va a cavallo e quel povero bambino a piedi! Bel cuore di padre!"

E il contadino, per dare ascolto alla gente, prese il figlio con sè, sull'asinello. Ma ugualmente la gente non taceva: "Povero asinello, con due uomini sul groppone! Che barbarie!"

Il povero uomo, che aveva una pazienza da santo e voleva soddisfare tutti, pensò che non gli rimaneva più che una soluzione e disse: "Figlio mio, vedi bene che la gente ci critica. Prendiamo noi questo povero asinello sulle spalle!"

E così fecero. Ed ecco che la gente rideva, rideva: "Oh, guarda quei pazzi! Portano l'asino sulle spalle!"

Allor finalmente il contadino ed il figlio si convinsero che se vuoi dare ascolto alla gente perdi tempo e pazienza.

E proseguirono il cammino come meglio piaceva a loro.

BY CARLO CATTANEO

A Proverb

Dove manca natura, arte procura.

CHAPTER 2

Small Advertisements

ADVERTISING is the process of disseminating information for commercial purposes. There are different forms of advertising and of advertising media such as the press, shop windows, radio and television, hoardings. Small advertisements or *piccola publicità* are one of the most popular forms of advertising in shop windows, newspapers, trade and technical journals, magazines and periodicals. The advertisements or *inserzione* or *annunzio* are published in large numbers in newspapers on the middle pages, ranging from houses, furniture and jewellery for sale or wanted, to jobs and marriage offers. The cost of the newspaper advertisements varies from 50 to 150 lire per word.

An Italian advertisement is written as if it were a telegram in order to save cost. The advertisements are grouped in the columns of the *piccola pubblicità* under the following main headings:

Offerte impiego. Situations vacant (white collar).
Offerte lavoro. Situations vacant (manual labour).
Domande impiego. Situations wanted (white collar).
Domande lavoro. Situations wanted (manual labour).
Offerte affitto camere. Rooms to let.
Domande affitto camere. Rooms wanted.
Vendite case. Houses for sale.
Vendite terreni. Building plots for sale.
Occasioni. Bargains.
Commerciali. Miscellaneous.
Auto, cicli. Cars, motor-cycles.
Mobili. Furniture.
Matrimoniali. Marriage offers.

9

Most advertisements will be found to start with a word like *cerco*, I want, or *cerchiamo*, we want. When an advertisement starts with *compero*, I buy, or *vendo*, I sell, it is assumed that the words mean, "I offer to buy" or "I offer to sell". Frequent use is made in advertisements of the infinitive tense of verbs which is an alternative form of the imperative. If you want to say, "ring up" or "write to", you use the infinitive: *telefonare* or *scrivere a*.

Vocabulary I

abbisognaci, we want
abbisognami, I want
acquisto, I (offer to) buy
assumo, I (offer to) employ
cerco, I want
cercasi, wanted (singular—from *si cerca*)
cercansi, wanted (plural—from *si cercano*)
compero or *compro*, I (offer to) buy
consegne rapide, quick delivery (plural)
contanti, cash
indirizzare, address to
informazioni telefonando al . . ., ring up for information to . . .

ottima retribuzione, excellent remuneration
ottime condizioni, in excellent condition
ottimo stato, in excellent condition
perito, expert
pratico, experienced
precisare, specify
pretese, wage or salary required
scrivere a, write to
sotto costo, below cost
telefonare, ring up
vendo, I sell
vendiamo, we sell
vendesi, for sale (singular)
vendonsi, for sale (plural)

The "staff finder" notices usually start with a word designating trade, profession or qualification, such as:

apprendista, apprentice
autista, driver
camionista, lorry driver
capomastro, clerk of works
cassiere, cashier
chimico, chemical scientist
commesso, shop assistant
commissionario, commission agent
computista, book-keeper
contabile, accountant
custode, watchman
dattilografa, typist
direttore, manager
domestica, maidservant

fattorino, messenger, delivery man
fatturista, invoice clerk
funzionario bancario, bank clerk
gerente, manager, agent
impiegato, clerk
laureato, graduate
magazziniere, storekeeper
piazzista, salesman
portiere, doorkeeper
ragioniere, accountant
segretaria, secretary
stenodattilografa, shorthand typist
telefonista, telephone operator

When the age is given of either a male or a female person in a notice, it is usual to write the age figure followed by the suffix *-enne*, thus: *18enne*, eighteen years old; *21enne*, twenty-one years old; *35enne*, thirty-five years old; *47enne*; forty-seven years old.

Examples

Staff-finder notices dealing with situations vacant and wanted are phrased as follows:

1. Cassiere bancario trentenne pratico divisa estera e cambiali, dinamica presenza offresi; scopo miglioramento. Scrivere a . . .

Banking cashier, thirty years old, experienced in foreign currency and bills of exchange, full of drive, offers his services in order to better himself. Write to . . .

2. Giovane signora pratica lavori ufficio offresi mattinata. Telefonare . . .

Young lady, experienced in office work, offers to work mornings. Ring up . . .

3. Cercasi domestica tutto fare escluso (o incluso) cucina. Referenze controllabili. Telefonare . . . dalle ore 16 alle ore 18.

Maidservant wanted for all work excluding (or including) cooking. Genuine references. Ring up . . . from 16.00 hours to 18.00 hours.

Advertisements dealing with bargains:

1. Frigorifero, macchina da scrivere famiglia traslocando vendo. Telefonare . . .

Frigidaire, typewriter for sale owing to family moving. Ring up . . .

2. A metà valore vendo macchina da cucire nuovissima. Telefonare mattinata . . .

Brand new sewing machine for sale at half price. Ring up mornings . . .

3. Acquisto francobolli. Tutto pagamento immediato. Scrivere . . .
Stamps bought for immediate cash. Write . . .

4. Acquistiamo argenteria, oro, brillanti, massimo prezzo. Telefonare . . . o scrivere . . .

IFC-C

We buy silver, gold, diamonds at highest prices. Ring up . . . or write . . .

The following advertisements deal with houses to let or for sale or accommodation wanted:

1. Vendesi villa antica, termosifone, ampio terrazzo, garage 20 minuti auto da Torino, altitudine 400 m . . .
Old villa for sale, central heating, spacious terrace, garage, 20 minutes by car from Turin at a height of 400 m . . . (Address follows.)

2. Abbiamo camere mobilitate, ingressi scala—riservatezza. Telefonare . . .
We have furnished rooms (to let), entrance by staircase—complete privacy. Ring up . . .

3. Centralissima affittasi camera mobilitata con pensione—riservatezza, ambiente signorile. Telefonare . . .
Very central, furnished room with board, to let—complete privacy, good-class family. Ring up . . .

4. Cercasi camera d'affittare—centro, ambiente signorile. Telefonare . . .
Room wanted—central, good-class family. Ring up . . .

5. Cercasi affitto villino dieci camere circa raggio 20 km. Roma. Scrivere a . . .
Wanted small villa to rent, ten rooms, within about 20 km. radius of Rome. Write to . . .

Correspondence

The following letter to the editor of an Italian newspaper requests insertion of an advertisement. The letter concludes by asking for a reply by return of post.

Address . . .
Date . . .

Vogliate inserire sulla pagina della Vostra piccola pubblicità il seguente avviso:

(Here follows text of the advertisement.)

Attendo di conoscere a stretto giro di posta la tariffa d'inserzione.

Distinti saluti.

(Signature)

If the cost of inserting the advertisement is, for instance, L. 120.000, the last sentence may be replaced by the following:

Allego alla presente l'assegno bancario (*or* vaglia postale) per L. 120.000, tariffa d'inserzione.

Vocabulary II

giornata, day-time
oppure, or else
presenza, appearance, aspect
macchina (da) cucire, sewing machine
lavoro, work
patente, licence

veloce, fast
società petrolifera, oil company
volenteroso, eager
campo, field
essaminare, to consider, to examine
proprio, own
macchina da scrivere, typewriter

Exercises

I. Translate into English:

Dattilografa mezza giornata cercasi. Offresi autista, camionista oppure fattorino, bella presenza. Cameriera cerca famiglia signorile. Signorina pratica macchina cucire—lavori facili. Fattorino patente auto massimo 25enne importante società cerca. Ditta commerciale cerca dattilografa veloce, pratica lavori ufficio. Società petrolifera cerca giovane volenteroso. Traduttore inglese, francese offresi mezza giornata. Chimico laureato esperienza campo documentazione tecnica, esaminerebbe eventuali offerte. Azienda industriale cerca giovane laureato per proprio ufficio legale.

Appartamento elegantemente mobilitato affitasi. Villa con giardino, dieci camere, garage cerco. Signora vende Fiat Seicento perfettisima. Cerco appartamento affitto. Vendo televisore nuovissimo. Acquisto subito contanti da privato macchina da scrivere nuova. Apparecchio fotografico vendesi sotto costo.

II. Translate into Italian.

1. Typist, experienced in office work, offers to work evenings.
2. Driver wanted, reliable references, ring up.
3. Silver wanted, best prices paid, write to . . .
4. Villa for sale, twelve rooms, central heating, garage, 30 minutes by car from Rome. Ring up . . .
5. German, French translator offers to work half-days.
6. Important firm wants chemistry graduate.
7. Furnished room with board wanted, central. Ring up mornings
   . . .
8. Furnished rooms to let, good-class district.

III. Write brief answers in Italian to the following questions:

1. Cerca un appartamento mobiliato in affitto?
2. A che prezzo vuol vendere la Sua automobile?
3. Qual è il Suo indirizzo?
4. La Sua salute è in ottimo stato?
5. È pratico di ragioneria?
6. Presso quale ditta è impiegato?
7. Le piacerebbe lavorare mezza giornata?
8. Qual è la Sua qualifica?
9. Esaminerebbe un'offerta d'impiego?
10. Vuol acquistare una macchina da scrivere?

Vocabulary III

soffiare, to blow	*orologio*, clock
ingresso, entrance	*rassicurante*, reassuring
portiere, doorkeeper	*pista*, runway
in fretta, in a hurry	*voltarsi*, to turn round
rammarico, regret	*seguire*, to follow
aereo, plane	cenno, sign

L'Aeroporto

Luigi e Renzo sono arrivati all'aeroporto. Il vento soffia con forza e sventola le bandiere multicolori e gli ornamenti di carta colorata davanti alla sala d'ingresso. Luigi domanda al portiere:

—"Scusi, a che ora parte l'aereo per Nuova York, per favore?"

—"Alle tre meno un quarto, signore" risponde colui.

Luigi guarda in fretta l'orologio dorato sul frontispizio dell' edifizio e dice con rammarico:

—"Allora, l'aereo è partito giacchè sono le tre. Per carità cosa faremo adesso?"

—"Non si tormenti, signore", risponde in tono rassicurante il portiere "ci scusi perchè si sta riparando l'orologio. Sono le due e mezzo in punto. Guardi, l'aereo è sulla pista."

Luigi lo ringraziò e voltatosi a Renzo gli fa cenno di seguirlo.

A Proverb

Chia fa da sè fa per tre.

CHAPTER 3

Book-keeping

BOOK-KEEPING is called *tenere i conti*, which literally means to keep accounts. There are various methods of book-keeping, the most important of which are the single-entry and double-entry methods. Double-entry book-keeping was invented in the mercantile cities of northern Italy in the Middle Ages whence it spread to the world of commerce. The essence of double-entry book-keeping is that any posting made to the debit of one account must be also made to the credit of another account. In this way the sum total of all debits must balance the sum total of all credits in the two sets of accounts.

The Italian trader known as *commerciante* or *imprenditore commerciale* is obliged by law to keep a journal, an inventory list and a letter book. Keeping a ledger and other books like the cash register is optional. The trader's books or *libri sociali* must be kept in order of date, without blank spaces or spaces between lines, without marginal notes or erasures. When it is necessary to cross out a word or figure, the crossed out word or figure must remain legible. Compliance with these requirements is important because if the trader becomes insolvent but proves that he has kept the requisite books in order, he is entitled to a preventive composition or *concordato preventivo* with his creditors and thus avoids bankruptcy proceedings. Moreover, a bankrupt trader is liable to be sent to prison.

The *libri sociali* of any commercial concern must make the utmost possible use of original entries and they must be so devised that errors are prevented and localized. Furthermore, the various books must be suitably divided for the convenience of the counting house staff.

The accounting operation or *rilevazione contabile* shows whether an account receives or yields a benefit. The account of *conto* has two sides: the debit side or *voce dare* and the credit side or *voce avere*. An account is closed when the balance or *saldo* is determined and entered in the appropriate side of the account.

The journal or *giornale* contains details of all transactions in chronological order together with references to the pages of the ledger or account numbers in which the transactions are to be entered.

The ledger or *mastro* is the book in which the trader's transactions are recorded in a classified and permanent form. Popular in Italy is the *Giornal-Mastro*. Each page of the *Giornal-Mastro* contains the corresponding entries of both journal and ledger.

The purpose of a trial balance or *bilancio di verificazione* is to ascertain whether the sum total of the debit and credit sides in the ledger tallies with the sum total of the entries in the journal.

In Italian book-keeping practice, the right side of the profit and loss account is the credit side while the left side is the debit side. In the balance sheet, therefore, the assets or *l'attivo* are on the left side and the liabilities or *il passivo* on the right side, as can be seen from the following examples:

Example I

Conto perdite e profitti al 31 dicembre . . .

Dare	Lire	Avere	Lire
Spese	70.000.000	Introiti lordi	
Imposte e tasse	10.000.000	di esercizio	100.000.000
Utile lordo di			
esercizio	20.000.000		
	100.000.000		100.000.000

Example II

Bilancio al 31 dicembre . . .

Attivo	Lire	Passivo	Lire
Impianti, macchinari,		Capitale sociale	8.000.000
immobili e lavori		Riserva legale	2.000.000
in corso	20.000.000	Fondo ammortamento	4.000.000
Automezzi	5.000.000	Fornitori	40.000.000
Magazzini	4.000.000	Creditori	80.000.000
Titoli azionari	2.000.000	Residuo utile	
Disponibilità—cassa		esercizio 59	12.000.000
e banche	40.000.000	Utile lordo d'esercizio	20.000.000
Debitori	50.000.000		
Fornitori	45.000.000		
	166.000.000		166.000.000

Vocabulary I

ammortamento, amortization
attivo, assets
avere, credit side
azienda, firm
azione, share, stock
azionista, shareholder
bancarotta, bankruptcy
bilancio, balance-sheet
buono del tesoro, treasury bill
capitale versato, paid up capital
cassa, cash
cassiere, cashier
contabile, accountant
conto, account
conto perdite e profitti, loss and profit account
copialettere, letter-book
dossiere, file
esercizio, period, year
fondo ammortamento, amortization fund
fornitore, contractor, purveyor
gerente, manager
gestione, management
giornale, journal
giornal-mastro, journal-ledger
importo, amount

imposta, tax
introiti, receipts
libro degli inventari, inventory list
libro di riferenza, letter register
magazzini, stock-in-trade
mastro, ledger
merce, goods
netto ricavo, net proceeds
obbligazione, debenture, bond
partita doppia, double entry
partita semplice, single entry
passivo, debit-side
pratiche, file
provento, income
quota, rate
quota di interesse, interest rate
ripartizione, distribution
saldo, balance
scritturazione, posting, writing-up
spese, expenses
stanziamento, appropriation
titoli di stato, gilt edged
utile, profit
utile lordo, gross profit
utile lordo di esercizio, gross profit for the year
utile netto, net profit

Exercises

I. Translate into English:

Il libro giornale, il libro degli inventari ed il copialettere sono i libri obbligatori del commerciante italiano. I libri commerciali devono essere tenuti per ordini di data senza alcuno spazio in bianco e senza abrasioni. Tutte le operazioni del commerciante sono esposte nel libro giornale e poi riportate nel libro mastro. Il conto è diviso in due sezioni, una per la voce dare ed una per la voce avere. Il saldo è la differenza fra il dare e l'avere. Il saldo si determina quando si chiude il conto.

La società a responsabilità limitata deve rispondere per le obbligazioni sociali solo col capitale sociale. I soci di un'azienda hanno diritto agli utili, al voto e alla ispezione dei libri sociali. Il capitale dell'azienda è impiegato al raggiungimento dello scopo che essa persegue. Il capitale principale partecipa alla gestione aziendale mentre il capitale accessorio è quello di cui l'azienda può fare a meno. Le spese di questo anno sono aumentate rispetto all'anno passato di L. 200.000. Il bilancio salda con un utile lordo di L. 25.000. La quota d'interesse del capitale investito a norma di legge è di 4 per cento. Gli introiti sono aumentati rispetto all'anno passato nel complesso di L. 200.000 pari al 10 per cento. Lo stanziamento anticipato del fondo ammortamento viene effettuato in vista degli ingenti oneri che graveranno sugli esercizi futuri. La proposta del contabile circa la ripartizione dell'utile netto è state approvata. Il cassiere pagherà al Sig. Bruno Rossi la somma di L. 20.000. Il commerciante italiano tiene annotata tutta la sua corrispondenza nel copialettere. Il reddito è un incremento di capitale durante un periodo di tempo e si determina facendo la differenze fra i costi e ricavi di esercizio. Un commerciante reo di bancarotta è punito col carcere.

II. Write brief answers in Italian to the following questions:

1. Scrivete 4 sotto la colonna delle unità e 2 sotto la colonna delle diecine. Quanto ne avete?
2. Qual è lo scopo del capitale dell'azienda?
3. Quali sono i libri obbligatori del commerciante?
4. Come devono essere tenuti i libri sociali?
5. Dove sono esposte tutte le operazioni dell commerciante?
6. Quando si determina il saldo di un conto?
7. Quali sono i diritti dei soci?
8. Cosa s'intende per capitale circolante di un'azienda?
9. A che cosa partecipa il capitale principale?
10. Come si determina il reddito di un'azienda?

III. Translate into Italian:

The expenses have increased. The account is in order. The shareholders are joint owners (*comproprietari*) of the firm. They have a right to the profits. The partners of a firm have the right to inspect the books. The working capital (*capitale circolante)* has increased. The expenses for 1961 have diminished as compared with *(rispetto al)* 1960. The cashier will not pay the sum. The journal must be kept without erasures *(abrasione)* or blank spaces *(spazio in bianco)*. The file is in the accountant's office. The gross profit for the year has not been calculated yet. The distribution of the net profit has been approved. What is the purpose of the amortization fund? The correspondence is noted in the letter book.

Vocabulary II

cane, dog	*mungere*, to milk
mucca, cow	*scoraggiare*, to discourage
oca, goose	*disavventura*, misadventure
voglio, I want	*tentare*, to try
ispezione, inspection	*uscire*, to come out
farsi avanti, to go forward	*fretta e furia*, great haste
muso, face	*gridare*, to shout
ossa cotte, broken bones	*deputato*, deputy

Il Cane, la Mucca e l'Oca

Un cane, una mucca e una oca si presentano un bel giorno alle porte di una grande città. Il cane dice:

—"Voglio entrare. Voglio fare un'ispezione."

Ma più tardi si lamenta.

—"È impossibile vivere qui. Tutti mi volgiono battere."

Si fa avanti allora la mucca che dice:

—"Voglio entrare io."

Entra nella città. Passa un'ora, un'ora e mezzo e poi tutto in un momento ritorna col muso lungo e grida:

—"Ahi! Ahi! Ahi! Ho le ossa cotte. Tutti mi voglioni mungere. Non posso resistere in questa città."

L'oca per nulla scoraggiata dalle disavventure dei suoi amici tenta anche lei la propria fortuna. Entra nella città ma poco dopo esce in fretta e furia e grida:

—"Io non ho proprio voluto restare. Appena arrivata, mi volevano fare deputato."

A Proverb

Il denaro è fratello del denaro.

CHAPTER 4

Insurance

INSURANCE as we know it today has grown from small beginnings. North Italian merchants began to insure their goods early in the thirteenth century. At a later date the Lombards introduced into English usage the word policy from the Italian *polizza* which originally meant a promise. The earliest-known Italian policy dates from 1523.

An insurance policy or *polizza di assicurazione* is a contract by which one party called the insurer or *assicuratore* undertakes in consideration of a payment called premium or *premio* to secure the other party called the insured or *assicurato* against loss of property, life or any other risk by payment of a sum of money in the event of such an occurrence taking place. If goods are insured, for instance, for a sum which exceeds their value, then in the event of loss, payment is made for the value of the goods only. If the goods are underinsured, any loss is made good up to the limit of the insurance.

There are a great variety of insurance contracts and of the clauses embodied in such contracts. Depending on the risk or *rischio* insured, Italian policies are called chiefly:

1. *Polizza di assicurazione maritima.* Marine insurance policy.
2. *Polizza di assicurazioni incendio e furti.* Fire and theft insurance policy.
3. *Polizza di assicurazioni per danni indiretti causati da inattività conseguente ad incendio.* Policy of insurance against loss of profits as a result of fire.
4. *Polizza di assicurazione responsabilità civile verso terzi.* Third party liability insurance policy.
5. *Polizza di assicurazione infortuni individuale.* Personal accident policy of insurance.

6. *Polizza di assicurazione sulla vita.* Life insurance policy.
7. *Polizza di assicurazione per la invalidità e la vecchiaia.* Invalidity and old age insurance policy.

The contract of insurance is valid only if laid down in writing in the form of a policy stipulating the date on which the insurance commences and the date on which it ends, signed by both the insurer and the insured. It is, in fact, a contract of utmost good faith. The insurance comes into force on the midnight of the day the premium is paid.

The policy of insurance is subject to terms, conditions and extensions, arranged in clauses or *articoli* on the middle or back pages of each policy. The terms and conditions deal with the definition of the risk and the rights and liabilities of both insurer and insured. Such perils as enemy action, riots, acts of God, acts of gross negligence and fraud are excluded from the insurance. The insured has the duty to declare any alterations to the risk. If the risk ceases during the period of insurance, the insured is not exempt from the duty to pay premiums until he has notified to the insurer such cessation of the risk. The insurer has the duty to inform the insurer of any new insurances he has effected. If a loss occurs the insured has the duty to notify the insurer within 24 hours of such loss occurring and to safeguard any evidence of the loss. If the insured fraudulently exaggerates his loss, he forfeits any right to compensation.

The insurer cannot be held liable to pay compensation for a sum greater than the sum insured. The payment of a compensation is made in cash at the headquarters of the insurer or of the agent who issued the policy within fifteen days of the agreement on the amount of compensation. After a loss the insurer has the right to cancel the policy by giving thirty days' notice. He also has the right to inspect the risks insured at any time and to ask for information about the risks from the insured.

There is a comprehensive scheme of social insurance in Italy. The Istituto Nazionale Previdenza Sociale (I.N.P.S.) pays unemployment benefits called *indennitá e sussidi*, while the Istituto Nazionale Assicurazione contro le Malattie (I.N.A.M.) is responsible for the *prestazioni* or sickness benefits.

Vocabulary I

agente di assicurazione, insurance agent or broker
ammontare, amount
annesso (allegato), policy endorsement (enclosed)
assicurato, insured person
assicuratore, insurer
caso di forza maggiore, act of God
conteggio, computation
corrispondere, to remit
danneggiato, person sustaining loss
danno, damage, loss
decorrenza, start (of period)
esattore, premium collector
eseguire, to effect
esplosione, explosion
facoltà, authority, power
fare denuncia, to claim
firma, signature
frodo, fraud
furto, theft
incendio, fire

infortunio, accident
inondazioni, floods
legittima difesa, self-defence
lesione, injury
malore, sudden illness
per nessun titolo, on no account
polizza, policy
preavviso, notice
premio, premium
proroga, renewal
provvedimento, provision
quietanza, receipt
rata, rate, instalment
recesso, renouncement
riassicurazione, reinsurance
rimborso, repayment
risarcire, to compensate
scadenza, maturity date
sconto, discount
sinistro, loss
ubicazione, location
valore, value

Exercises

I. Translate into English:

Vi sono assicurazioni contro i danni terrestri, contro i danni marittimi e sulla vita dell'uomo. Il reddito delle società assicuratrici si determina facendo la differenze fra il totale dei premi e il totale dei pagamenti delle indennità. La polizza di assicurazione è un contratto in cui l'assicuratore si obbliga a risarcire i danni che possono derivare all'assicurato da casi fortuiti o da casi di forza maggiore come l'azione del fulmine, influence atmosferiche, infortuni sul lavoro. Di solito la prima rata del premio dev'essere pagata alla consegna della polizza. L'assicurato prudente legge attentamente la polizza e richiede, se del caso, la rettifica prima di firmarla. In molti casi di assicurazione la società assicuratrice ha focoltà di recedere dal contratto con preavviso di, per esempio, venti giorni. L'assicurato è tenuto a denunciare ciascun sinistro. Questa denuncia contiene tre punti: la narrazione del

EDIZIONE 1954

POLIZZA N. ....   AGENZIA ....

Sostituisce la Pol. N. ....   N. C. con Pol. ....

Anno di
fondazione
1 8 3 6

POLIZZA DI ASSICURAZIONE CONTRO I DANNI DELL' INCENDIO

La Compagnia con la presente Polizza, alle condizioni generali, speciali e particolari che seguono assicura contro i danni dell'Incendio..

....

a : ....

domiciliat.... in...

che agisc....... in qualità di _____ ....

le cose in seguito indicate e descritte per la somma di

Lire : ██

per la durata di.. a partire dalle ore ventiquattro

del giorno...sino alle ore ventiquattro...............................

LIQUIDAZIONE DEL PREMIO E DEGLI ACCESSORI

		RATA DA PAGARSI ALLA FIRMA DELLA POLIZZA	RATA ANNUALE
PREMIO NETTO..	L.		
ADDIZIONALI	»		
....	»		
....	»		
....	»		
TOTALE PREMIO ED ACCESSORI..........................	L.		
TASSE E IMPOSTE	»		
TOTALE COMPLESSIVO	L.		

Per il primo periodo decorrente dal................................ 19...... al................ 19........

l'Assicurato deve pagare L................... comprese le tasse

Per la residua durata contrattuale L.................... ....suddivise in

N..............rate annue di L.................... ciascuna, (oltre le tasse) che

scadranno nel.giorno.................... di ogni anno fino al 19......

L'Assicurato dichiara che le descrizioni, ubicazioni ed uso delle cose assicurate sono conformi alle proprie dichiarazioni e determinano la precisa qualità e natura del rischio, coerentemente alle quali vennero di comune accordo convenuti i relativi premi.

Fig. 1. Fire insurance policy of a British company operating in Italy

fatto, l'indicazione delle conseguenze ed il nome dei danneggiati. In ciò che riguarda l'indennità, la società la corrisponde per le conseguenze dirette ed esclusive dell'infortunio. Alla domanda, Che cos' è l'infortunio? si può rispondere come segue: l'infortunio è un evento dovuto a causa fortuita violenta ed esterna che produce lesioni corporali. Anche le lesioni riportate in occasione di legittima difesa sono comprese fra gli infortuni. In Italia l'assicurazione contro gli infortuni sul lavoro è organizzata dallo stato. Un principio ben noto dell'assicurazione è che a nessun titolo la società assicuratrice potrà essere tenuta a pagare all'assicurato una somma maggiore di quella assicurata. Molto spesso il pagamento dell'indennità è eseguito in contanti dalla società assicuratrice alla propria sede. Qualche volta i sinistri denunciati dall'assicurato possono dar luogo a procedure lunghe nel caso di discordia sul pagamento dell'indennità. Il premio dev' essere pagato nel giorno della scadenza fissato sulla polizza. Questo provvedimento vale anche per le rate successive del premio.

II. Translate into Italian:

The present contract of insurance is agreed *(è convenuto)* for a duration of six months. The mishap having taken place *(essendo avvenuto)*, the insured must take all the measures to diminish the consequences of the inactivity of his firm. The enclosure forms an integral part of the policy. The payment of the premium, due on *(dovuto a)* the signing of the present policy, has been made to the insurance agent. The insured declares that there are no risks capable of aggravating the dangers *(i pericoli)* of fire in insured warehouses *(magazzini)*. The insuring company has the right *(facoltà)* of withdrawing in case of loss. The insured must announce every loss. The premium must be paid on the date of maturity. The company does not compensate damages caused by fire found to be the result *(verificatosi in occasione di)* of an act of God. Their risks are only insurable under special conditions *(a condizione)*.

III. Write brief answers in Italian to the following questions:

1. Qual è la definizione delle polizze di assicurazione?
2. Contro quali rischi è possibile assicurarsi?
3. Quando si paga la prima rata del premio?

4. Che cosa deve contenere la denunzia?
5. Che cos'è l'infortunio?
6. Qual è il principio basilare dell'assicurazione?
7. Com'è eseguito il pagamento dell'indennità?
8. Quando ha facoltà recedere dal contratto la società assicuratrice?
9. È obliggato l'assicurato di fare denuncia di ciascun sinistro?
10. Come si determina il reddito delle società assicuratrice?

Correspondence

When a client writes to an insurance company wishing to enter into a contract of insurance, he specifies the nature of the property to be insured, its value and the contingencies insured against. In the following letter, a client requests cover for baggage and personal effects valued at L. 100.000.000 against the risk of fire and theft in view of his journey to Italy:

Spett. Ditta "Società Assicurazioni Italiana", Milano.

10 marzo 19 . . .

In vista del mio prossimo giro d'Italia per terra e per mare dal primo aprile al quindici maggio, vogliate assicurare il mio bagaglio ed effetti personali per un importo di L. 100.000.000 contro i rischi dell'incendio e del furto.

In attesa di una Vostra gentile risposta circa il premio di assicurazione da pagare, Vi invio i miei distinti saluti.

(Signed)

The insurance company answers accepting the client's proposals. The client is asked to pay L. 1.500.000 as a premium for the policy requested.

Prot. No. 232   12 marzo 19 . . .

Oggetto: Polizza di assicurazioni contro i rischi di incendio e furto.

Egregio Signore,

con riferimento alla Sua lettera del 10 m.c. siamo lieti di poter.le communicare che abbiamo emesso una polizza alle condizioni specificate nella Sua lettera.
Voglia rimetterci a stretto giro di posta l'importo di L. 1.500.000 essendo il premio di assicurazione per la polizza da Lei desiderata.

                              Gradisca i nostri migliori saluti.

                                                    (Signature)

Vocabulary II

scommessa, bet	*scomodo*, uncomfortable
camminare, to walk	*piombare*, to sink like lead
scommettere, to bet	*sonno*, sleep
muoio, I die	*addormentare*, to fall asleep
scoppiare a ridere, to burst into laughter	*convoglio*, train
fiasco, flask	*graffiare*, scratch
ferrovia, railway	*velocità*, speed
rasserenare, to brighten	*afferrare*, to seize
binario, rail-track	*carabiniere*, policeman

La Scommessa

Mario Bruno e tre giovani amici camminavano lentamente sulla strada deserta non lontano dalla bella città di Pisa.
—"Scommettete che non muoio anche se mi passa un treno sopra" disse Mario Bruno ai tre amici che scoppiarono a ridere e gli risposero in coro:
—"Scommettiamo. Si fa un gran fiasco di vino bianco."
Cosi Mario Bruno si recò insieme ai tre amici lungo la ferrovia Pisa–Roma. Il tempo si era rasserenato e il sole appariva chiaro fra le nuvole in movimento. Si mise sui binari nella posizione alquanto scomoda ma secondo lui necessaria per vincere la scommessa, e attese con pazienza il passaggio dei treni. Aspettarono un buon tratto di tempo, ma nè da una parte nè dall'altra arrivavano locomotive. I tre

IPC-D

amici decisero quindi di andarsene a casa, visto che i fumi dell'alcool li stavano facendo piombare in un sonno profondo e che la notte si avvicinava a grandi passi. Si addormentò anche Mario Bruno e dal sonno profondissimo non lo svegliarono neanche i convogli che gli passarono senza neanche graffiarlo alla velocità di novanta chilometri orari.

Il sole si levava sui monti grigi quando Mario Bruno si svegliò afferrato dalla decisa mano di un grosso carabiniere. Naturalmente Mario Bruno vinse la scommessa.

A Proverb

La prima pioggia è quella che bagna.

CHAPTER 5

Banking

THE earliest known banks in Italy were publicly owned deposit banks established in cities like Genoa, Piacenza, Venice, Siena, Lucca and Florence. Records from Genoa and Venice go back to the twelfth century. The Casa di San Giorgio in Genoa was founded in 1148. These banks provided a system of bank money in exchange for various forms of metallic currency. The Mediterranean merchants introduced the word bank from the Italian *banco* or bench on which the money was counted.

At a later date the medieval money-lending Lombards in the north pioneered the business of commercial banking. They gave the name to Lombard Street in the city of London. In central Italy the Banco di Santo Spirito was founded in Rome in 1605 and the Monte dei Paschi bank started business in Siena in 1624. Two further important banks were established in the second half of the nineteenth century. The Credito Italiano appeared in 1870 and the Banco di Roma in 1880.

Modern Italian banking is based on the concept of a financing institution making loans and purchasing various kinds of securities. Unlike the British joint-stock banks, Italian banks are closely associated with industry. The Istituto Mobiliare Italiano is a major credit institution providing medium- and long-term finance for industry.

At the top of the Italian banking system is the central Banca d'Italia which alone has the right to issue paper money or *carta moneta*. The Banca d'Italia controls the volume of monetary circulation and hence the level of investment in industry. It also exercises control over the liquidity ratio of the other banks in the country.

The banks coming under the Banca d'Italia fall into three groups.

First there are the Banco di Roma, Credito Italiano and Banca Commerciale Italiana which are essentially deposit banks. Next come the credit institutions for the medium- and long-term finance of industry like the Istituto Mobiliare Italiano, Banco di Napoli, Banco di Sicilia, Banca Nazionale del Lavoro. The third group is formed of small popular savings banks like the *Banche popolari cooperative, Casse di risparmio, Casse rurali e agrarie* which take short-term deposits, and banks like the *Istituto di credito fondiario* or *Istituti di credito agrario* which take long-term deposits.

The operations carried out by the banks may be active, passive or auxiliary. Active operations are the discounting of bills, transactions in securities and foreign exchange. Passive operations are deposits, the re-discounting of bills. Auxiliary operations are the safe-keeping of securities, cashing dividends, the issuing of cheques and letters of credit.

Bills of Exchange

In Italian practice a bill of exchange or *cambiale* is an unconditional written instrument or *titolo a ordine determinato*. It is an instrument to which there are three parties, the drawer or *traente*, the payee or *prenditore* and the drawee or *trattario* who, if he accepts, becomes the acceptor or *accettante*. The bill of exchange must be an order to pay a determined sum, that is *ordine di pagare una determinata somma*. It must show the place and date of payment and bear the requisite stamp or *bollo*.

Bills of exchange belong to three categories called *la tratta, il pagherò* and *la tratta all ordine proprio*. These bills are negotiated when they are transferred. The endorsement is called *girata*, the endorser *girante* and the endorsee *giratario*.

The *tratta* will usually contain the following words:

> A vista pagate per questa cambiale al Sig. M. B. di Torino la somma di Lit. venticinquemilioni.
>
> P.M.

or

Pay to Sig. M. B. of Torino at sight the sum of twenty-five million Italian Lire.

The *pagherò* is worded as follows:

A sei mesi data pagherò per questa cambiale al Sig. M. B. di Torino la somma di Lit. sessantamilioni.

or

Six months after date, I will pay Sig. M. B. of Torino the sum of sixty million Italian Lire.

The *tratta all'ordine proprio* contains the words:

A sei mesi data pagate per questa cambiale all'ordine mio proprio la somma di Lit. settantamilioni.

or

Six months after date pay to my order the sum of seventy million Italian Lire for value received.

Examples

La tratta

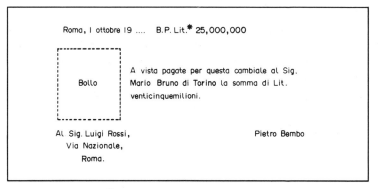

Roma, I ottobre 19 ....   B.P. Lit.* 25,000,000

Bollo

A vista pagate per questa cambiale al Sig. Mario Bruno di Torino la somma di Lit. venticinquemilioni.

Al Sig. Luigi Rossi,   Pietro Bembo
Via Nazionale,
Roma.

*B.P. Lit. stands for Buono per Lire Italiane.

Il pagherò

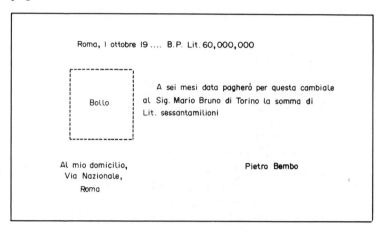

La tratta all'ordine proprio

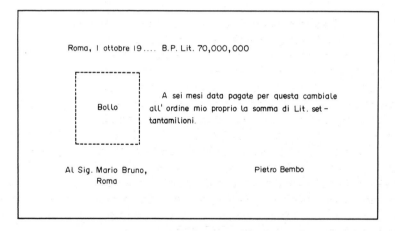

Cheques

A cheque or *assegno bancario* is a bill of exchange drawn on a banker and payable on demand. When a cheque is presented the banker must pay if he has funds belonging to the drawer at hand. The

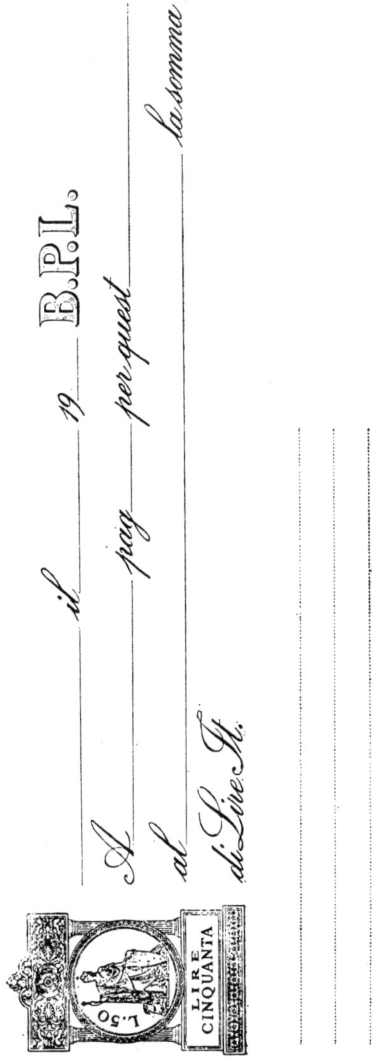

FIG. 2. Bill of exchange

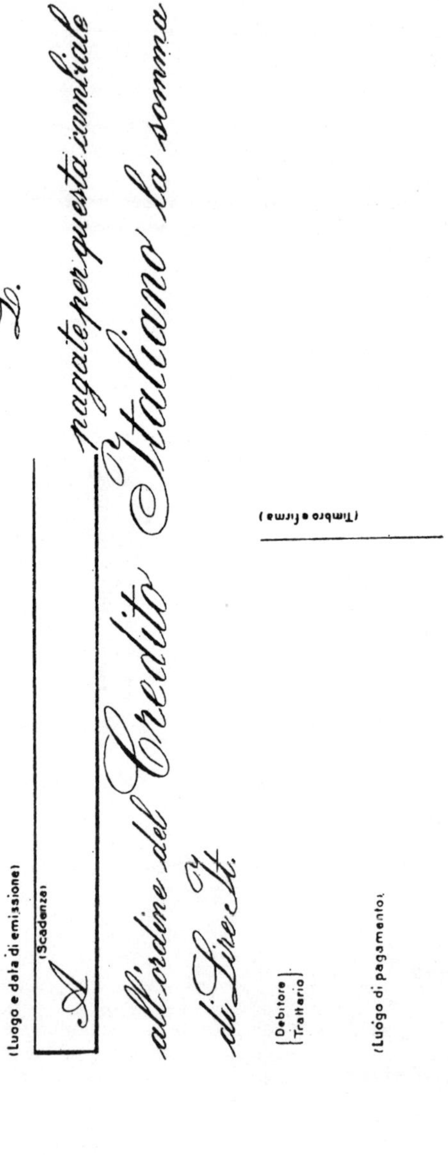

(Luogo e data di emissione)

(Scadenza)

A

all'ordine del Credito Italiano

di Lire It.

[Debitore
(Trattario)]

(Luogo di pagamento)

(Timbro e firma)

pagate per questa cambiale la somma

L.

N° 6486   (Provincia)

Fig. 3. Bill of exchange

banker's authority to pay the cheque is revoked by countermand of payment or by notice of the customer's death.

Three types of cheque are popular in Italy. The ordinary cheque or *assegno bancario* may or may not be crossed or *sbarrato*. The bank draft or *assegno circolare* is issued by banks specially empowered by law and it is payable to bearer at sight. It is negotiable by simple endorsement. The traveller's cheque or *assegno turistico* may be cashed at any bank abroad for the equivalent foreign currency. The *assegno turistico* is not negotiable and valid for six months only as a rule.

Vocabulary I

accettante, acceptor
accreditare, to credit with
addebitare, to debit
assegno, cheque
assegno sbarrato, crossed cheque
assegno turistico, traveller's cheque
avallante, guarantor
avallo, guarantee
banconota, banknote
beneficiaro, payee
biglietto di banca, banknote
bollo, stamp, seal
cambiale, bill of exchange
cambiare, to exchange
cambio, exchange
cassa, bank
cedola, dividend warrant
chiusura dei conti, closing the books
conteggio, computation
conto, account
conto corrente, current account
conto deposito, deposit account
correntista, current account holder
corso legale, legal tender
denaro, money
effetti, securities
effetti in portafoglio, securities on hand
girante, endorser
girare, to endorse
incassare, to cash
incasso, collection

interesse, interest
lettera di credito, letter of credit
libretto di assegni, cheque book
libro di cassa, cash book
moneta, coin
percepire, to cash
portatore, bearer
prenditore, payee
prospetto, statement
ricavo, proceeds
riporto, amount carried forward
risconto, rediscount
riscossione, collection (of bills, etc.)
saggio dello sconto, discount rate
scheda, register, form
schedino, index
scoperto di conti, overdraft
sottoscrivere, to undersign
talloncino, coupon, slip
tasso d'interesse, rate of interest
titoli, securities
titolo, instrument, paper
tratta, bill of exchange
trattario, drawee
valuta, paper money
valuta estera, foreign currency
verificare, to audit, to check
versamento, payment
vigente, in force
(a) vista, (at) sight

Exercises

I. Translate into English:

La Banca d'Italia emette carta moneta. In Italia vi sono banche d'interesse pubblico, istituti di credito di diritto pubblico e istituti di credito raccoglitori del risparmio. Il bilancio di un'azienda è un prospetto delle attività e delle passività di quella azienda in un dato momento. Le operazioni di banca si classificano a seconda degli oneri e dei lucri in operazioni attive, operazioni passive e operazioni accessorie. Il ragioniere riporta il saldo in un conto nuovo. L'assegno bancario è buono se ragolarmente girato. Il mercante imprudente trae un assengo per una somma superiore alla provvista di fondi. Giuridicamente il conto corrente è un contratto che regola i rapporti fra banchieri e clienti. La banca ha ritirato i suoi biglietti dalla circolazione. Ho ricevuto da un cliente un effetto a saldo. He detto al ragioniere di non riportare il saldo. La banca è un istituto di credito dove si fanno operazioni su effetti commerciali. Il suo assegno può essere pagabile a vista o in un termine non maggiore di sei giorni. Il saldo della presente rivalutazione è stato impiegato a copertura delle perdite subite negli esercizi precedenti. L'assegno deve sempre indicare la somma da pagarsi e deve essere dato e sottoscritto dal traente. Ho scritto il mio nome sul dorso della cambiale. La girata condizionata limita l'ordinaria responsibilità del girante. Il cassiere registra a debito tutti gli introiti di qualsiasi natura. Il contabile divide il giornale in due volumi. Il negoziante apre un conto Cassa di Risparmio. C'è un ammanco di cassa. Il contabile accredita il saldo al conto corrente.

II. Translate into Italian:

The bank is a credit institution *(istituto di credito)*. The current account is a contract *(contratto)* between banker and client. The rate of interest has been changed *(cambiato)*. I have lost my cheque book. Where can I cash this traveller's cheque? What is the rate of exchange today? I am sorry *(mi rincresce)* but this cheque is not payable at sight. The accountant checks thoroughly *(esaurientemente)* the current accounts. The balance sheet of this firm shows a small net profit for the year. The balance has been credited to the new account. The bank draft is negotiable by endorsement *(trasmissibile con girata)*. The bill of exchange states: six months after date pay to my order the sum of ten thousand Italian lire.

III. Write brief answers in Italian to the following questions:

1. Qual è l'ordinamento bancario in Italia?
2. Qual è la classificazione delle operazioni di banca?
3. Il conto corrente è un contratto?
4. Come sono classificati i conti correnti a seconda del contenuto?
5. Quando è valido l'assegno bancario?
6. L'assegno circolare è pagabile a vista?
7. È trasferibile la cambiale?

Correspondence between a Bank and its Clients

A firm of wool importers Ditta Affix, writes to the Banca di Milano asking for an advance to be guaranteed by wool stored at Genoa. The bank replies agreeing to provide the advance subject to the customary conditions.

Spett. Banca di Milano   1 ottobre 19 . . .

La sottoscritta Ditta Affix chiede alla spett. Banca di Milano che le sia concessa una sovvenzione di L. 1.000.000 per tre mesi garantita da una partita di lana depositata a Genova del valore di L. 5.000.000, come risulta da warrant No. 32 qui incluso.

In attesa di una Vs/ risposta a stretto giro di posta, vogliate gradire i ns/ distinti saluti.

I alleg.

Ditta Affix.

Spett. Ditta Affix   4 ottobre 19 . . .

Con riferimento alla Vs/ lettera del 1 c.m., vi communichiamo che possiamo concedervi la sovvenzione richiesta di L. 1.000.000 per tre mesi sulla partita di lana depositata a Genova alle seguenti condizioni: tasso d'interesse 5% per tre mesi; provvigione 2%; tassa erariale 1%.
In attesa di Vs/ adesione, vi inviamo is ns/ distinti saluti.

                                                                        Banca di Milano

Spett. Bnca di Milano   8 ottobre 19 . . .

In risposta alla Vs/ lettera del 4 c.m., siamo lieti di communicarvi che accettiamo le condizioni specificate.
Gradite frattanto i ns/migliori saluti.

                                                                        Ditta Affix

A textile firm, "Mercury & Co. Ltd.", informs the Banca di Londra that its representative Mr. John Hunter is visiting Milan and Turin in November. The letter asks the bank for a letter of credit in favour of Mr. John Hunter up to the sum of lire 800,000. The sums of money which Mr. John Hunter will cash by virtue of the letter of credit will be refunded by bill of exchange payable at sight in London.

The bank sends a letter of credit in favour of Mr. John Hunter in the sum of lire 800,000 addressed to the Banca Lombarda in Milan and the Banco di Torino in Turin.

Mercury & Co. Ltd. thankfully acknowledges receipt of letter of credit.

Spett. Banca di Londra   18 novembre 19 . . .

Il Sig. John Hunter, ns/ rappresentante, visiterà nel prossimo mese di novembre le città di Milano e Torino per la propaganda dei prodotti tessili della ns/ ditta Mercury & Co. Ltd.
Con la presente Vi preghiamo di volerci rimettere una lettera di

credito in favore del Sig. John Hunter fino alla concorrenza di L. 800.000. Le somme che il Sig. John Hunter preleverà in virtù della Vs/ lettera di credito, Vi saranno rimborsate dalla ns/ ditta Mercury & Co. Ltd. per mezzo di tratto a vista pagabile in Londra.

Nell' attesa di un Vs/ cortese riscontro, Vi salutiamo ben distintamente.

Ditta Mercury & Co. Ltd.

Spett. Ditta Mercury & Co. Ltd.   20 novembre 19 . . .

Qui inclusa abbiamo favore di rimetter Vi la lettera di credito da Voi richiestaci con pregiata vostra del 18 novembre a favore del Vs/ rappresentante Sig. John Hunter.

La lettera stressa per la somma di L. 800.000 è indirizzata alle banche qui sotto specificate:

Banca Lombarda, Milano, Corso Umberto

Banca di Torino, Torino, Piazza della Repubblica

Siamo ben certi che il Vs/ rappresentante Sig. John Hunter troverà presso le banche suddette la massima sollecitudine.

Mentre, per ns/ tranquilità, Vi preghiamo di un breve cenno di riscontro, vogliate ricevere i sensi della ns/ considerazione.

Banca di Londra

Spett. Banca di Londra   23 novembre 19 . . .

A riscontro della pregiata Vs/ in data 20 c.m.

Vi ringraziamo sentitamente per averci potuto favorire con la lettera di credito da noi richiestaVi a favore del ns/ rappresentante Sig. John Hunter per la somma di L. 800.000.

Gradite i ns/ migliori saluti.

Ditta Mercury & Co. Ltd.

Vocabulary II

arricchire, to grow rich	*afferrare*, to pick up
mantenere, to keep	*chierica*, tonsure
matrigna, stepmother	*massaia*, housewife
capacitarsi, to convince oneself	*sfaccendare*, to bustle
piacere, to like	*ali*, wings
parroco, parson	*nozze*, wedding
ragguardevole important	*straccio*, scrap
cappone, capon	*troncone*, stump
beffardamente, mockingly	*mangiare*, to eat
tagliare, to cut	

Il Dottore e il Cappone

C'era un agricoltore arricchito, il quale manteneva il figlio agli studi in città. La cosa poco piaceva alla matrigna, che non poteva capacitarsi si spendessero tanti denari per l'ambizione di avere un figlio dottore. Quando il giovane fu addottorato, il padre dètte un gran pranzo invitando il parrocco e gli altri uomini ragguardevoli. Fu portato a tavola un cappone magnifico: la matrigna beffardamente disse al giovane:

—"Tu che hai studiato, vedi se sai tagliare il cappone per grammatica."

E il giovane:

—"Súbito, madre."

Afferrò il coltello e incominciò:

—"La cresta è giusto sia data al signor parroco, che è padre spirituale e porta la chierica. La testa dobbiamo darla al babbo, ch'è il capo della famiglia. Le gambe alla mamma, che è tanto brava massaia e corre sempre su e giù per la casa a sfaccendare. Poi daremo alle sorelle le ali, perchè presto usciranno di casa volando a nozze. E questo straccio di trancone buono a nulla me lo mangerò io."

By Franco Sacchetti
(From *Curiosità e capricci della lingua
italiana* by Dino Provenzal)

A Proverb

Non dir quattro se non l'hai nel sacco.

CHAPTER 6

Carriage of Goods on Land

AN ITALIAN carrier of goods or *spedizioniere* may dispatch or receive goods on behalf of third parties. If he carries goods in his own name he is called commission agent or *commissionario*. Whether the carrier is *spedizioniere* or *commissionario*, he must observe the clauses of the *Codice Civile*, which oblige the carrier to comply with the instructions of the consignor or *committente* and which lay down his rights. Payment for carriage of goods if not covered by an agreement must be effected in accordance with the professional tariffs or the usual terms obtaining in the place from where the goods are dispatched.

The carrier of goods must possess a licence or *patente* issued by the local provincial authorities. He must have the penal certificate or *certificato penale* and good-conduct certificate or *certificato di buona condotta* and must prove that he has the juridicial capacity and the necessary knowledge to carry out his trade. The carrier must comply with customs regulations and the laws affecting public health and safety.

The carriage of goods on land is by railway or road.

Three-quarters of the Italian railway network belong to the State and come under the Ministry of Transport. The rest of the railways are in the hands of private enterprise being operated as a concession. The railways undertake to carry goods in accordance with the tariffs in force and the sender's instructions. The railways are responsible for loss or damage. The sender must pay the carriage cost and present the carriage note or *lettera di vettura* with every consignment. The *lettera di vettura* shows: the names and addesses of consignor and consignee; type of goods and their value; list of documents, if any, accompanying the goods; itinerary and any special services.

Road haulage is carried out by a contractor or *imprenditore*. The haulage charge depends on whether the goods are dispatched in parcels or *collettame* or whether a whole truck, *carro completo*, is hired.

All motor-vehicles in Italy are subject to the payment of a road tax or *tassa di circolazione* except for new motor vehicles which are exempt for the first six months. The driver of a lorry must have a second-grade driving licence or *patente di guida di secondo grado* and he must be at least twenty-one years of age. The driver of a motor-train or *autotreno* must be accompanied by another man.

Italian roads are well built and are two-thirds the length of British roads. Italy has a larger number of motor-roads than Britain. The longest Italian motorway, the Autostrada del Sole, is 738 kilometres long and links Milan to Bologna, Florence, Rome and Naples. The second longest Italian motorway links Naples to Bari over a distance of 240 kilometres.

Vocabulary I

assegno (contro), (collection) cash on delivery
autocarro, lorry
autostrada, motor road
autotreno, motor-train
avviso di arrivo, notice of arrival
balla, bale
bollettini, note
bollettino di consegna, delivery note
bollettino di spedizione, consignment note
bombola (per gas), (gas) bottle
botte, cask
caricare, to load
carico, load
carro, truck
carta d'imballaggio, packing paper
cartone, cardboard
cassa, case
collettame, parcels
collo, parcel
commissionario, commission agent
committente, consignor
consegna, delivery
dazio, customs duty

destinatario, consignee
destinazione, destination
distinta, list, schedule
ferrovia, railway
fragile, fragile
imballaggio, packing
imprenditore, contractor, haulier
incatramare, to tar
inviare, to send
lettera di vettura, carriage note
mandare (per ferrovia), to send (by rail)
marcatura, labelling
mercanzia, merchandise
merce, goods
mittente, sender
patente, licence
patente di guida, driving licence
peso lordo, gross weight
peso netto, net weight
porto affrancato, carriage paid
porto assegnato, carriage unpaid
porto compreso, carriage included
posa piano, handle with care
provenienza (luogo di), origin (place of)

sacco, sack, bag
scaricare, to unload
scatola, box, tin
spedire, to dispatch
spedizione, consignment
spedizioniere, forwarding agent
tariffa, tariff, charge
tassa, tax
trasporto, transport
trasporto automobilistico, road haulage
trasporto ferroviario, railway transport
vagone, wagon, truck
vettura, railway carriage

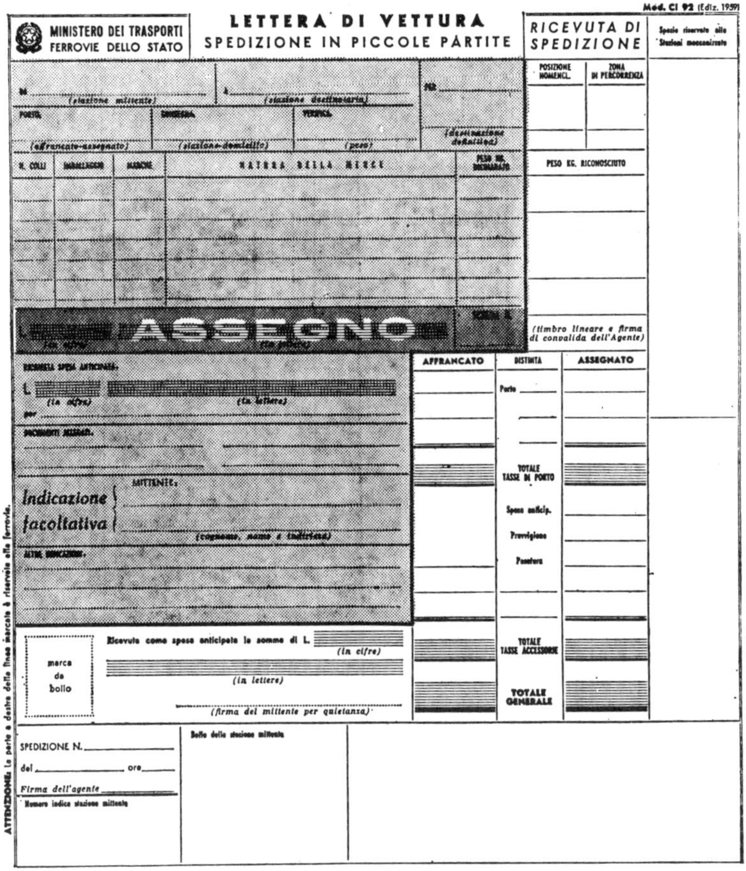
Mod. Cl 92 (Ediz. 1959)

MINISTERO DEI TRASPORTI
FERROVIE DELLO STATO

LETTERA DI VETTURA
SPEDIZIONE IN PICCOLE PARTITE

RICEVUTA DI SPEDIZIONE

(stazione mittente)
(stazione destinataria)
(affrancato-assegnato)
(stazione-domicilio)
(peso)
(destinazione definitiva)

N. COLLI | IMBALLAGGIO | MARCHE | NATURA DELLA MERCE | PESO KG. DICHIARATO

POSIZIONE NOMENCL.
ZONA DI PERCORRENZA
PESO KG. RICONOSCIUTO

ASSEGNO
(in cifre)
(in lettere)

(timbro lineare e firma di convalida dell'Agente)

L.
(in cifre)
(in lettere)
per

Indicazione facoltativa
MITTENTE:
(cognome, nome e indirizzo)

AFFRANCATO | DISTINTA | ASSEGNATO
Porto
TOTALE TASSE DI PORTO
Spese anticip.
Provvigione
Presaturo
TOTALE TASSE ACCESSORIE
TOTALE GENERALE

marca da bollo
Ricevuto come spese anticipate la somma di L.
(in cifre)
(in lettere)
(firma del mittente per quietanza)

SPEDIZIONE N.
del ore
Firma dell'agente
Numero indice stazione mittente
Bollo della stazione mittente

ATTENZIONE: La parte a destra della linea marcata è riservata alle ferrovie.

FIG. 8. Carriage note

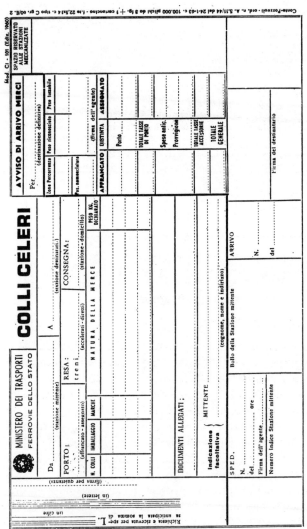

FIG. 9. Railway advice note

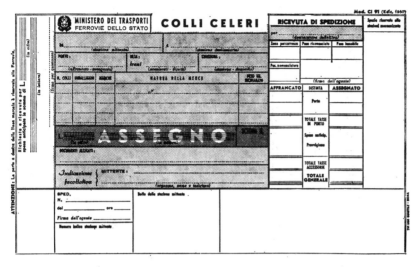

Fig. 10. Railway certificate of posting

Exercises

I. Translate into English:

L'azienda della ferrovie dello stato italiano è dotata di autonomia amministrativa e ha quattordici compartimenti. I viaggiatori sono tenuti a presentare il biglietto agli agenti delle ferrovie all'entrata nella stazione o nelle carrozze. I prezzi dei viaggi di corsa semplice non sono fissi. Ho un biglietto di andata e ritorno ordinario.

I prezzi di trasporto delle merci nelle ferrovie dipende dalla distanza, dal peso, dalla qualità delle merci, dalla celerità, e finalmente dalla responsabilità della ferrovia. La letters di vetura è il documento adatto alle spedizioni ferroviarie.

I trasporti in autocarro o autotreno si fanno da imprenditori. Ogni conducente di autoveicoli deve essere in possesso di una patente di guida. Chi guida veicoli deve essere idoneo per condizioni fisiche e psichiche, dice il Codice della Strada. Ogni autoveicolo deve essere munito di una licenza di circolazione. Il Codice Civile italiano regola gli obblighi e i diritti dello spedizioniere. Il mittente ha l'obbligo di pagare il prezzo di trasporto mentre il destinatario quello di ritirare le merci entro i limiti di tempo prestabiliti. In caso di perdita o averia delle merci trasportate si rimborsa il porto pagato. A causa della sua fragilità questa merce deve essere imballata con la massima cura. La carta d'imballagio è fatta con cellulosa di paglia o canapa, mentre i cartoni sono delle carte a forte spessore. Il cartone incatramato è ricoperto di catrame.

II. Translate into Italian:

Transport charges depend directly on distance, weight and quality of goods. Road haulage in Italy is carried out by contractors. The packing and labelling of parcels is of great importance. The driver's licence has been suspended and he has to pay a heavy fine for the motoring offence. New cars are exempted from paying the road tax for the first six months. I am sorry but I have lost my ticket. Special tickets are issued on the occasion of exhibitions and fairs. The new Italian Highway Code came into force a few years ago and it consists of 146 clauses.

Here is the list of the enclosed documents. The place and date of delivery are indicated in the letter. These charges are not applicable. The value of the goods is not marked on the parcels. The name and the address of the consignee must be shown in the railway consignment note.

III. Answer briefly in Italian the following questions:

1. Da chi sono condotti i trasporti automobilistici in Italia?
2. Quale è il documento relativo alle spedizioni ferroviarie?
3. Quali sono gli obblighi degli spedizionieri?
4. Gli imballaggi e la marcatura dei colli sono importanti o no?
5. Da che dipende il prezzo di trasporto delle merci nelle ferrovie italiane?
6. Che cosa succede in caso di perdita o avaria delle merci trasportate?
7. Quali sono le norme salienti del Codice della Strada?

Vocabulary II

terremoto, earthquake	lastricato, flag-stone
immane, huge	*crollare*, to collapse
sciagura, misfortune	*sprofondare*, to sink
abitante, inhabitant	*scomparire*, to disappear
scossa, tremor	*superstite*, survivor
in rovina, in ruins	*impazzire*, to madden
sonno, sleep	*fitto*, thick
seppellire, to bury	*polvere*, dust
macerie, rubble	*schiacciare*, to crush
cimitero, graveyard	*scampo*, escape
viscere, bowels	*cieco*, blind
contrarre, to contort	*ira*, wrath
ruggire, to roar	*catasta*, heap
gemere, to groan	*luccicare*, to glitter
belva, beast	*benigno*, benign
ferito, wounded	*squarcio*, gash

Il Terremoto di Messina

Un'immane sciagura accadde il 28 dicembre del 1908 in Sicilia. Un terrible terremoto distrusse Messina e causò la morte di circa ottanta mila dei suoi abitanti. Ecco una descrizione autentica di questo quadro terrificante di distruzione:

Una scossa tellurica di potenza titanica trasformava in pochi istanti in rovina la bella città immersa in sonno tranquillo, una città di contoquaranta mila abitanti, seppellendo sotto le macerie delle case quasi due terzi della popolazione. Messina cessava di esistere, trasformata in pochi secondi in un immenso cimitero. Era un'altra Pompei. La terra tremava nelle su eviscere, si contraeva in convulsioni nervose, ruggiva, gemeva come una belva ferita. Le case, le chiese, i monumenti, i lastricati, tutto crollava, sprofondava, si polverizzava e scompariva nell'abisso di questo inferno.

Da tre giorni superstiti impazziti, intossicati dal fumo e dalla fitta polvere, feriti e orrendamente mutalati, schiacciati dalle case crollate, cercavano scampo alla cieca ira degli elementi scatenati e invocavano soccorso.

La città pareva una caotica catasta di rovine informi. Un fumo denso oscurava la vista del mare che il giorno prima luccicava nel sole benigno di dicembre. La città s'intravvedeva appena negli squarci delle fiamme e pareva senza vita.

A Proverb

Il monde è fatto a scale: chi le scende e chi le sale.

CHAPTER 7

Merchant Shipping

ITALIAN navigators and merchants have a long and colourful tradition of seafaring. In the Middle Ages the maritime cities of Venice and Genoa vied with each other in establishing colonies in the Levant and on the shores of the Black Sea. The rival city of Pisa won for herself trading enclaves on the North African coast from Tunis to Tripoli.

Warehouses, shops, piers, wharfs and other harbour installations were built in these colonies which enjoyed considerable tax and duty exemptions and were governed by a consul aided by a council of elders. In modern times the consul was to become the name of a diplomatic representative.

The Italian colonies became so flourishing that their citizens could afford to build mansions and erect churches and monuments, besides sending untold riches to the mother cities. Their argosies pioneered the basic rules of merchant shipping and the complex procedure involved in loading and unloading operations.

In view of Italy's long seaboard and many ports, merchant shipping plays a big role in her coastal and foreign trade. The merchant traffic consists of tramps with changeable ports of call, that is *navi da carico con scalo variable*, and cargo boats with regular ports of call, known as the *navi da carico con scali fissi*.

A ship's ballast space and some of its superstructure is called gross tonnage or *stazza lorda*. Gross tonnage less the space occupied by the machine rooms, crew quarters and other space not used for cargo is the net tonnage or *stazza netta*. The space available in a ship for the stowage of goods is called *netta portata*.

The master of an Italian ship must be conversant with the law as set down in the *Codice di navigazione* as well as with mercantile law which is codified in the *Codice di commercio*. The master must start the voyage on time and must take proper care of crew and equipment. He manages the ship and navigates her by employing a pilot. He takes cargo as quickly as possible and stows it properly. He signs the bill of lading or *polizza da carico* for all he has taken on board his ship. He delivers the cargo on arrival at destination to the person or persons named in the bill of lading.

The ship's master has the power to discipline his crew, to tranship in cases where it is in the interests of his owners, to jettison goods overboard to lighten the ship in cases of danger. The master is responsible for the ship's papers or *libri di bordo* and those usually carried are: certificate of registry, ship's log book, charter party and bills of lading, agreement with the seamen, bill of health, inventory of the cargo or invoices giving particulars of the cargo.

The contract of affreightment or charter party, known in Italian as the *contratto di noleggio*, is an agreement by which a shipowner places the whole ship or a part of it at the disposal of the charterer or *noleggiatore* for a certain voyage or for a certain time. The contract of affreightment must show the name or description of the ship, the names of the shipowner and charterer, the name of the ship's master, place and time of loading and unloading, the rates of freight, whether whole or part of the ship is chartered, compensation to be paid in case of delay, clauses exonerating the shipowner from liability for loss caused by act of God, blockades, embargoes, perils of the seas.

Bills of Lading

The bill of lading is a document acknowledging the shipment of goods. It is a symbol of goods at sea. The bill is generally signed by the master and shipper who is already acquainted with the conditions of transport. The format and layout of the bill varies from one shipping company to another, but all bills contain the following information: bill and journey reference numbers; date, name of ship and master; port of shipment and destination; detailed information about the markings, quality and quantity of parcels, weight, value and contents; freight rates, primage, taxes and commission. The freight must be paid before the consignment of the goods, unless otherwise agreed to. The

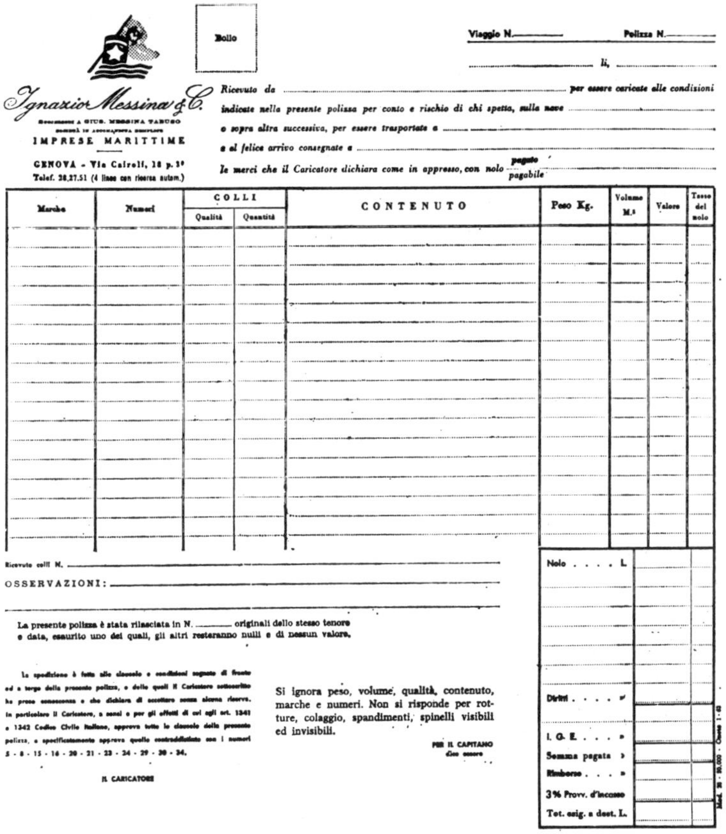

Fig. 11. Bill of lading

freight is also fully due and earned whether the ship reaches its destination or not.

The bill of lading is subject to general and special conditions of transport. The conditions are arranged in clauses on the back of each bill and deal with the rights, duties, liabilities and exclusions from liability of master, shipowner and shipper.

In accordance with the stipulated conditions, the liability of the master and shipping company commences only after the stowage of the

FLOTTA LAURO
NAPOLI - Via Nuova Marittima
(Palazzo Lauro)

Polizza N. _____   _____, li _____ 19____   **Viaggio N.** _____

Sono state caricate da _____ alle condizioni della presente polizza

trascritte qui sotto e a tergo, per conto e rischio di chi spetta, sul piroscafo _____ Cap. _____

per essere trasportate a _____ ed al felice arrivo consegnate a _____ le merce

che il caricatore dichiara come in appresso:

Il nolo _____ pagato _____ come da distinta.

MARCHE	NUMERI	COLLI Quantità	COLLI Qualità	DICHIARAZIONE DEL CONTENUTO	VALORE dichiarato	PESO	VOLUME	TASSO del nolo	LIQUIDAZIONE DEL NOLO

LIQUIDAZIONE DEL NOLO:

Diritto fisso di polizza L. _____
Cappa . . . . . » _____
Diritti . . . . . » _____
Bolli . . . . . » _____

Nolo incassato . . . . » _____
Nolo esigibile a destino » _____
Assegno . . . . . » _____
Provvig. d'incasso » _____

Totale esigibile a destino L. _____

M/2

Ricevuto Colli N. _____

Rilasciato N. _____ polizze firmate, delle quali una sola adempie le altre restano senza valore.

Dice essere senza responsabilità per marche e numeri, senza responsabilità per il peso, volume, qualità e contenuto, rottura, colaggio, spandimento visibile e non stabile.

La medesima spedizione è fatta alle clausole e condizioni segnate di fronte ed a tergo della presente polizza, delle quali il caricatore ha preso conoscenza e che dichiara di accettare senza riserva alcuna.

p. IL CAPITANO   IL CARICATORE

ARTI GRAFICHE G. D'AGOSTINO - NAPOLI

Fig. 12. Bill of lading

goods in the hold of the ship. The master and shipping company reserve the right to check weight, value and contents of parcels both at loading and unloading. They expressly exclude liability for any insurable risks, for loss caused by act of God, quarantine, pirates, riots and strikes, shipwreck, etc. Moreover, the shipping company excludes liability for any errors of negligence on the part of the master and his crew or pilot. The captain has the right, without incurring any liability, to enter and leave ports without a pilot and to deviate from the route. The shipper is liable to the shipowner for any damages or expenses arising from missing customs papers, health bills, etc.

The general conditions of transport also stipulate that the shipowner or shipowner's agent delivers the goods to whomsoever presents the bill of lading.

Bills of lading may be split up for convenience into several delivery orders or *ordini di consegna*.

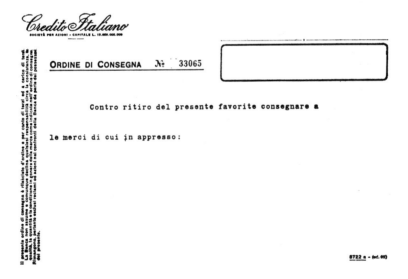

FIG. 13. Delivery of order form

Vocabulary I

armatore, shipowner
avaria, damage, average
avaria generale, general average
avaria particolare, particular average
banchina, wharf
bandiera, flag
barca, boat
bastimento, ship
boccaporto, hatchway
(a) bordo, (on) board
calata, wharf
cantiere, shipyard
capitano marittimo, ship's master
caricatore, shipper
carico medio, average load
carico per peso proprio, dead load
certificato di iscrizione della nave, ship's
  registry
certificato santario, health bill
chiatta, lighter
controstallia, demurrage
costo, assicurazione e nolo, C.I.F.
equippagio, crew
fare gettito, to jettison
franco a bordo, F.O.B.
giornale di navigazione, ship's logbook
inventario di bordo, inventory of the cargo
libri di bordo, ship's papers
linea di carico, load line
marina mercantile, merchant navy
mettere in chiatte, to load in lighters
motoscafo, motor-boat
nave, ship
nave da carico, cargo boat
nave in zavorra, ship in ballast
noleggiare, to charter
noleggiatore, charterer

noleggio, affreightment, charter party
noleggio a tempo, time charter party
noleggio a viaggio, voyage charter party
nolo, freight
nota di pegno, dock warrant
ordine di consegna, delivery note
ordine di imbarco, shipping order
pilota, pilot
polizza di carico, bill of lading
portata della nave, ship's carrying capacity
porto, harbour
rada, roadstead
registro di classificazione, certificate of
  character
responsabilità, liability
ricuperabile, recoverable
rimorchiatore, tug
ritenere, to withhold
rotta, route
salvataggio, salvage
salvezza, safety
sbarco, unloading
scalo, port of call
scaricamento, unloading
scialuppa da salvattagio, lifeboat
stazza, tonnage
stazza lorda, gross tonnage
stazza netta, net tonnage
stivaggio, stowage
stivatore, stevedore
traffico marittimo, shipping
trasbordo, transhipment
varare, to launch
via di mare, by sea
via marittima, sea route
zavorra, ballast

Exercises

I. Translate into English.

Il giornale di navigazione e l'inventario di bordo sono libri di bordo che ogni capitano di una nave italiana deve tenere. Il bastimento naviga sotto bandiera neutrale. La merece è stata caricata a Genova sopra una nave che accetta soltanto merce a carico generale. La polizza di carico non è un documento di trasporto ma un titolo rappresentativo della proprietà delle merci, e deve contenere le seguenti indicazioni: natura, qualità e quantità della merce caricata i nomi del caricatore e del destinatorio, il nome e la nazionalità della nave, e il nolo. La nave riceve il carico lungo la calata. In questo caso il contratto è intervenuto fra l'armatore ed il neoleggiatore. Benchè la nave che ha gettato l'àncora nel porto sia vecchia è ancora atta alla navigazione. I cantieri di Trieste hanno varato una petroliera della portata di 20.000 tonnellate. Il bastimento in alto mare bate bandiera italiana. Il contratto di noleggio dà diritto al nolo sino al luogo di naufragio. Il noleggiatore vuole procurare un carico completo per la nave. Purtroppo il carico è stato danneggiato per difetto nello stivaggio prima dell'arrivo al porto indicato. La polizza di assicurazione marittima protegge la nave durante il viaggio da un porto all'altro. Non crediamo che questa nave sia capace di tenere il mare. Non possiamo determinare la responsabilità dello speditore. Qualche volta la polizza di assicurazione marittima autorizza la deviazione della rotta. Ci sembra che dobbiamo pagare il nolo in anticipo. Qualche polizza di carico può essere frazionata in due o tre ordini di consegna. Le merci devono essere trasportate lungo bordo della nave per cura del caricatore. L'imbarco e lo stivaggio delle merci sono effettuate a rischio dei caricatori. Il capitano ha focaltà di entrare ed uscire dai porti senza pilota practico. L'armatore consegna le cose incaricate a chi presenta la polizza di carico. Il possessore di una polizza non ha diritto di mutare il luogo di destinazione della merce. Il nolo è pagabile nella moneta stipulata in polizza.

II. Translate into Italian:

The ship sails under neutral flag. The bill of lading is being checked by the ship's master. The unloading of the goods has started. This policy of marine insurance makes no provision for deviation. The ship is not seaworthy. The Italian cargo boat has cast anchor in the harbour. The master has the right to deviate from his route. The delivery order is an important document. The shipowner reserves the right *(si riserva il diritto)* to delay departure of the ship. The master must keep the ship's books. In this case the freight is not recoverable. The loading of goods is done at shipper's risk. The ship flying the Italian flag has left *(è uscita da)* the roads.

III. Answer briefly in Italian the following questions:

1. Quali sono i libri di bordo che il capitano della nave deve tenere?
2. Come si chima la ricevuta che il capitano rilascia per la merce caricata?
3. Quali sono le indicazioni che deve contenere la polizza di carico?
4. È possibile frazionare la polizza di carico in vari ordini di consegna?
5. A chi consegna l'armatore le cose incaricate?
6. Dove riceve il carico la nave?
7. In che moneta è pagabile il nolo?
8. La polizza di assicurazione marittima autorizza la deviazione dalla rotta o no?
9. Quale facoltà ha il capitano?
10. Come può essere danneggiato il carico di una nave?

Vocabulary II

rena, sand	*accorgersi*, to notice
sedia a sdraio, deck-chair	*spumoso*, foamy
ombrellone, parasol	*grido*, shout
bagnante, bather	*scintillare*, to sparkle
bagnato, wet	*patino*, dinghy
sorvegliare, to watch	*galleggiare*, to float
tutti quanti, all together	*specchio*, mirror
scomparire, to vanish	*bagnino*, beach attendant

Sulla Spiaggia

Stavo seduto nella rena dietro la sedia a sdraio del mio amico. Da una parte erano le cabine da bagno con i tetti rossi e verdi; da l'altra parte qualche ombrellone multicolore sulla spiaggia dava riparo ai bagnanti. A piedi nudi il mio amico sorvegliava i ragazzi che giocavano nella rena bagnata e non pareva essersi accorto della mia presenza. Ad un tratto un ragazzone coi capelli neri domandò, "Si va in mare?" "Sì, sì andiamo" risposero tutti quanti in coro. Cominciarono a correre attraverso la spiaggia verso il mare. Li vidi gettarsi l'uno dopo l'altro e scomparire come pesci nel'acqua verdastra e spumosa, tra gridi di gioia.

Il mare era calmo e scintillava comse se fosse composto di mille pezzetti di vetro e di specchio, orlati di spuma che riflettevano le nuvole bianche e il cielo brillante. Qualche barca o patino galleggiava sonnolento sull'acqua scossa dai bagnanti presso la riva. Da lontano si udiva, portata dalla brezza, la voce melodiosa di un bagnino che era seduto presso un tavolinetto accanto alla sua tenda. "Ecco", mi dissi, "un quadro di benessere, di gioia e di pace."

A Proverb

Chi va piano va sano e va lontano.

CHAPTER 8

The Sale of Goods

GOODS pass from seller to buyer by virtue of a contract or *contratto*. A contract of sale and purchase of goods is called in Italian *contratto di compra-vendita*. Parties to the contract, the *soggetti*, are the seller or *venditore* and the buyer or *compratore*. The subject-matter of the contract, the *oggetto*, consists of the goods and price. It is customary to give a description of the goods and an account of their origin and brand. Reference to a sample or *campione* may be made. If the buyer already has a sample the contract may specify that the quality is as per sample or *qualità come al compaione*. If the buyer and seller have in mind a commonly known sample then reference may be made to quality as per standard sample or *qualità come al campione tipo*.

If after the complete performance of the contract or *completa perfezione*, the buyer finds the goods to be defective then he must lodge a statement called *denunzia* two days after receiving the goods. Such a *denunzia* is made if the defect is visible on examination. If the defect is hidden the *denunzia* must be made within two days of the discovery of such a defect.

A transaction for the sale and purchase of goods has three phases. First, the seller has to offer the goods at a price. Secondly, the buyer has to accept them at that price. Thirdly, the goods have to pass from the seller to the buyer. Once the goods pass to the buyer he assumes full responsibility for them. As for the conditions of payment, they vary according to practice. Payment may be ready cash or *pagamento a contanti*. If the buyer is given a certain time within which to make the payment then it is called *pagamento a respiro*. Another form of payment is by instalments or *pagamento a rate*. In certain cases partial payment is made when a deposit or *caparra* is given to be followed by the residue. If the seller makes certain allowances for the payment then it is called *pagamento con concessione di abbuoni*.

Important documents involved in the transaction for the sale and purchase of goods are the request notice or *buono di richiesta*, the delivery note or *bollettino di consegna*, the dispatch notice or *avviso di spedizione* and the invoice called *fattura* or *conto*. Examples of these documents are given below.

Example I

The following request notice concerns an order for 50 quintals of wheat flour to be sent by rail:

Spett. Ditta Carrara   Milano 3/10/19 . . .
   Piazza Repubblica
   Torino

Favorite spedirci q. li 50 di farina di frumento a ½ ferrovia G.V.—pagamento in c/c.

                              p. Ditta Affix
                              Mario Bruno

Example II

The delivery note states that 20 quintals of phosphates have been delivered to a firm's courier, sig. Aldo Rossi.

Casa Lombarda   Milano 9/4/19 . . .
   Milano   Spett. Ditta Marco Polo
                      Corso Umberto, Modena

Eccovi il bollettino di consegna delle merci consegnate al V/ corriere sig. Aldo Rossi:

Quantità	Marche e numeri	Peso			Descrizione
		Lordo	Tara	Netto	
q.li 20	V.T. 65	q.li 20	q.li 0,40	q.li 19,60	Concimi fosfatici

Example III

The following dispatch notice concerns the dispatch of 50 quintals of wheat flour by rail:

Spett. Sig. Mario Bruno   Torino 5/10/19 . . .
   Dita Affix
     Via Zerbini
     Milano

Ci pregiamo informarvi di avervi inviato q. li 50 di farina di frumento a ½ ferrovia G. V.

                          p. Ditta Carrara
                          Dino Vanoni

Example IV

Here is an invoice for the following quantities of fertilizers: 35 quintals of phosphates and 25 quintals of nitrates dispatched by rail. The terms of payment are 50 per cent cash and 50 per cent 30 days after date:

Casa Lombarda   12/4/19 . . .
   Milano   Alla Spett. Ditta Marco Polo
                           Corso Umberto, Modena

Vi diamo fattura delle merci ordinateci a ½ piazziste e speditevi a ½ ferrovia G. V. a v/ spese. Pagamento 50% contanti e 50% a 30 giorni data.

Marche e numeri	Quantità	Descrizione	Prezzo unitario	Importo totale
TV–33	q.li 35	Concimi fosfatici	3.000.000	105.000.000
SP–14	q.li 25	Concimi azotati	2.000.000	50.000.000
				155.000.000
		Imposta entrate 2%		3.100.000
				158.100.000
		S. E. & O.		

Example V

The following selling agent's invoice account relates to the purchase of 30 quintals of wheat at 2.000 lire per quintal on the instructions of a wholesale grain merchant:

Conto di costo e spese

Marche e numeri	Quantità	Merce	Importo	Totale
TA	q. 30	Frumento a L. 2.000.000 il quintale		60.000.000,–
		Competenze e spese:		
		Spese di trasporto	4.000.000	
		Spese varie	2.000.000	
		Commissione 2%	1.200.000	
		L.		7.200.000,–
		L.		67.200.000,–

Example VI

The following invoice relates to the sale of 30 quintals of wheat on the merchant's instructions:

Conto di netto ricavo

Marche e numeri	Quantità	Merce	Importo	Totale
TA	q. 30	Frumento a L. 2.500.000 il quintale Competenze e spese: Spese di trasporto Spese varie Commissione 2%	1.200.000 300.000 1.500.000	75.000.000
			L.	3.000.000
		Netto ricavo	L.	72.000.000

R I C E V U T A

Le fatture richiamate nella presente dovranno essere pagate il giorno...............

.... , ...

£it.

chè a mezzo del **Credito Italiano**

N.............. *del* .... *di £it.*...................

? .... , ... *» . »* ....

£it. _____

Riceviamo la somma di

ci avete versata *a saldo / in conto* *delle nostre fatture*

per le quali è stata corrisposta l' J.G.E.

Spett. ....

....

.... *(* .... *)*
Provincia

Bollo

Firma

(La presente deve essere allegata alle sopramenzionate fatture)

FIG. 14. Bank's receipt for payment of invoices

Vocabulary I

accusare ricevuta di, to acknowledge receipt of
acquirente, purchaser
acquisto, purchase
atto di compravendita, conveyance sale
avviso di consegna, notice of delivery
bolletta, bill, receipt
bolletta doganale, bill of entry
bollettino dei prezzi, price list
bollettino di consegna, delivery note
bollettino di spedizione, consignment note
buono di richiesta, request note
campione, sample
caparra, earnest
carico di, charge of
commissione, purchase
comprare to buy
compratore, buyer
compravendita, bargain, deed of sale
concorrenza, competition
conti di compra, purchases account
conto di netto ricavo, selling agent's invoice account
conto di vendita, sales account
contrassegno, mark sign
contratto di compravendita, agreement for sale and purchases
costo, cost
debito, debt
diritto di bollo, stamp duty

fattura, invoice
fattura consolare, consular invoice
fattura doganale, customs invoice
fatturare, to invoice
impegnare, to pledge
libro copialettere, invoice copy-book
modulo, coupon form
pagamento, payment
pagamento a contanti, cash payment
pagamento a rate, payment by instalments
pagare, to pay
pegno, pledge
percentuale, percentage
prezzo, price
quietanza, receipt
quietanzare, to receipt
ribasso, fall (in prices)
ricevuta, receipt
(a) richiesta, (on) request
rimessa, remittance
rispedire, to forward
sopperire, to provide for
spese di senseria, brokerage expenses
tara, tare
vendita, sale
vendita a rate, hire-purchase
vendita al minuto, retail sale
vendita all'asta, auction sale
vendita all'ingrosso, wholesale
vendita su campione, sale by sample
venditore, seller

Exercises

I. Translate into English:

La fattura ordinaria è un documento relativo alla compravendita. La merce acquistata è di primissima qualità. I prezzi sul mercato mondiale hanno subito un notevole rincaro. Il venditore deve spedire le merci secondo le modalità del contratto di compravendita. Il bollettino di consegna è un documento commerciale. Lo scope del buono di richiesta è di sopperire alla deficienza di merce. Il pagamento a contanti è sempre fatto a pronta cassa, mentre il pagamento a respiro è fatto in un certo periodo di tempo. Il venditore dev'essere sempre in grado di soddisfare le esigenze del compratore. Il contabile ha portato l'ammontare della fattura a debito del conto del compratore. Vi ringraziamo per lo sconto accordatoci. Ho messo sul tavolo il libro delle fatture di vendita. La fattura dice che i prezzi sono soggetti alle variazioni del mercato e che gli imballaggi non restituti saranno addebitati entro tre settimane. Le condizioni di vendita sono buone. Spesso accade che la concorrenza porta al ribasso di prezzi. È importante indicare il prezzo sotto il quale le merci devono essere vendute. Questi acquisti sono stati fatti a caso. Le spese di raccomandazione sono a carico del committente. In questo caso la merce viaggia per conto e rischio del commissionario.

II. Translate into Italian:

Please pay on receipt of goods. Do not send money in anticipation. I have heard that the conditions of sale are good. The prices on the world market have fallen. The invoice is a commercial document. The contract says that the payment is by instalments. The discount is 3 per cent. The forwarding note has been dispatched. The buyer must receive the goods according to the conditions of the contract.

III. Give brief answers in Italian to the following:

1. Che cosa è la compravendita?
2. Quali sono gli elementi necessari per la validità del contratto di compravendita?
3. Che forme di pagamento ci sono?
4. Quali sono gli elementi del costo delle merci?
5. Enumerare i documenti relativi alla compravendita.
6. Come deve consegnare il venditore le merci?
7. Quali sono le condizioni di vendita più importanti in Italia?

Vocabulary II

siffatto, such
campagna, countryside
capitare, to arrive

guardare, to gaze at
stillarsi, to rack
cervello, brains

avvicinare, to approach
dentro, inside
di traverso, askance
prendersi a gabbo, to laugh at
aggrinzare, to wrinkle

stappare, to uncork
replicare, to retort
all'improviso, suddenly
davvero, really

L'Agente di Cambiavalute

A Firenze, sul Ponte Vecchio, c'erano un tempo molte agenzie di cambiavalute, e naturalmente in questi locali non si vedeva merce alcuna, sia perchè i denari occupano poco spazio sia perchè siffatta merce non si espone con piacere. Un tale Pippo da Brozzi, che veniva dalla campagna, capitando sul Ponte Vecchio guardava in quelle botteghe vuote, e si stillava il cervello, e non riusciva a capire che cosa mai vi si vendesse.

E vedendo un padrone sulla porta, un tal Tonto da Bagnone, Pippo gli si avvicinò e, salutandolo con molta grazia gli domandò:

—"Volete farmi il favore di dirmi cosa si vende qui dentro, nella vostra bottega?"

Tonto lo misurò di traverso, e, parendogli che fosse up tipo da predersi a gabbo, rispose:

—"Ci si vendono teste di asino, galantuomo."

Pippo aggrinzò il naso come se gli avessero stappato all'improviso una bottiglia d'ammoniaca, e poi, pronto, replicò:

—"Si vede che ne avete davvero un bello smercio, chè per quanto io guardi non v'è rimasta che la vostra."

By Francesco D. Guerrazzi

A Proverb

La parola è d'argento, il silenzio è d'oro.

CHAPTER 9

Companies and the Stock Exchange

Companies

THE Italian Code of Commerce requires companies to keep proper books of account giving a true and fair view of the company's affairs. The companies are also required to keep a register of members or *libro dei soci*, and books containing the statutory reports on the meetings and deliberations of the members, of the executive committee and of the company committee, or *collegio sindacale*, which is a committee charged with controlling the proper administration of the company and compliance with the memorandum and articles of association. The memorandum of the company must show the name, domicile and objects of the company as well as the liability of the members and the amount of share capital if any. The articles of association stipulate the way the profits are to be distributed at the end of each accounting year, but the actual distribution is carried out only after the general meeting of the members or *assemblea generale dei soci*.

A general partnership where the members have unlimited liability is called *società in nome collettivo*. A limited partnership having both general and limited partners is known as a *società in accomandita semplice*. In the *società in accomandita per azioni*, however, the limited partners have shares which represent their sole liability.

The joint-stock company or *società anonima* may be registered or unregistered, that is *registrata* or *non registrata*. A company limited by shares is according to Italian law a *società anonima a responsabilità limitata al capitale* while a company limited by guarantee is defined as a *società anonima a responsabilità limitata ad una certa somma oltre le azioni.* The unlimited company now rare in Italy is called *società anonima a responsabilità illimitata.*

A widespread form of commercial enterprise company in Italy is the co-operative society or *società cooperativa.* Each co-operative society has its trustees or *sindaci,* management staff and membership body called the *assemblea.*

The Stock Exchange

The oldest and leading stock exchange in Italy is the Milan stock exchange or *borsa valori di Milano* founded in 1808. Today the exchange has a membership of over 100 *agenti di cambio.*

The Italian Stock Exchange is governed by rules fixed by law and the Treasury supervises its work. Every two years a directing committee of the *agenti di cambio* is elected by the general assembly to act as mediators in disputes and publish the official lists.

The Milan stock exchange deals in national, communal and provincial securities. A small number of transactions are for cash. The bulk of the transactions are for the account or *a termine.* Transactions such as option dealings are called *a premio.* Settlement is at the end of the month through the clearing houses. The *agenti di cambio* are required by the *Codice Civile* to keep a stamped register or *libro bollato* in which they enter daily all their transactions as well as the contango rates or *riporti sui titoli.*

In addition to Milan Italian stock exchanges operate at Turin, Genoa, Rome, Naples, Venice, Palermo, Trieste, Florence and Bologna.

Vocabulary I

acciai, steel shares
accomandante, limited partner
accomandatario, general partner
adunanza, meeting
agente di cambio, stockbroker
agricoli, agricultural shares
alimentari, food shares
amministratore, director
apertura, opening

assemblea, assembly
assicurativi, insurance shares
attivo sociale, company's assets
atto di costituzione, memorandum of association
automobilistici, motor shares
bancari, banking shares
borsa, exchange
borsa valori, stock exchange

capitale sociale, share capital
certificato di azioni, share certificate
certificato provvisorio, scrip
chimici, chemical shares
chiusura, close
collegio, committee
collegio sindacale, company committee
colmare, to make up
contanti, cash
cottimista, jobber
debiti sociali, company's debts
direttore, manager
disposizione, disposal, order
dividendo, dividend
elettrici, electrical shares
emissione, issue
fiacco, dull
finanziari, financial shares
fondi pubblici, public funds
gestione contabile, accounting
illimitato, unlimited
immobiliari, property shares
impresa, enterprise
interesse, interest
libro dei soci, register of members of shareholders
manifatturieri, manufacturing shares
meccanici, engineering shares
metallurgici, metallurgical shares
minerari, mining shares
obbligazione, debenture, bond

pari (alla), par (at)
per intero, fully
petroliferi, oil shares
prospetto, prospectus, schedule
quota, quota
quotare, to quote
redatto, drafted
rendiconto, statement of assets and liabilities
rialzo, rise (in prices)
ribasso, fall (in prices)
ripartire, to divide, to distribute
riparto di azioni, allotment of shares
sbilancio, balance deficit
società, company
società anonima, joint-stock company
società in accomandita per azioni, partnership limited by shares
società in accomandita semplice, limited partnership
società in nome colletivo, general partnership
socio, partner, member of a company
statuto sociale, article of association
tessili, textile shares
titoli, securities
titoli di stato, gilt-edged
titolo, instrument, paper
trasporti, transport shares
versare, to pay down

Exercises

I. Translate into English:

I soci della società in accomandita semplice si chiamano accomandatari e accomandanti. La responsabilità del socio accomandante è limitata alla quota versata. La responsabilità del socio accomadantario è illimitata. Le società anonime italiane si constituiscono per atto pubblico. L'assemblea dei soci e il collegio sindacale sono organi sociali della società anonima. L'azionista è un comproprietario della società e puo prendere parte alle assemblee dei soci. L'obbligazionista è un creditore della società. La forma e il contenuto dei bilanci sono a norma delle disposizioni del Codice Civile. Il bilancio compilato dall'amministratore dev'essere approvato dall'assemblea dei soci. L'utile netto d'esercizio si determina dallo sbilancio del conto dei profitti e delle perdite. La situazione alla fine del periodo della gestione contabile risulta dal rendiconto. L'utile netto si ripartisce secondono le disposizioni dello statuto sociale. Il pagamento dei dividendi si effetua per via di cedole.

La borsa valori, fiacca all'inizio è rimasta ferma alla chiusura. Quando il mercato è povero d'affari, i prezzi dei valori sono generalmente calmi. Pochi titoli italiani sono quotati all'estero. I fondi pubblici sono fermi. La borsa era agitata all'apertura. Le perdite dei chimici sono contenute tra 2 e 4 punti. I meccanici e automobilistici sono richiesti. Il membro della borsa valori che opera per conto proprio si chiama cottismista o jobber. Non tutti i titoli sono ammessi a quotazione officiale. Nel mercato dei premi i prezzi sono ammessi a quotazione officiale. Nel mercato dei premi i prezzi sono cedenti. La borsa di Londra ha chiuso al ribasso mentre a Milano il mercato è poco animato dopo due giorni di buoni guadagni. L'emissione del certificato provvisorio di azioni è stato effettuato. La società ha deciso di fare un riparto di azioni.

II. Translate into Italian:

All members of a general partnership have unlimited liability. A partnership limited by shares is a commercial enterprise. Joint-stock companies can issue debentures. The payment of dividends is made to shareholders. The balance sheet is drawn up by the company director. The deficit of the profit and loss account has been made up. The debentures are issued at par. Stock prices are firm. Textile and manufacturing shares are in demand. A few Italian securities are quoted on the London stock exchange. Different classes of shares are quoted abroad. The shares are fully paid up. The share certificate has already been issued.

III. Answer briefly in Italian the following questions:

1. Quali sono le varie specie di azioni?
2. L'atto costitutivo della società anonima è importante o no?
3. Che cosa è il rendiconto?

4. Quali sono gli organi sociali di una società anonima?
5. È limitata la responsabilità dei soci nella società in nome collettivo?
6. Da chi è redatto il bilancio?
7. Come risulta l'utile netto d'esercizio?

Vocabulary II

pastore, shepherd
aspro, rough
disagiato, hard
nonostante, in spite of
lasciare, leave
pianura, plain
sconfinato, boundless
polveroso, dusty
battere, to beat
bruciare, to burn
gregge, flock
pecora, sheet
avvicinarsi, to approach
fettina, small slice
arrostire, to roast
fetta, slice
fustagno, fustian
ripararsi, to shelter

campanaccio, bell
collo, neck
fitto, thick
scampanellìo, ringing
bisacca, saddle-bag
viveri, food
bidone, can
fucile, shotgun
sparare, to shoot
volpe, fox
lupo, wolf
tentare, try
magro, thin
cacciare, to chase away
gelo, frost
ovile, sheep run
trascorrere, to pass (time)

Pastore Italiano

La vita del pastore italiano è aspra, disagiata e piena di avversità. Nonostante ciò egli è contento del suo destino, e ama il suo lavoro.

In primavera, all'inizio di maggio o più tardi, i pastori lasciano le grandi pianure sconfinate e polverose, quando il sole batte ed il vento brucia la terra, e ritornano ai pascoli alti e freschi dei loro paesi di montagna. Due o tre cavalli ed il fedele cane seguono ogni gregge. Le pecore portano campanacci al collo che danno un fitto e continuo scampanellìo. I cavalli trasportano i pochi bene dei pastori: le bisacce variopinte con i viveri, i bidoni per il latte ed il fucile per sparare alle volpi ed ai lupi. Guai alla volpe o al lupo che tentasse avvicinarsi al gregge!

Il pranzo dei pastori è quanto mai frugale: una fettina di formaggio bianco arrostito al fuco e una fetta di pane. Essi si corpono con mantelli di fustagno per ripararsi dal freddo, dal vento e dalla pioggia.

Nel tardo autunno quando la neve copre di bianco i colli e il sole si leva pallido sui monti grigi, i lupi magri e feroci cacciati dalla fame e dal gelo, si avvicinano all'ovile. I cani da pastore li sentono da lontano ed entrano in uno stato di agitazione. I pastori sanno cosa significa questa agitazione, si mettono in guardia e si preparano a fare ritorno alla pianura dove trascorrono l'inverno fino alla primavera.

A Proverb

A caval donato non is guarda in bocca.

CHAPTER 10

Commercial Correspondence

WHEN merchants and clients separated by a distance greater than the range of vision or sound wish to communicate with each other, they send messages. In Roman times already such messages were delivered by word of mouth or by letter. The messenger carried letters on foot or on horse. Later in medieval Italy the practice grew among merchants of passing letters from messenger or *corriere* to messenger, that is to say from post to post. Thus the postal system came into being.

Today the Italian postal system, *Poste e telegrafi*, offers the commercial world an efficient and reliable service for the transmission of letters, postcards, parcels, money orders, telegrams, etc., for the country or abroad.

Commercial correspondence, as a means of communication, makes possible business transactions in its multiple forms. The post is used extensively by Italian merchants and clients as a means of communicating the offer or acceptance of goods, demand for payment or acknowledgement of receipts, the advertising of new products or price lists. When it is desired to convey certain information to a large number of people then a circular letter or *lettera circolare* is used. Widespread resort is also had to secret codes or ciphers called *cifrari* for confidential information transmitted by letter or telegram. The codes which are mutually known are an important means of economy in telegrams.

Offices have an established way of handling the commercial correspondence of a firm in order to fulfil practical and legal requirements. All incoming letters are stamped with a capital R for "*ricevuto*" as well as with the date of arrival. The reference book or *libro protocollo* is used for entering details of all incoming and outgoing mail. Italian offices are obliged to keep a letter-book or *copialettere* which is a commercial book in which all copies of letters are kept. The letter-book is subject to stamp duty and must be endorsed as correct by the local magistrate or *pretore*.

Vocabulary I

affrancatura, postage
argomento, subject, topic
avviso di ricevimento, notice of receipt
busta, envelope
cartella, folder
cartolina illustrata, picture postcard
cartolina postale, postcard
cifrario, code
circolare, circular letter
copialettere, letter-book
corrispondenza, correspondence
dattiloscrivere, to type
espresso, express post
far proseguire la posta, to forward the post
fermo posta, poste restante
firma, signature
fonogramma, written telephone message
francobollo, postage stamp
lettera, letter

libro protocollo, reference book
manoscritto, handwritten
modulo per telegramma, telegram form
pacco ordinario, ordinary parcel
per l'estero, for abroad
per l'interno, for the country
porto assegnato, postage unpaid
posta, post
pratiche, file
protocollo, reference
raccomandare, to register
risposta, reply
rubrica, reference, title
sopratassa, surcharge
stampe, printed matter
tariffe postali, postal charges
telegramma, telegram
ufficio postale, post office
vaglia, postal order
(per) via aerea, by air

Commercial Letter Writing

An Italian commercial letter usually has the name and address of the sender and the date on the right-hand side, and the name and address of the addressee on the left-hand side. A reference number or letters, where correspondence is heavy, and a heading of the subject-matter are useful.

The letter proper need not begin with "Dear Sir" though its counterpart, "Egregio Signore", is sometimes used. The letter can start directly with an introductory sentence or paragraph followed by the subject-matter. The writer concludes with a courtesy phrase or sentence, rather than with a terse "Yours faithfully". The signature must be handwritten because a typed signature has no value.

The writer of a good commercial letter must be conversant with and fluent in the usage of commercial phrases and abbreviations. His exposition of the subject-matter must be accurate, clear and concise.

Some Standard Beginnings of Letters

Abbiamo il piacere di . . . We are pleased to . . .

Abbiamo l'onore di communicare . . . We are honoured to inform . . .

A riscontro della pregiata Vs. in data . . . In answer to your letter of . . .

Con riferimento alla pregiata Sua del . . . With reference to your letter of . . .

Con riferimento alla Sua richiesta del . . . With reference to your request of . . .

Con riferimento alla Vs. del . . . With reference to your letter of . . .

Ho ricevuto la Sua gradita del . . . I received your letter of . . .

In possesso della stimata Sua del . . . Having received your letter of . . .

In riscontro alla Sua del . . . In reply to your letter of . . .

In risposta alla . . . In reply to . . .

In seguita alla visita Vs. di . . . Following your visit of . . .

La ringrazio della Sua lettera del . . . I thank you for your letter of . . .

Qui allegata (or *allegato*) *ho l'onore di rimetterLe* . . . Herewith enclosed I have the honour to send you . . .

Ricevemmo a suo tempo la pregiata Vs. in data . . . We duly received your letter dated . . .

Riferendomi alla stimata Sua del . . . Referring to your letter of . . .

Siamo ben lieti di poterVi communicare . . . We are glad to be able to inform you . . .

Vi accusiamo ricevuta di . . . We acknowledge receipt of . . .

Vi confermiamo che . . . We confirm that . . .

Vi ringraziamo della pregiata Vs. di . . . We thank you for your letter of . . .

Standard Endings of Letters

Ci è grata l'occasione per presentarVi i ns. distinti saluti. We take the opportunity to send you our kind regards.

Con distinti saluti. With kind regards.

Con rinnovati molto cordiali ringraziamenti. With renewed and most cordial thanks.

Con tutta stima. Respectfully.

Con tutta stima Vi salutiamo. We greet you respectfully.

Cordiali saluti. Cordial greetings.

Cordialmente Vi (or La) salutiamo. We greet you cordially.

Distintamente. Regards.

Distintamente salutiamo. Kind regards.

Distinti saluti. Kind regards.

Gradisca frattanto i miei migliori saluti. Please accept in the meantime my best regards.

Gradite i ns. migliori saluti. Please accept our best regards.

Gradite i ns. più distinti saluti. Please accept our kindest regards.

Ho l'onore di essere, I have the honour to be,
    Sue dev. mo.   Yours faithfully.

In attesa della Sua gradita visita, distintamente salutiamo. Looking forward to your welcome visit, we send our kind regards.

In attesa di una Sua gentile risposta, distintamente salutiamo. Awaiting your kind reply, we send our kind regards.

La prego di gradire i miei ringraziamenti. Please accept my thanks.

Le presento i miei distinti saluti. I send you my kind regards.

Mi è gradita l'occasione per porgerLe i miei distinti saluti. I take the opportunity to send you my kind regards.

Nell'attesa di un Vs. cortese riscontro, Vi porgo i miei distinti saluti. Awaiting your kind acknowledgement, I send you my kind regards.

Presento i miei ossequi, dichiarandomi, Sending you my respects, I am,
    Suo dev. mo.   Faithfully Yours.

Ricevete i ns. devoti saluti. Accept our kind regards.

Vi porgiamo i ns. distinti saluti. We send you our kind regards.
Vi prego di ricevere l'assicurazione del mio profondo rispetto, Please accept my deepest regards.
Vi salutiamo. Greetings.
Vi salutiamo distintamente. Kind greetings.
Vogliate gradire l'espressione dei ns. omaggi. Please accept our respects.
Vogliate ricevere i sensi della ns. considerazione. Please accept our kind regards.

Festive occasions, anniversaries, the presentation of gifts and so on are accompanied by various greetings. Here are a few:

AugurandoLe un lieto Natale . . .	Wishing you a merry Christmas . . .
Auguri	Greetings or Good wishes
Auguri sinceri	Sincere greetings
Buon Anno	Happy New Year
Buon Natale	Happy Christmas
Buon viaggio	Have a good journey
Buona fortuna	Good luck
Buone Feste	Happy Holidays
Cento di questi giorni	Many happy returns of the day
Con auguri natalizi . . .	With Christmas greetings . . .
Con mille buoni auguri	With a thousand good wishes
Mille auguri	A thousand greetings
Tanti auguri	Many greetings
Un felice Nuovo Anno	A happy New Year
Un felicissimo Natale	A very happy Christmas
Un lieto Natale	A merry Christmas

Miscellaneous Model Letters

In the following letter a customer writes to the fruit firm "Frutta Citrica" of Palermo stating his requirement for 100 cases of oranges to be dispatched by goods train. He ends the letter by asking whether this consignment is available:

5 febb. 19 . . .

Spett. Ditta "Frutta Citrica",
    Palermo.

Oggetto: Fornitura 100 cassette Arance Siciliane

Ho l'onore di comunicare alla Spett. Ditta "Frutta Citrica" che mi occorre la fornitura di 100 cassette di Arance Siciliane a ½ ferrovia P.V. alle condizioni specificate nella Vs. circolare del 10 m.s.
    Vogliate quindi informarmi a stretto giro di posta della possibilità di questa fornitura.

Gradite i miei migliori saluti,
(Signature)

The firm "Frutta Citrica" answers that it is able to fulfil the customer's order for 100 cases of oranges, specifying the charges for which the customer is responsible:

Prot. No. 12.   10 febb. 19 . . .

Oggetto: Fornitura 100 cassette Arance Siciliane

Egregio Signore,

con riferimento alla Sua lettera del 5 m.c. siamo lieti di poterLe comunicare che la nostra ditta "Frutta Citrica" puo accordarLe la fornitura di 100 cassette Arance Siciliane alle condizioni specificate nella ns. circolare del 10 dicembre a.s. Le spese d'imballo, di trasporto e di contrassegno sono a Suo carico.
    AugurandoLe il migliore successo, Le porgiamo i ns. distinti saluti.

(Signature)

When dispatching the invoice, the firm supplying the oranges sends an accompanying letter specifying a discount of 3 per cent 30 days after date.

Prot. No. 12.   12 febb. 19 . . .

Oggetto: Fornitura 100 cassette Arance Siciliane

Egregio Signore,

qui acclusa Le rimettiamo la ns. fattura No. 150 relativa alla Sua commissione "Frutta Citrica" No. 20 evasa in data odierna.

Un soprasconto del 3 per cento le spetta contro pagamento 30 giorni data.

Con stima.
(Signature)

A customer orders a book from a bookshop and encloses a cheque for 80.000 lire:

Spett. ditta Libreria Delfino,   Roma,
    Milano,   Piazza Esedra,
      Piazza Repubblica.   4 aprile 19 . . .

Volgliate inviarmi una copia del Manuale Didattico di F., editore M., a stretto giro di posta contro assegno per l'importo di lire 80.000 qui accluso.

Distinti saluti
(Signature)

The bookshop replies expressing regret for not stocking the book in question owing to the fact that it does not specialize in technical books. It recommends two bookshops in Milan specializing in this line. The cheque for 80.000 lire is returned:

Libreria Delfino,
Milano,
10 aprile 19 . . .

Gentile Signore,

La ringraziamo della Sua attenzione. Ci duole però di non poterLa accontentare perchè la nostra Casa ha pochi libri tecnici non avendo la specializzazione per tal genere di libri. Vi sono altre librerie a Milano specializzate in questo campo come la CIC, e la ABA. Le rimettiamo quindi il Suo assegno per l'importo di lire 80.000

1 alleg.   Con stima.
                                                       (Signature)

Mr. John Hunter intends to visit Rome and he therefore writes a letter to Albergo Gloria inquiring whether he can book a room from 20th to 25th March. He also wants to know the price.

Ill.mo Sig. Direttore,   Londra,
    Albergo Gloria,   Inghilterra,
        Roma.   4 febb. 19 . . .

Essendo mia intenzione visitare Roma nel mese di marzo dal 20 al 25, voglia comunicarmi se ha la possibilità di alloggiarmi per questo periodo.

Vorrei anche sapere i prezzi che Lei pratica in questa stagione.

In attesa di una Sua gentile risposta, Le invio i miei distinti saluti.

                                        (Signature)

The Albergo Gloria replies that it can book a room for Mr. John Hunter from 20th to 25th March and then specifies the various charges as follows: room L. 9.000; heating L. 500; bath L. 2.000; breakfast L. 4.000; luncheon L. 6.000; dinner L. 8.000.

                              Albergo Gloria, Roma
                              15 febb. 19 . . .

In risposta alla Sua lettera del 4 febb. u. s., siamo lieti di comunicarLe che presso l'Albergo Gloria abbiamo la possibilità di alloggiarLa per le notti dal 20 al 25 marzo.

I prezzi a persona al giorno sono i seguenti: pernottamento L. 9.000; riscaldamento L. 500; bagno L. 2.000; prima colazione L. 4.000; seconda colazione L. 6.000; pranzo L. 8.000.

Restando in attesa di averLa presto nostro ospite La salutiamo distintamente.

(Signature)

Mr. John Hunter now writes to the Albergo Gloria booking a room from 20th to 25th March at the prices indicated in the letter of 15th February. He concludes by asking for a letter of acknowledgement.

Londra,
Inghilterra,
20 febb. 19 . . .

Ill.mo Sig. Direttore,

in vista della mia prossima visita a Roma voglia riservare una camera nel Suo Albergo per le notti del 20 al 25 marzo alle condizioni specificate nella Sua lettera dal 15 m.c.
Per mia tranquillità La prego di un breve cenno di riscontro

Con stima
(Signature)

The Albergo Gloria writes back confirming that a room has been booked for Mr. John Hunter from 20th to 25th March.

Albergo Gloria, Roma,
Prot. 15   26 febb. 19 . . .

Oggetto: prenotazione camera

Gentile Signor Hunter,

con riferimento alla Sua lettera del 20 febb. u.s. La informiamo che abbiamo riservato una camera nel ns. Albergo Gloria per le notti del 20 al 25 marzo.
Grati della Sua attenzione, La salutiamo cordialmente.

(Signature)

Letter of Introduction

The letter introduces Mr. John Hunter who is a representative in Milan. It concludes with anticipated thanks for help given.

Il latore della presente, Sig. John Hunter, è il nostro rappresentante a Milano. Ci prendiamo la libertà di pregarVi di ascoltare quanto Vi dirà.

Vi ringraziamo in anticipo della Vs. assistenza, e Vi salutiamo ben distintamente.

(Signature)

Letter of Invitation

The following letter invites a couple to dinner on Saturday, 5th January, at eight o'clock. The letter points out that there is an excellent trolley-bus which leaves the Piazza Esedra at a quarter to eight and that the host will be waiting at the bus stop. The host looks forward to the visit.

Gentile Signore Bianchi,

sarò ben lieto se Lei e Sua Moglie potranno venire da me a pranzo sabato prossimo 5 gennaio alle ore otto.

C'è il filobus alle otto meno un quarto da Piazza Esedra ed io verrei alla fermata per accoglierLi.

In attesa della Loro gradita visita, invioLoro i miei più distinti saluti.

(Signature)

Letter Accepting the Invitation

The letter thanks for the invitation and confirms acceptance. In conclusion thanks are expressed again for the invitation.

Gentile Signor Rossi,

mille grazie del gentile invito per sabato prossimo. Mia Moglie ed io siamo ben lieti di accettare e può attenderci per le otto.

Con molti ringraziamenti per il Suo gentile invito, rimango Suo

> dev. mo.
> (Signature)

Letter Turning Down the Invitation

The letter gives thanks for the kind invitation but expresses regret for having to turn down the invitation owing to a promised visit to friends at Siena. Thanks are expressed again in conclusion.

Gentile Signor Rossi,

grazie infinite del Suo gentile invito per sabato prossimo. Ci rincresce molto di non poter venire perchè abbiamo promesso di andare da nostri amici a Siena.

Con rinnovati ringraziamenti, La saluto cordialmente.

> (Signature)

A proverb

Dal dire al fare c'è di mezzo il mare.

CHAPTER 11

Translation Techniques

Model Translations

THE Italian saying that a translator is a traitor, *traduttore traditore*, focuses attention on the central problem of translating, which is how to find the right meaning—translating is a form of writing and at the same time a search for meaning. The aim of the translator is to keep the structure, meaning and flavour of the original in such a way that it may be read as if it were issued from the pen of an English writer.

There are two basic methods of translating both of which are suited to the utility of translations. The first method is to translate word for word, phrase for phrase, meaning for meaning keeping in this way as closely as possible to the structure of the original. This literal approach is best suited for commercial, technical and scientific literature where the danger of ambiguity is at a minimum.

The second method of translating is more fundamental and is based on rethinking the original in English terms. The translator has to penetrate deeply into the meaning of the original text. He translates not words, phrases, clauses of sentences, but rather units of thought. When he is confronted with a passage of uncertain meaning he takes a calculated risk. This second approach is pre-eminently used in translating literary works.

A good translator is strictly impartial and must not allow his own emotions or bias to creep into the translation. If a translation is subjected to such extraneous influences then it becomes inaccurate and distorted.

The professional translator cannot hope of being proficient unless he is speedy, accurate and versatile. These qualities can be acquired with practice and with observing some of the principles listed below:

(a) Find the general meaning of the text to be translated first. Then find the meaning of each sentence before it is translated.

(b) Look out for idiomatic constructions and have ready their English equivalents. For instance, the translation of *far buon viso a cattivo giuoco* is "to make the best of a bad job" or of *ce ne vuole* is "it takes a great deal of trouble".

(c) Beware of the "false friends" which lurk on every page. For instance, *fattoria* means "farm" and not "factory"; *attualmente* means "at present" and not "actually"; *acconto* means "deposit" and not "account".

(d) Always determine the exact meaning of a word by reference to its context. In the counting-house, *conto* means "an account". In the trading-house *conto* means "an invoice". In the café, *conto* means "a bill".

(e) Remember that the word order in Italian is not always the same as in English. Sometimes the tail of an Italian sentence forms the head of the equivalent English sentence.

(f) Long sentences in Italian are best cut up into shorter sentences in English and vice versa.

(g) In your translation use a short word for a long one when you have the choice and avoid strange and unusual words.

(h) Translate by being clear without being scarce.

For practical purposes translations fall into the following categories according to the treatment of the original:

1. *Report.* When the translator makes a report on an article, circular, correspondence, etc., he uses his own words to give the gist of the original. The report is therefore only a translated account of the original which if lengthy can be put in indirect speech.

2. *Summary.* The summarized translation of an original is an abridged version keeping the same mood and tense. A summary is usually longer than a report because it is more detailed and in the same mood and tense as the original.

3. *Summary with excerpts.* This type of translation is also an abridged version of the original in the same mood and tense with the addition of translated passages of importance placed between quotation marks. The textual passages quoted should be no shorter than a complete sentence.

4. *Text excerpts.* When doing text excerpts, the translator gives extracts of noteworthy passages not shorter than a sentence. The passages omitted from the original should be shown by three or four dots. If the translator is faced with translating an important document which nevertheless has to be shortened, he may show in footnotes the gist of the passages omitted.

5. *Single excerpt.* Sometimes the translator may decide to do a single excerpt of some noteworthy passage and ignore the rest or just give the gist of what has been omitted in a footnote. This type of translation is best suited for an article or circular where the main information is concentrated in an introductory or concluding paragraph.

6. *Text.* A textual translation is the fullest execution of the original, the type of translation most suited for the examination room and for the translation of the long array of technical and commercial documents. The full use of abbreviations is allowed in a textual translation provided it does not cause ambiguity.

Examples

Report

I petroli dell'Africa hanno costituito uno dei principali motivi d'interesse e di attività europea in quel continente. Le società commerciali europee hanno escavato dei pozzi, costruito delle raffinerie e creatod egli oleodotti.

Gli esperti hanno gia redatto il progetto di un oleodotto dall'Africa all'Europa. Attualmente questo progetto è passato dalla fase di semplice idea a quella di studio vero e proprio. Navi specializzate faranno dei rilievi e dei sondaggi nel Mediterraneo per risolvere il problema di posare a grandi profondità i tubi dell'oleodotto.

A report in *Il Messaggero* states that European oil companies operating in Africa are planning to build a pipeline linking Africa to Europe. Plans are well advanced and ships will shortly investigate the possibility of laying the pipeline at great depths in the Mediterranean.

(From *Il Messaggero*)

Summary

Il piano di rinascità della Sardegna costituisce il primo esperimento di programmazione globale nell'ambito regionale; esso prevede 400 miliardi di investimenti aggiuntivi in tredici anni e stabilisce alcuni criteri direttivi per tutta la spesa pubblica da eseguirsi in Sardegna. Il piano è stato elaborato dalla Regione, i cui organi tecnici hanno operato d'intesa con la Cassa per il Mezzogiorno, la quale eserciterà anche una attività di assistenza e di controllo nella progettazione esecutiva degli interventi. Nella fase di elaborazione del piano, la Regione ha consultato anche i sindacati dei lavoratori e dei datori di lavoro.

The plan for the economic revival of Sardinia provides for an investment of 400 milliard lire over a period of 13 years. The Board for the South has co-operated with the Regional authorities in drafting the plan. The Board will also help in and control the implementation of the plan. The regional authorities consulted the trade unions and employers when drafting the plan.

(From *24 Ore*)

Summary with excerpts

Le prime rappresaglie della Francia nei confronti di Monaco metteranno fra breve tempo in difficoltà le banche del Principato. Il governo di Parigi ha infatti vietato ad alcuni istituti di credito monegaschi di avere rappresentanti o di concludere operazioni finanziarie nel territorio francese: ventidue delle ventotto banche esistenti a Monaco (ma la cui clientela si trova nella grande maggioranza in Francia) sono interessate al provvedimento. Alcune di esse potrebbero essere costrette a cessare completamente la propria attività. Soltanto i sei istituti di credito monegaschi graditi dal governo francese potranno continuare a lavorare.

La battaglia delle banche è il primo risultato della guerra fredda franco-monegasca. Le altre conseguenze cominceranno a farsi sentire in ottobre, quando spirerà il preavviso semestrale per la denuncia della convenzione franco-monegasca.

France's reprisal against Monaco's banks will cause difficulties. "The Paris government has in fact banned a number of Monaco credit institutions from having representatives or carrying out financial transactions on French territory." Twenty-two of Monaco's twenty-eight banks are affected and some of them could be obliged to end completely all activities. Only six of Monaco's banks will be able to continue operations in France.

"The battle of the banks is the first result of the cold war between France and Monaco. The other consequences will start making themselves felt in October when the six month notice ending the agreement between France and Monaco expires."

(From *Corrier della Sera*)

Un aumento dei costi, non ancora recuperato da un aumento di produttività, non puo fare a meno di creare qualche difficoltà per le vendite all'estero, ma sopratutto di quelle merci che si trovavano al limite della copertura dei costi con i ricavi.

An increase in costs not compensated by an increase in productivity, cannot but create difficulties for sales abroad and above all for those goods which are at the limit of the costs cover and proceeds . . .

Facendo la differenza tra i valori delle importazioni e delle esportazioni si ricava il disavanzo della bilancia commerciale.

Passage omitted

Bisogna poi ricordare che la bilancia commerciale non è che una parte della bilancia dei pagamenti, la quale comprende anche le partite invisibili. Le compensazioni delle partite visibili ed invisibili trovano espressione nella situazione valutaria.

. . . One must then remember that the trade balance is only part of the balance of payments which includes also the invisible entries. The compensation of visible and invisible entries finds expression in the monetary situation.

(From *Corriere della Sere*)

Uscirono dalla valle e cominciarono a salire sulla collina. I campicelli sulla collina erano separati l'uno dall' altro da siepi verdi e il vento soffiava tra le cime degli alberi.

They came out of the valley and climbed up into the hills, where the little fields were parted with green hedges and the wind blew in the tree tops.

Si sedettero uno accanto all'altro nell'erba alta e guardarono il fiume laggiù che serpeggiava argenteo tra i prati tranquilli. Videro gli uccelli che volavano altissimi nel cielo d'estate, e nuvole bianche che percorrevano il grande campo azzurro. Insetti si arrampicavano con lenta ostinazione sui fili d'erba e sugli steli dei fiori. Le api ronzavano in un cespuglio vicino mentre giù nella valle le vacche bianche e nere aspettavano ai cancelli per essere munte.

They sat down side by side in the long grass and looked down to the river winding silvery through peaceful meadows. They saw birds flying far above in the summer sky, and white clouds crossing the great expanse of blue. Insects climbed the blades of grass and the stalks of flowers with slow determination. Bees buzzed in a nearby bush, and down in the valley the black and white cows stood in the gateways waiting to be milked.

Qui nella calma della campagna i due borghesi si sentivano tranquilli. Le loro reazioni erano più basse. Qualche ora prima si erano bisticiati ma adesso stavano zitti e si sentivano contenti. Il tema della loro disputa sembrava senza importanza

Here in the calm countryside the two townspeople felt peace. Their reactions became slower, steadier, their voices softer. Earlier they had been quarrelling, but now they became silent and content. The subject of their argument seemed insignificant in comparison with the beauty of the

in quel bel paesaggio e nel piacevole	landscape and the pleasant heat of the
tepore del sole di giugno.	June sun.

A Proverb

Idee nuove, uomini vecchi; fiori freschi e rami secchi.

Abbreviations of Commercial Terms and Organizations

The following list gives abbreviations currently used in Italian commercial correspondence, circulars, price lists, journals and other publications. When writing, the student should exercise his discretion in using abbreviations, and he should avoid them altogether where they are likely to confuse the reader. Some abbreviations stand for the singular and plural. For instance, L. stands either for *lira* in the singular or *lire* in the plural. But pag. is used for the singular *pagina* while pagg. is used for the plural *pagine*.

Full point after an abbreviation should not be used where it is not required.

Signore and dottore, if not abbreviated, drop the *e* before a name or title thus, Signor Bruno or Dottor Bruno.

Abbre- viation	Italian	English or Latin
a ½	a mezzo	by means of
ag.	agosto	August
alleg.	allegato	enclosure
alt.	altitudine	altitude
apr.	aprile	April
art.	articolo	article
avv.	avvocato	lawyer
c.a.	corrente anno	of this year
cat.	categoria	category
Cav.	Cavaliere	Cavalier (title)
cfr.	confronta	cross-refer
C.I.F.	(cost, insurance and freight)	C.I.F.
c/o	conto	account
cod.	codesto	this
coll.	collettame	parcels
Comm.	Commendatore	Italian title

Abbre-viation	Italian	English or Latin
corr.	corrente	current
C.V.	cavallo vapore	Horse-power
dest.	destinazione	destination
dic.	dicembre	December
dir.	direttore	director
div.	divisione	division (admin.)
dott.	dottore	Dr.
ecc.	eccetera	etc.
es.	esempio	example
esig.	esigibile	payable
etto	ettogrammo	hectogramme
febb.	febbraio	February
f.m.	fine mese	end of month
F.O.B.	(Free on board)	F.O.B.
genn.	gennaio	January
giu.	giugno	June
G.V.	grande velocità	by passenger train
I.G.E.	imposta generale sull'entrata	purchase tax
inform.	informazione	information
ing.	ingegnere	engineer
isp.	ispettore	inspector
L.	lire	lire
Lit.	lire italiane	Italian lire
ll.	loro	they or their
loc.	località	locality
lu.	luglio	July
m.	mio	my
magg.	maggio	May
mar.	marzo	March
min.	minuto	minute
mq.	metro quadrato	square metre
N.B.	nota bene	take note
nov.	novembre	November
ns.	nostro	our
o.d.g.	ordine del giorno	agenda
ott.	ottobre	October
pag.	pagina	page
pagg.	pagine	pages
p/c	pronto cassa	ready cash
preg.	pregiata	esteemed—i.e. letter
prot.	protocollo	reference
prov.	provvigione	commission
P.S.	poscritto	P.S. (post scriptum)
P.V.	piccola velocità	by goods train
q.li	quintali	quintals

Abbre- viation	Italian	English or Latin
S/	Suo	your
s.a.	scorso anno	of last year
S. A.	società anonima	limited company
S. E. & O.	salvo errori e omissioni	errors and omissions excepted
sett.	settembre	September
Sig.	signore	Mr.
sig.ra	signora	Mrs.
sig.na	signorina	Miss
soc.	società	company
S.p.A.	società per azioni	joint-stock company
spett.	spettabile	honourable
spett. ditta	spettabile ditta	Messrs.
tel.	telefono	telephone
t/m	tara per merce	tare per goods
tot.	totale	total
u.s.	ultimo scorso	ultimo, last (of time)
v.s.	vostro, vostra	your
Vs/	Vostra lettera	your letter
V.S.	voi signori	gentlemen

Italian Weights, Measures and Sizes

Weights

t. (tonnellata)	= 1.000 kg.
q. (quintale)	= 100 kg.
mag. (miriagrammo)	= 10 kg.
kg. (chilogrammo)	= 1 kg. (1 kg. = 35 oz.)
hg. (ettogrammo)	= 0,1 kg.
dag. (decagrammo)	= 0,01 kg.
g. (grammo)	= 0,001 kg.
dg. (decigrammo)	= 0,1 gr.
cg (centigrammo)	= 0,01 gr.
mg. (milligrammo)	= 0,001 gr.

Long Measures

mam. (miriametro)	= 10.000 m.
km. (chilometro)	= 1.000 m. (1 km. = 1094 yd)
hm. (ettometro)	= 100 m.
dam. (decametro)	= 10 m.
m. (metro)	= 1 m.
dm. (decimetro)	= 0,1 m.
cm. (centimetro)	= 0,01 m.
mm. (millimetro)	= 0,0001 m.

Measures of Capacity

mal. (mirialitro)	= 10.000 l.
kl. (chilolitro)	= 1.000 l.
hl. (ettolitro)	= 100 l.
dal. (decalitro)	= 10. l.
l. (litro)	= 1 l. (1 l. = 1,76 pt)
dl. (decilitro)	= 0,1 1.
cl. (centilitro)	= 0,01 l.
ml. (millilitro)	= 0,001 l.

Sizes

Women's clothes:	40	42	44	46	48	50	
(English equivalents)	C-2	D-2	E-2	F-2	G-2	H-2	
Men's clothes:	46	48	50	52	54	56	
(English equivalents)	36	38	40	42	44	46	
Shirt collars:	36	37	38	39	40	41	42
(English equivalents)	14	14½	15	15½	16	16½	17
Shoe sizes:	34	35	36	37	38	39	
(English equivalents)	1	2	3	4	5	6	
Shoe sizes:	40	41	42	43	44	45	
(English equivalents)	7	8	9	10	11	12	

IFC-H

Hat sizes: 53   54   55   56   57   58
(English equivalents)   6½   6⅝   6¾   6⅞   7   7⅛

Hat sizes: 59   60   61
(English equivalents)   7¼   7⅜   7½

Organizations

A.G.I.P	Azienda Generale Italiana Petroli
ALITALIA	Linee Aeree Italiane
A.N.A.S.	Azienda Nazionale Autonoma Strade
A.N.I.C.	Azienda Nazionale Idrogenazione Combustibili
C.N.E.L.	Consiglio dell'Economia e del Lavoro
E.N.A.L.	Ente Nazionale Assistenza Lavoratori
E.N.I.	Ente Nazionale Idrocarburi
E.N.I.T.	Ente Nazionale Industrie Turistiche
FS/FFSS	Ferrovie dello Stato
I.B.I.	Istituto Bancario Italiano
I.N.A.M.	Istituto Nazionale Assicurazione contro le Malattie
I.N.P.S.	Istituto Nazionale Previdenza Sociale
I.R.I.	Istituto Riscostruzione Industriale
RAI– TV	Radiotelevisione Italiana
S.N.A.M.	Società Nazionale Metanodotti

Trade Unions

G.G.I.L	Confederazione Generale Italiana Lavoratori
C.I.S.A.L.	Confederazione Italiana Sindacati Autonomi Lavoratori
C.I.S.L.	Confederazione Italiana Sindacati Lavoratori
C.I.S.N.A.L.	Confederazione Italiana Sindacati Nazionali Autonomi Lavoratori
U.I.L.	Unione Italiana del Lavoro
U.N.S.A.	Unione Nazionale Sindacati Autonomi

Political Parties

B.R.	Brigate Rosse
M.S.I.	Movimento Sociale Italiano
P.C.I.	Partito Comunista Italiano
P.D.C.	Partito della Democrazia Cristiana
P.L.I.	Partito Liberale Italiano
P.R.I.	Partito Repubblicano Italiano
P.S.D.I.	Partito Social-Democratico Italiano
P.S.I.	Partito Socialista Italiano
P.S.I.U.P.	Partito Socialista Italiano di Unità Proletaria

Newspapers

Corriere della Sera	*L'Osservatore Romano*
La Stampa	*L'Avanti*
Stampa Sera	*L'Unità*
Il Messaggero	*Paese Sera*
Il Tempo	*La Nazione*
Il Popolo	*Il Resto del Carlino*
24 Ore	*Il Giornale d'Italia*
Il Giorno	*La Gazzetta del Popolo*
Il Mattino	*La Voce Repubblicana*
Il Secolo D'Italia	*Momento Sera*

Press Agency

A.N.S.A.	Agenzia Nazionale Stampa Associata

CHAPTER 12

Computers: hardware and software

THE ITALIAN primacy in book-keeping, banking and insurance does not extend to computers and data processing. Computer hardware and software were imported mostly from the United States and so has basic terminology. New Italian words have been coined and invented and many adapted for use in computer operations. In a few instances Italian words are used alongside English terms.

Words that have been imported intact such as directory, bound and restore (used as a noun) have become feminine. The plural of these terms are often unchanged. Computer, flag (additional information added to data), file, start or system are all masculine. File in the singular is il file but in the plural i files. Start acquires the *lo* definite article in the singular and *gli* in the plural. Mask is used as an alternative to maschera, while flow is used for flow-charting. Byte, chip, pathname and hardware are also currently used in computer manuals.

Data processing is called *elaborazione dei dati*. A computer or *calcolatore elettronico* is an electronic device which deals with input data, that is *fa la gestione delle entrate*, puts the data into storage or *salvataggio*, operates on the data according to programme or *programma* and the result is output or *uscita*. A word processor, a type of automated typewriting, is *un elaboratore di testi* which has a keyboard or *una tastiera* and keys or *tasti*. To type is *battere il tasto* or *digitare*. The display or screen is called *il video*, a terminal is *un terminale* which can be linked or *associato* or unlinked, that is *dissociato*. To de-activate a terminal is *disattivare un terminale* and to link a printer is *associare una stampante*. The printout is called *la stampa*. A phase is known as *una fase* and to commence a phase is *lanciare una fase.* To load a disk is *montare un disco* and to unload a disk is *smontare un disco.* Computer users or *utenti* are divided into small users, that is to say *piccoli utenti,* and large users *grossi utenti.* Computer systems being used in Italian commerce and trade are based on a standard organization. The firms marketing the computers aim at making their customers independent in computer operations and at providing sufficient information to enable the customers to deal with any problems which may arise during operations.

Computer hardware is called *componenti di macchina* and also hardware while software is generally known as *programmatura.* Disks are called *dischi.* A hard disk is a *disco fisso* and a floppy disk is a *disco mobile.* The storage disk is *disco di salvataggio* which is used for daily storage, that is *salvataggio giornaliero* or monthly storage, or *salvataggio mensile.* Various archive storages are called *salvataggi degli archivi.*

Flowcharting is simply called flow. A sample computer installation flowcharting is given below, using the codes as they appear in a SICIT Spa. instruction manual.

Vocabulary

accodare, to line up
associare, to link (up), to connect
azzerare, to zeroize
base dati, database
calcolatore elettronico, computer
codice, code
comparire, to appear
componenti di macchina, hardware
digitalizzare, to digitize
digitare, to type
disattivare, to de-activate
disco, disk
disco fisso, hard disk
disco mobile, floppy disk
dissociare, to disconnect
elaborare, to process
elaboratore, processor
elaboratore di testi, word processor
elaborazione dei dati, data processing
elencare, to list
eseguire, to carry out
file (archivio), file

formattare, to format
lato, side
lotto, batch
maschera, mask
meccanizzare, to computerize
memoria centrale, central memory
montare, to load, to fit
ottimizzare, to optimize
piastrina, chip
programmatura, software
progressivo, running total
pulire, to clean
pulsante, switch
richiesta, request
riga, line
salvare, to store, to save
salvataggio, storage
segnalazione, signalling
segnale, signal
sistema, system
sistemista, systems expert
smontare, to unload, to take off

Flow installazione

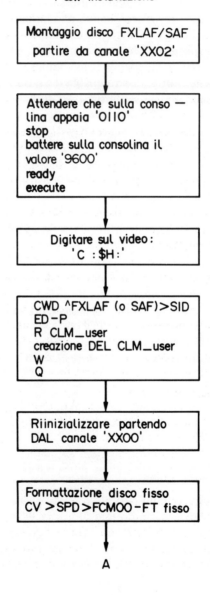

Montaggio disco FXLAF/SAF
partire da canale 'XX02'

Attendere che sulla conso —
lina appaia 'OIIO'
stop
battere sulla consolina il
valore '9600'
ready
execute

Digitare sul video:
'C : $H:'

CWD ^FXLAF (o SAF)>SID
ED-P
R CLM_user
creazione DEL CLM_user
W
Q

Riinizializzare partendo
DAL canale 'XX00'

Formattazione disco fisso
CV >SPD>FCM00-FT fisso

A

spia, warning light	*tasto*, key
stampa, printout	*telescrivente*, teleprinter
stampante, printer	*terminale*, terminal
stampante in parallelo, linc printer	*utente*, user
tabulato, tabulation	*video*, display, screen
tastiera, keyboard	

Exercises

I. Translate into English:

I tasti più importanti sono sul lato destro della tastiera. Per chiudere il lavoro è necessario disattivare tutti i terminali Sul vido compare la richiesta del nome della stampante da associare. I codici delle operazioni di servizio sono elencati in ordine alfabetico. La richiesta della data compare sul terminale pilota. Ogni comando può essere digitato solo dopo che è apparso il segnale. Il cursore luminoso si posiziona sulla riga successiva. Bisogna evitare gli errori operativi accidentali o di malfunzionamento dell' elaboratore. E necessario smontare il disco fisso, montare il disco mobile e digitare il codice. Si consiglia di prendere nota delle ultime segnalazioni apparse sul video. Il tabulato che viene stampato durante la fase mensile deve essere conservato con cura. I sistemisti devono cautelare i piccoli utenti da situazioni che possono rendere futile il lavoro nella sala dei calcolatori elettronici. Il programma prevede varie possibilità. Occore stampare il libro giornale ed altre schede contabili ed azzerare i progressivi mensili dei clienti o fornitori e dei conti. Gli archivi vengono puliti nella fase mensile. Il commando è: sospendere il lavoro se si verificano delle anomalie nel corso dell' elaborazione. La normale procedura di fine lavoro è stata eseguita. Non è necessario dividere il salvataggio dei vari archivi su più dischi. La creazione distinta del file maschera è stata fatta per ottimizzare lo spazio di memoria centrale.

II. Translate into Italian:

One of the disks contains part of the archive. The operative system (sistema operativo) is an important directory. The correct sequence (sequenza) has not been checked. The generalized (generalizzata) documentation is contained in one of the files. All the lines have to be eliminated. The codes of the service operations (operazioni di servizio) are listed on the display. Check (use the infinitive) that the red key is still down (abbassato). The printout of the day's accounting entries (movimenti contabili) has been carried out (eseguita). It is advisable (si consiglia) to stop work if anomalies arise (si verificano) during processing. It is necessary (è necessario) to vary the pathname of the files. We must not carry out a whole (una intera) evening phase.

III. Answer briefly in Italian the following questions:

1. Dove sono posti i tasti più importanti?
2. Quando is può digitare il comando?
3. Dove appare la richiesta della data?
4. In che ordine sono elencati i codici?
5. Che cosa è necessario fare per chiudere il lavoro?
6. Quando vengono puliti gli archivi?
7. Perchè è stata fatta la creazione distinta del file maschera?

A Proverb

Ogni medaglia ha il suo rovescio.

Bibliography

General

Landogna, F. *Storia d'Italia.*
Leonardo, *Almanacco di educazione popolare.* Ministero della Pubblica Educazione.
Popescu, J. *An Elementary Italian Grammar.* P. R. Macmillan.
Provenzal, D. *Curiosità e capricci della lingua italiana.* ERI. Edizioni RAI.
Zingarelli, N. *Vocabolario della lingua italiana.* Bietti & Reggiani.

Specialized

Caspis, G. *Sintesi di computisteria.* Vallardi.
Caspis, G. *Sintesi di pratica commerciale.* Vallardi.
Caspis, G. *Sintesi di ragioneria generale ed applicata.* Vallardi.
Manganelli, B. *Calcolo e contabilità aziendale.* Vallardi.
Manganelli, B. *Le imprese bancarie.* Vallardi.
Manganelli, B. *Società commerciali.* Vallardi.
Maragoni, F. A. *Dizionario commerciale fraseologico.* Hoepli.
Motta, G. *Dizionario commerciale.* Signorelli.
Santagata, M. A. *Moderna corrispondenza commerciale italiana.* Hoepli.
Sicit SpA—*Instructions on Computer Operations.*
Spinelli, N. *Dizionario commerciale.* Vols. I and II. E.L.I.T.
Tobia, M. *Sintesi di merceologia.* Vallardi.

Newspapers

Corriere della Sera.
Il Messaggero.
24 Ore.

Commercial Vocabulary

ITALIAN–ENGLISH

(Masculine nouns are indicated by *m* and feminine nouns by *f*.)

A

abbassamento, *m.* lowering
abbassare, to lower
abbisognare, to need
abbonamento, *m.* subscription
abbonarsi, to subscribe
abbreviazione, *f.* abbreviation
abbuono, *m.* allowance
abitudine, *f.* custom
abolire, to abolish
abolizione, *f.* abolition
abrogare, to abrogate
abrogazione, *f.* abrogation
abusare, to abuse
abuso, *m.* abuse
accantonare, to put to reserve
accaparramento, *m.* buying up
accaparrare, to buy up
accedere, to accede, to adopt
accendere, to open (an account)
accennare, to point out; to mention
accertabile, ascertainable
accertamento, *m.* settlement (of an account)
accertare, to ascertain
accessorio, accessory
accettabile, acceptable
accettante, *m.* acceptor
accettare, to accept
accettazione, *f.* acceptance

acchiudere, to enclose
accidente, *m.* accident; mishap
accodare, to line up
accoglienza, *f.* reception
accogliere, to receive, to welcome
accomandante, *m.* limited partner
accomandatario, *m.* general partner
accomodamento, arrangement
accomodare, to arrange
accompagnare, to accompany
accontentare, to satisfy
accontentarsi (di), to be satisfied (with)
acconto, *m.* deposit
accordare, to grant, to open (an account)
accordo, *m.* agreement; covenant, deal
accreditamento, *m.* crediting
accreditare, to credit with
accreditato, accredited; qualified
accumulare, to accumulate
accumulazione, *f.* accumulation
accusa, *f.* accusation; charge
accusare, to accuse; to acknowledge
acquirente, *m.* buyer
acquistare, to buy
acquisto, *m.* purchase
adattare, to adapt; to fit
adatto, fit, suitable
addebitamento, *m.* debiting
addebitare, to debit
addebito, *m.* debit
addetto, *m.* employee

101

addizionale, additional
addizionare, to add
addizione, *f.* addition
adempimento, *m.* fulfilment
adempire, to fulfil
adempito, fulfilled
adequato, adequate
aderire, to comply with
adesione, *f.* assent
adoperarsi, to try
adottare, to accept; to adopt
adozione, *f.* acceptance; adoption
adulterare, to adulterate
adulterazione, *f.* adulteration
adunanza, *f.* meeting
adunarsi, to assemble
aereo, *m.* plane
affare, *m.* affair, business
affermare, to affirm
affermativo, affirmative
affermazione, *f.* affirmation
affidare, to entrust
affidarsi, to rely on
affidavit, *m.* affidavit
affittare, to lease; to rent
affitto, *m.* lease; rent
affittuario, *m.* leaseholder
affluenza, *f.* affluence
affondare, to sink
affrancare, to frank; to stamp
affrancatura, *f.* postage
affrettare, to hasten
affrontare, to face
agente, *m.* agent
agente di cambio, *m.* stockbroker
agenzia, *f.* agency
agevolare, to facilitate
agevolezza, *f.* ease; facility
aggio, *m.* premium
aggiornare, to postpone; to update
aggiudicare, to adjudge
aggiudicazione, *f.* adjudication; award
aggiungere, to add
aggiunta, *f.* addition; rider
aggiustare, to adjust
aggravare, to worsen
aggravio, *m.* burden; charge
agire, to act
agrario, agrarian

agricoli, *m.* agricultural shares
alienare, to alienate
alimentari, *m.* food shares
aliquota, *f.* rate; share of payment
alla pari, at par
allegare, to enclose
allegato, enclosed
allegazione, *f.* allegation
alleggerire, to lighten
almanacco, *m.* almanac
alterare, to alter; to change
alterazione, *f.* alteration
alternativa, *f.* alternative
alto, high
ambiguità, *f.* ambiguity
ambito, *m.* ambit, range
ammanco, *m.* deficit
ammenda, *f.* fine
ammendare, to fine
amministare, to administer
amministrativo, administrative
amministratore, *m.* director
amministrazione, *f.* administration; board
    of directors
ammissione, *m.* admission
ammontare, to amount
ammontare, *m.* amount
ammortamento, *f.* amortization
ammortizzare, to amortize
ampliare, to amplify
ampliazione, *f.* amplification
amplificamento, *m.* amplification
anagrafe, *f.* register office
analisi, *f.* analysis
analizzare, to analyse; to scan
àncora, *f.* anchor
ancoraggio, *m.* anchorage
ancorarsi, to cast anchor
andante, instant
angolo, *m.* corner, angle
annata, *f.* year
annesso, annexed, enclosed
annesso allegato, *m.* policy endorsement
anno, *m.* year
annotare, to note
annuale, yearly
annualità, *f.* annuity
annualmente, yearly
annuario, *m.* directory

annullabile, voidable
annullamento, , *m.* cancellation
annullare, to cancel
annunziare, to inform, to advertise
annunzio, *m.* advertisement
annuo, annual
anonimo, anonymous
antecedente, antecedent
anteriore, previous
anticipare, to anticipate; to advance
anticipato, in advance
anticipazione, *f.* advance
anticipo, *m.* anticipation
antiparte, *f.* preferential share
aperto, open
apertura, *f.* opening.
appaltare, to lease
appaltatore, *m.* contractor
appalto, *m.* lease
apparecchio, *m.* apparatus
appartenenza, *f.* appurtenance
appellare, *f.* appurtenance
appellare, to appeal
appello, *m.* appeal
appendice, *f.* appendix
applicare, to apply
applicazione, *f.* application
apporre, to affix
apportare, to contribute
apprendere, to learn
apprendista, *m.* apprentice
appresso, after, as below
apprezzare, to appreciate; to estimate
approdare, to land
approdo, *m.* landing-place
approfittare, to profit (by)
appropriare, to appropriate
approssimativo, approximate
approssimazione, *f.* approximation
approvare, to approve
approvazione, *f.* approval
approvvigionamento, *m.* provisioning
approvvigionare, to provision
appuntamento, *m.* appointment
appuramento, *m.* verification
aprile, April
aprire, to open (an account)
arbitraggio, *m.* arbitrage, mediation
arbitrario, arbitrary

arbitro, *m.* adjudicator; mediator
archivio, *m.* archive
area, *f.* area; surface
area fabbricabile, *f.* building plot
arenamento, *m.* stranding
arenare, to strand
argento, *m.* silver; silver money
argomento, *m.* subject; topic
armamento, *m.* armament; rigging
armare, to arm; to rig
armatore, *m.* shipowner
armeggio, *m.* rigging
arredare, to furnish
arrestare, to arrest
arresto, *m.* arrest
arretrati, *m.* arrears
arricchimento, *m.* enrichment
arricchire, to enrich
arrischiare, to risk; to hazard
arrischiato, risky
arrivare, to arrive; to attain; to reach
arrivi, *m.* supplies
arrivo, *m.* arrival
arsenale, *m.* arsenal; stockpile
articolo, *m.* article; commodity
artificiale, artificial
ascensione, *f.* ascent
ascensore, *m.* lift
asciugare, to dry; to wipe
aspettative, *f.* expectation
aspetto, *m.* aspect
aspirante, *m.* candidate (for a job)
aspirare, to aim at
aspirazione, *f.* aim; aspiration
asse, *f.* axis; axle
assegnamento, *m.* assignment
assegnare, to assign; to earmark; to allot
assegnatario, *m.* allottee
assegnato, unpaid
assegnazione, *f.* allotment
assegno, *m.* allowance; cheque
assegno bancario, *m.* cheque
assegno circolare, *m.* bank draft
assegno sbarrato, *m.* crossed cheque
assegno turistico, *m.* traveller's cheque
assemblea, *f.* general meeting; assembly
assente, absent
assentire, to agree; to admit
assenza, *f.* absence

asserire, to assert
asserzione, *f.* assertion
assestamento, *m.* adjustment
assestare, to adjust
assicurabile, insurable
assicurare, to assure; to insure
assicurativi, *m.* insurance shares
assicurato, *m.* insured person
assicuratore, *m.* insurer
assicurazione, *f.* assurance; insurance
assistenza, *f.* assistance; attendance
associare, to link up
associarsi, to join
associato, *m.* partner
associazione, *f.* association; society
assoluto, absolute
assolvere, to acquit
assorbire, to absorb
assortimento, *m.* assortment
assortire, to assort
assumere, to assume; to take up; to employ
asta, *f.* auction
astenersi, to abstain; to refrain
astensione, *f.* abstention
attardamento, *m.* delay
attardarsi, to delay
attenuamento, *m.* attenuation
attenuante, attenuating
attenuare, to attenuate
attenzione, *f.* attention
attesa, *f.* expectation; awaiting
attestare, to attest; to certify
attestazione, *f.* attestation
attività, *f.* activity; assets' side
attivo *m.* assets
attivo, active
atto, *m.* act; deed
atto di costituzione, *m.* memorandum of association
attore, *m.* actor
attrezzatura, *f.* equipment; rigging
attrezzo, *m.* tool
attribuire, to attribute; to impute
attribuzione, *f.* attribution; authority
attuale, current; present
attualità, *f.* actuality; reality
attuare, to carry out
auditore, *m.* listener

audizione, *f.* audition
augurare, to wish
augurio, *m.* wish
aula, *f.* hall; room
aumento, *m.* increase
ausiliare, auxiliary
auspicare, to augur
auspicio, *m.* auspices
autenticare, to authenticate
autenticazione, *f.* authentication
autenticità, *f.* authenticity
autentico, genuine
autista, *m.* driver
auto, *m.* motor-car
autocarro, *m.* motor-lorry
automatico, automatic
automazione, *f.* automation
automezzo, *m.* motor vehicle
automobile, *f.* motor-car
automobilistici, *m.* motor shares
autonomia, *f.* autonomy
autonomo, autonomous
autoparco, *m.* car park
autorità, *f.* authority; power
autorizzare, to authorize
autorizzazione, *f.* authorization
autoscafo, *m.* motor-boat
autostrada, *f.* motor way
autotreno, *m.* motor-train
avallante, *m.* guarantor
avallare, to guarantee
avallo, *m.* guaranty
avanzo, *m.* advance
avaria, *f.* damage; loss; average
avaria generale, *f.* general average
avaria particolare, *f.* particular average
avariare, to damage
avere, *m.* credit side
aviazione, *f.* aviation
avvalersi, to make use of
avvalorare, to strengthen; to utilize
avvenire, to happen
avvenire, *m.* future
avventore, *m.* customer
avventura, *f.* adventure; affair
avventurarsi, to venture
avversario, *m.* opponent
avvertenza, *f.* attention; preface
avvertimento, *m.* warning

avvertire, to warn; to inform
avviare, to start
avvisare, to notify; to advertise
avviso, *m.* notice; advertisement
avvocato, *m.* lawyer
azienda, *f.* firm; business
aziendale, pertaining to a firm
azionare, to move; to drive
azionario, pertaining to shares
azione, *f.* action; share
azionista, *m.* shareholder
azzardo, *m.* risk
azzerare, to zeroize

B

babordo, *m.* port-side
bacino, *m.* dock
badare, to pay attention
bagaglio, *m.* luggage
balla, *f.* bale
bambola, *f.* **(per gas)** *f.* (gas) bottle
banca, *f.* bank
bancabile, bankable
bancari, *m.* banking shares
bancario, banking
bancarotta, *f.* bankruptcy
bancarottiere, bankrupt
banchiere, *m.* banker
banchina, *f.* quay; wharf
banco, *m.* bank
bancogiro, *m.* bank clearing
banconota, *f.* banknote
bandiera, *f.* flag
baratteria, *f.* barratry
baratto, *m.* barter
barca, *f.* boat; barge
basare, to base
base, *f.* base; basis
base dati, database
basso, low
bastare, to be enough
bastimento, *m.* ship
beneficenza, *f.* charity; benevolence
beneficiare, to benefit
beneficiario, *m.* payee
beneficio, *m.* profit; gain; benefit
benefico, beneficent

benemerenza, *f.* merit
benemerito, *m.* worthy person
beneplacito, *m.* convenience; approval
benessere, *m.* well-being
benevolenza, *f.* favour
beni, *m.* property, goods
benintenso, of course; well understood
benservito, *m.* testimonial
biasimare, to blame
biasimo, *m.* blame
bidone, *m.* can; drum
biglietto, *m.* ticket; note
biglietto all'ordine, *m.* promissory note
biglietto di banca, *m.* banknote
bilancia, *f.* scales
bilancia del commercio, *f.* balance of trade
bilanciare, to weigh; to balance
bilancio, *m.* balance-sheet
bilancio statale, *m.* budget
bilaterale, bilateral
bilione, *m.* billion (a thousand million)
bimensile, bi-monthly
binario, *m.* railway-track
bisognatario, *m.* referee
bisogno, *m.* need; want
bisticciare, to quarrel
bisticcio, *m.* quarrel
bivio, *m.* cross-roads
bloccare, to block up; to blockade; to freeze (prices)
blocco, *m.* blockade; block
bocca, *f.* mouth
boccaporto, *m.* hatchway
bollare, to stamp; to seal
bolletta, *f* bill; receipt
bolletta doganale, *f.* bill of entry
bollettino, *m.* bulletin
bollettino commerciale, *m.* trade report
bollettino dei cambi, *m.* exchange list
bollettino dei prezzi, *m.* price list
bollettino di consegna, *m.* delivery note
bollettino di spedizione, *m.* consignment note
bollo, *m.* stamp, seal
bollo postale, *m.* postmark
bonificazione, *f.* allowance; discount
borderò, *m.* memorandum; bordereau
bordo, *m.* side (of a ship)
borsa, *f.* exchange

borsa valori, *f.* stock exchange
botte, *f.* cask; barrel
bottega, *f.* shop; warehouse
bottegaio, *m.* shopkeeper
bottiglia, *f.* bottle
bottino, *m.* booty
bottone, *m.* button
brevettare, to patent
brevetto, *m.* patent
brogliaccio, *m.* day book
brutto, ill favoured; ugly
buca, *f.* hole
buca delle lettere, *f.* letter-box
buio, dark
bullettino, *m.* bulletin (of news)
buon mercato, cheap
buono, *m.* bond
buono del tesoro, *m.* treasury bill
buono di cassa, *m.* cheque
buono di consegna, *m.* delivery note
buono di incasso, *m.* money-order
buono di richiesta, *m.* request note
buonsenso, *m.* common sense
burla, *f.* jest; hoax
bussola, *f.* compass; bearings
busta, *f.* envelope
busta-paga, *f.* pay packet
buttare, to throw; to fling

C

cablogramma, *m.* cablegram
cabotaggio, *m.* coasting trade
cadere, to fall
caduta, *f.* fall; failure
calata, *f.* wharf; pier
calcolare, to calculate
calcolatore elettronico, *m.* computer
calcolatrice, *f.* computer
calcolo, *m.* calculation
calendario, *m.* calendar
calmo, calm
calo, *m.* short weight
cambiale, *f.* bill of exchange
cambiamento, *m.* alteration; change
cambiare, to change
cambiario, pertaining to bills of exchange
cambiavalute, *m.* money-changer

cambio, *m.* exchange (money)
cambio marittimo, *m.* bottomry
campione, *m.* sample
campo, *m.* field
canapa, *f.* hemp
cancelleria, *f.* stationery
cantiere, *m.* shipyard
caparra, *f.* earnest
capitale, *m.* capital, stock
capitale circolante, *m.* working capital
capitale sociale, *m.* stock capital
capitale versato, *m.* paid-up capital
capitalizzazione, *f.* capitalization
capitolo, *m.* chapter
capo, *m.* chief
capoluogo, *m.* main town
capomastro, *m.* clerk of works
cappa, *f.* primage
carato, *m.* carat
carattere, *m.* character
caratteristica, *f.* characteristic
carena, *f.* hull
carenare, to careen (a ship)
carestia, *f.* scarcity
carica, *f.* charge; appointment
caricamento, *m.* charging; loading
caricare, to charge; to load
carico, *m.* cargo; charge; load
carità, *f.* charity
caro, dear
carro, *m.* truck; van
carta, *f.* map; paper
carta bianca, *f.* carte blanche
carta da imballagio, *f.* packing paper
carte di bordo, *f.* ship's papers
carteggio, *m.* documents; papers
cartella, *f.* share certificate
cartellino, *m.* card; ticket
cartolina illustrata, *f.* picture card
cartolina postale, *f.* postcard
cartone, *m.* cardboard
casa, *f.* firm; house
caso, *m.* case; act
caso di forza maggiore, act of God
cassa, *f.* bank; board; cash
cassaforte, *f.* safe
cassazione, *f.* supreme court of appeal
cassetta, *f.* small box
cassiere, *m.* cashier

castelletto, *m.* credit register
catalogo, *m.* catalogue
catrame, *m.* tar
causa, *f.* cause; lawsuit
causare, to bring
cautela, *f.* caution
cauto, cautious
cauzione, *f.* bail
cedente, *m.* assignor
cedere, to assign
cedibile, assignable
cedola, *f.* coupon; dividend warrant
celare, to conceal
celerità, *f.* speed
cenno, *m.* sign; order; acknowledgement
cento, hundred
centrale, *f.* head office
centrale, central
centralino, *m.* telephone exchange
centralizzazione, *f.* centralization
centro, *m.* centre
cercare, to search; to want
cercasi, wanted (in adverts.)
cerchio, *m.* circle
certezza, *f.* certainty
certificare, to certify
certificato, *m.* certificate
certificato di azioni, *m.* share certificate
certificato provvisorio, *m.* scrip
certificazione, *f.* certification
certo, certain; sure
cessare, to cease
cessazione, *f.* cessation
cessionario, *m.* assignee
cessione, *f.* assignment
chiamare, to call
chiaramente, clearly
chiarezza, *f.* clearness
chiarire, to clarify; to explain
chiatta, *f.* lighter
chiave, *f.* key
chiedere, to ask
chiglia, *f.* keel
chimici, *m.* chemical shares
chimico, *m.* chemical scientist
chiudere, to close
chiusura, *f.* closing
ciclo, *m.* cycle
cifra, *f.* figure

cifrare, to cipher
circa, about
circolare, to circulate
circolare, *f.* circular letter
circolazione, *f.* circulation
circostanza, *f.* circumstance
citare, to quote
citazione, *f.* quotation
classe, *f.* class
classificare, to classify
classificazione, *f.* classification
clausola, *f.* clause
cliente, *m.* client
clientela, *f.* clientele
codice, *m.* code
codice della strada, *m.* highway code
codicillo, *m.* codicil
cognome, *m.* surname
collaudare, to test
collaudo, *m.* test
collazionamento, *m.* checking
collazionare, to check
collega, *m.* colleague
collegio, *m.* committee
collegio sindacale, *m.* company committee
colletta, *f.* collection
collettame, *m.* parcels
collettivo, joint
collezione, *f.* collection
collo, *m.* parcel
collocamento, *m.* placement; sale
collocare, to place; to sell
colloquio, *m.* conversation
colmare, to fill up
colorare, to colour
colorazione, *f.* colouring
colore, *m.* colour
colpa, *f.* fault
colpevole, guilty
colpevolezza, *f.* guilt
colpire, to hit; to affect
colpo, *m.* blow
coltivare, to cultivate
coltivatore, *m.* grower
coltivazione, *f.* cultivation
comandante, *m.* commandant
comando, *m.* order
comitato, *m.* committee

commerciale, commercial
commerciante, *m.* trader; merchant
commerciare, to trade
commercio, *m.* trade; commerce
commesso, *m.* clerk; shop assistant
commissario, *m.* commissary
commissionario, *m.* commission agent
commissione, *f.* commission; message
committente, *m.* consignor
comodità, *f.* commodity; convenience
comodo, *m.* convenience
comparire, to appear
compensare, to compensate
compensazione, *f.* compensation
compenso, *m.* compensation
comperare, to buy
competente, competent
competenza,*f.* authority; competence; fee
competere, to compete
competitore, *m.* competitor
compilare, to compile
compilazione, *f.* compilation
compito, *m.* task
complessivo, as a whole
complesso, *m.* complex
completare, to complete
completo, whole
componenti di macchina, *m.* hardware
componimento, *m.* arrangement
comporre, to settle
comportare, to allow
composto, compound
compra, *f.* purchase
comprare, to purchase
compratore, *m.* purchaser
compravendita, *f.* deed of sale
comprendere, to understand, to include
compromesso, *m.* compromise
compromettere, to compromise
computare, to compute
computista, *m.* book-keeper
comune, common; joint
comunicare, to communicate
comunicazione, *f.* communication
concedente, *m.* grantor
concedere, to grant
concernare, to concern
concessionario, *m.* grantee
concessione, *f.* concession

concetto, *m.* concept
conchiudre, to conclude
conciliare, to conciliate
concordare, to agree
concordato, *m.* agreement
concorrente, *m.* competitor
concorrenza, *f.* competition
concorrere, to compete
concorso, *m.* competition
condividere, to share
condizionale, conditional
condizionare, to condition
condizione, *f.* condition
condotta, *f.* behaviour
conducente, *m.* driver
condurre, to lead, to manage
conferenza, *f.* lecture
conferimento, *m.* bestowal
conferire, to bestow
conferma, *f.* confirmation
confermare, to confirm
confezionare, to manufacture
confezione, *f.* manufactured article
confidare, to entrust
confidenza, *f.* confidence
confidenziale, confidential
confidenzialmente, confidentially
confine, *m.* border, frontier
confisca, *f.* confiscation
confisscare, to confiscate
conflitto, *m.* conflict
conformare, to conform
conforme, in conformity (with)
conformità, *f.* conformity
confrontare, to confront
confronto, *m.* confrontation
confusione, *f.* confusion
congedare, to dismiss
congettura, *f.* conjecture
congiungere, to connect
congiuntura, *f.* conjuncture
congiunturale, conjunctural
congratulare, to congratulate
congratulazioni, *f.* congratulations
congruo, suitable
coniare, to coin
coniazione, *f.* coinage
conoscenza, *f.* acquaintance
conoscere, to know

consecutivo, consecutive
consegna, *f.* delivery
consegnabile, deliverable
consegnare, to deliver
consegnatario, *m.* consignee
consegnatore, *m.* consignor
conseguente, consequential
conseguenza, *f.* consequence
conseguire, to attain
consenso, *m.* consent, assent
consentire, to consent; to enable
considerare, to consider
considerazione, *f.* consideration
consigliare, to advice; to counsel
consiglio, *m.* advice
consistere, to consist of
consolare, consular
consulato, *m.* consulate
console, *m.* consul
consolidare, to consolidate
consolidazione, consolidation
consorzio, *m.* trust
constatare, to find, to ascertain
consueto, customary
consuetudine, *f.* custom
consultare, to consult
consultazione, *f.* consultation
consumare, to consume
consumatore, *m.* consumer
consumo, *m.* consumption
consuntivo (bilancio) amended (balance)
contabile, *m.* accountant
contabilità, *f.* accountancy
contanti, *m.* cash
contare, to count; to rely on
contatto, *m.* contact
conteggio, *m.* computation
contenuto, *m.* contents
contingenza, *f.* contingency
conto, *m.* account
contrabbandare, to smuggle
contrabbandiere, *m.* smuggler
contrabbando, *m.* smuggling
contradittorio, contradictory
contraente, contracting
contraffare, to counterfeit
contrare, to contract
contrasegnare, to countersign
contrassegno, mark; sign

contrattare, to negotiate
contrattazione, *f.* bargain
contratto, *m.* contract
contrattuale, contractual
contravvenire, to infringe
contravventore, *m.* infringer
contravvenzione, *f.* infringement
contribuente, *m.* taxpayer
contribuire, to contribute
contributo, *m.* contribution
controllare, to control
controllo, *m.* control
controllore, *m.* controller
controparte, *m.* counterpart
contropartita, *f.* counter item
controstallia, *f.* demurrage
controversia, *f.* controversy
controvertere, to controvert
convalidare, to endorse; to confirm
convenire, to agree
conversazione, *f.* conversation
conversione, *f.* conversion
convertibile, convertible
convertibilità, *f.* convertibility
convertire, to convert
convocare, to convene
convocazione, *f.* convocation
convoglio, *m.* convoy, train
cooperativa, *f.* co-operative
cooperazione, *f.* co-operation
copia, *f.* copy
copialettere, *m.* letter-book
copiare, to copy
coprire, to cover
corporazione, *f.* corporation
corredato, enclosed
corredo, *m.* package
correggere, to correct
corrente, *f.* current; stream
corrente, current
correntista, *m.* current account holder
correzione, *f.* correction
corriere, *m.* messenger
corrispetivo, *m.* compensation
corrispondente, *m.* correspondent
corrispondenza, *f.* correspondence
corrispondere, to correspond; to remit
corrompere, to corrupt
corruzione, *f.* corruption

corso, *m.* course; rate
corso legale, *m.* legal tender
corte, *f.* court
cortesia, *f.* courtesy
cosa, *f.* thing
costare, to cost
costituire, to form
costo, *m.* cost; charge
costoso, costly
costringere, to compel
costruire, to build
costruttuore, *m.* builder
costruzione, *f.* building
costume, *m.* custom
cottimista, *m.* jobber; piece worker
credere, to believe
credito, *m.* credit
creditore, *m.* creditor
crisi, *f.* crisis
critico, critical
crollare, to collapse
crollo, *m.* collapse
cura, *f.* care; solicitude
curare, to care
custode, *m.* custodian; keeper; watchman
custodia, *f.* custody
custodimento, *m.* keeping
custodire, to keep; to preserve

D

danaro, *m.* money
danneggiare, to damage
danno, *m.* damage; loss
dannoso, harmful
dare, *m.* debit side
darsena, *f.* dock
data, *f.* date
datare, to date
dato, *m.* datum
dato, fixed; given
datore, *m.* employer
dattilografa, *f* typist
dattilografia, *f* typewriting
dattiloscritto, typewritten
dattiloscrivere, to type
daziabile, dutiable
daziare, to charge duty on

daziere, *m.* customs officer
dazio, *m.* duty
debitamento, duly; regularly
debiti sociali, *m.* company's debts
debito, *m.* debt
debito, due
debitore, *m.* debtor
decade, *f.* period of ten days
decadenza, *f.* forfeiture
decidere, to decide
decifrare, to decipher
decima, *f.* tenth part
decimale, decimal
decisione, *f.* decision
decisivo, decisive
deconto, *m.* pass-book
decorrenza, *f.* start of period
decorrere, to start from; to lapse
decorso, *m.* lapse of time
decretare, to decree
decreto, *m.* decree
decurtare, to reduce
decurtazione, *f.* reduction
dedurre, to deduct
deduzione, *f.* deduction
deferire, to defer
deficiente, deficient
deficienza, *f.* deficiency
deficit, *m.* deficit
definire, to define
definitivo, final
definizione, *f.* settlement
delega, *f.* delegation; proxy
delegare, to delegate
delegazione, *f.* delegation
denaro, *m.* money
denominare, to denominate
denominatore, *m.* denominator
denominazione, *f.* denomination
denunzia, *f.* denunciation
denunziare, to denounce
deperibile, perishable
deperimento, *m.* decay
deperire, to decay
deporto, *m.* backwardation
depositante, *m.* depositor
depositare, to deposit
depositario, *m.* depositary
deposito, *m.* deposit

depressione, *f.* depression
deprezzamanto, *m.* depreciation
deputato, *m.* deputy
derivare, to derive
deroga, *f.* derogation
derogare, to derogate
destinare, to address
destinatario, *m.* addressee
destinazione, *f.* destination
destituire, to dismiss
detentore, *m.* holder
determinare, to determine
determinazione, *f.* determination
detrimento, *m.* detriment
dettagliante, *m.* retailer
dettagliatamente, in detail
dettaglio, *m.* detail; retail trade
dettare, to dictate
dettatura, *f.* dictation
deviare, to deviate
deviazione, *f.* deviation
devotissimo, yours faithfully
diagramma, *m.* diagram
diario, *m.* diary
dichiarare, to declare
dichiarazione, *f.* declaration
dicitura, *f.* wording
diecina, *f.* ten
difetto, *m.* defect
difettoso, faulty
diffalco, *m.* deduction
differenza, *f.* difference
differenziale, *m.* differential
digitare, to type
dilatorio, delaying
dilazionare, to delay
dilazione, *f.* delay
diluire, to water down
dimensione, *f.* size
diminuire, to diminish
diminuzione, *f.* diminution; fall
dismissioni, *m.* resignation
dipartimentale, departmental
dipartimento, *m.* department
dipendente, *m.* employee
dipendere, to depend
diramare, to send out
direttamente, directly
diretto, direct

direttore, *m.* manager
direzione, *f.* management
dirigere, to manage
diritto, *m.* law; duty
diritto, straight; upright
disaccordo, *m.* disagreement
disapprovare, to disapprove
disapprovazione, *f.* disapproval
disattivare, to deactivate
disavanzo, *m.* deficit
discarica, *f.* unloading
discendere, to decline; to fall
discesa, *f.* decline, fall
disco, *m.* disk
disco fisso, *m.* hard disk
disco mobile, *m.* floppy disk
discreditare, to discredit
discredito, *m.* discredit
discrezione, *f.* discretion
discussione, *f.* discussion
discutere, to discuss
discutibile, questionable
disonore, *m.* dishonour
dispiacere, to displease
disponibile, available
disponibilità, *f.* availability
disporre, to dispose
disposizione, *f.* disposal
disputa, *f.* dispute
dissociare, to disconnect
distanza, *f.* distance
distinta, *f.* list; bill
distinto, distinguished
distribuire, to distribute; to deliver
distribuzione, *f.* distribution
ditta, *f.* concern; firm
dividendo, *m.* dividend
dividere, to divide
divieto, *m.* prohibition
divisione, *f.* division
documentazione, *f.* documents
documento, *m.* document
dogana, *f.* customs
doganale, pertaining to customs
doganiere, *m.* customs man
dolo, *m.* fraud
doloso, fraudulent
domanda, *f.* demand; request
domandare, to ask

domestica, *f.* maidservant
domicilio, *m.* residence
doppiare, to double
doppio, double
dorso, *m.* back
dose, *f.* dose
dotare, to endow
dottrina, *f.* doctrine
dovere, to owe
dovere, *m.* duty
dozzina, *f.* dozen
dubbio, *m.* doubt
dubbioso, doubtful
dubitare, to doubt
duplicare, to duplicate
durante, during
durare, to last
durata, *f.* duration
durezza, *f.* hardness
duro, hard; steady

E

eccedente, exceeding
eccedenza, *f.* excess
eccedere, to exceed
eccessivamente, exceedingly
eccessivo, excessive
eccesso, *m.* excess
eccettuare, to except
eccezionale, exceptional
eccezionalmente, exceptionally
eccezione, *f.* exception
economia, *f.* economy
economico, economic
economista, *m.* economist
economizzare, to economize
effetti, *m.* bills; effects; securities
effetti in portafoglio, *m.* securities on hand
effettivo, actual, real
effetto, *m.* effect
effettuare, to effect; to accomplish
efficace, effective
eguale, equal
elaborare, to elaborate; to process
elaboratore, *m.* processor
elaborazione, *f.* processing
elasticità, *f.* elasticity

elastico, elastic
eleggere, to choose; to elect
elemento, *m.* element
elencare, to list
elenco, *m.* list
elettrici, *m.* electrical shares
elevare, to raise
elevato, high
eliminare, to eliminate
eliminazione, *f.* elimination
eludere, to elude
embargo, *m.* embargo
emettere, to issue
emigrare, to emigrate
emigrazione, *f.* emigration
emissione, *f.* issue; *m.* emission
emittente, *m.* issuer
emporio, *m.* emporium
energia, *f.* energy
energico, energetical
ente, *m.* corporation; organization
entità, *f.* entity
entrare, to enter
entrata, *f.* admission; input
entrate, *f.* assets
enumerare, to enumerate
enumerazione, *f.* enumeration
epoca, *f.* period
equazione, *f.* equation
equilibrio, *f.* equilibrium
equipaggiare, to equip
equipaggio, *m.* crew
equivalare, to be equivalent
equivalente, equivalent
equivoco, *m.* ambiguity
equo, equitable
erariale, fiscal
erario, *m.* treasury
erede, *m.* heir
eredità, *f.* heritage
ereditare, to inherit
erroneamente, erroneously
erroneo, erroneous
errore, *m.* error
esagerare, to exaggerate
esagerazione, *f.* exaggeration
esame, *m.* examination
esaminare, to consider; to examine
esattamente, exactly

esattezza, *f.* accuracy
esatto, exact
esattore, *m.* premium collector
esazione, *f.* premium collection
escludere, to exclude
esclusione, *f.* exclusion
esclusivamente, exclusively
esclusivo, exclusive
esecutivo, *m.* executive
esecutore, *m.* executor
esecuzione, *f.* execution
eseguire, to execute
esempio, *f.* example
esemplare, exemplary
esentare, to exempt
esente, exempt
esenzione, *f.* exemption
esercitare, to exercise
esercizio, *m.* period, year
esigente, exacting
exigenza, *f.* exigency
esigere, to exact
esigibile, payable
esistenza, *f.* existence
esistere, to exist
esito, *m.* issue; result
esonerare, to exonerate
esorbitante, exorbitant
espediente, *m.* expedient
esperienza, *f.* experience
esperimentare, to experiment
esperimento, *m.* experiment
esperto, *m.* expert
esponente, *m.* exponent
esporre, to expose
esportare, to export
esportatore, *mn.* exporter
esportazione, *f.* export
espositore, *m.* exhibiter
esposizione, *f.* exhibition
esposto, *m.* account; statement
espressamente, expressedly
espressione, *f.* expression
espresso, express
essenziale, essential
estendere, to increase; to extend
estensione, *f.* extension
estero, foreign
esteso, extensive

estinto, redeemed
estrarre, to extract
estratto, *m.* abstract; extract
etichetta, *f.* label
evadere, to evade
evasione, *f.* evasion; business reply
evasivo, evasive
evento, *m.* event
eventuale, eventual; possible
eventualità, *f.* eventuality
eventualmente, eventually
evidente, clear
evidenza, *f.* evidence
evitare, to avoid

F

fabbrica, factory
fabbricabile, manufacturable
fabbricante, *m.* manufacturer
fabbricare, to manufacture
fabbricato, *m.* building
fabbricazione, *f.* manufacturing
faccenda, *f.* business
facilitare, to facilitate
facilitazione, *f.* facility
facoltà, *f.* authority; power
facoltativo, optional
facsimile, *m.* facsimile
fallimentare, pertaining to bankruptcy
fallimento, *m.* bankruptcy
fallire, to go bankrupt
falsificare, to falsify
falsificatore, *m.,* forger
falsificazione, *f.* forgery
falso, false
fama, *f.* fame
fatto, *m.* fact
fattore, *m.* factor
fattorino, *m.* delivery man; messenger
fattura, *f.* invoice
fatturare, to invoice
fatturazione, *f.* invoicing
fatturista, *m.* invoice clerk
favore, *m.* favour
favorevole, favourable
favorire, to favour
favorita, *f.* letter

fede, *f.* faith
fedeltà, *f.* loyalty
feriale, ordinary
fermo, *m.* stability
fermo, firm
ferrovia, *f.* railway
ferroviario, pertaining to a railway
fiacco, dull
flachezza, *f.* dullness
fideiussione, *f.* suretyship
fideiussore, *m.* sponsor
fido, *m.* credit
fiducia, *f.* confidence
fiduciario, fiduciary
fiducioso, confident
fiera, *f.* fair.
figura, *f.* appearance; figure
figurare, to appear
filiale, *f.* branch office
filigrana, *f.* watermark
filo, *m.* thread, wire
finanza, *f.* finance
finanziare, to finance
finanziari, *m.* financial shares
finanziario, financial
finanziere, *m.* financier
fine, *f.* end
finire, to finish
fino, fine
firma, *f.* signature
firmare, to sign
fiscale, fiscal
fisco, *m.* fisc, public treasury
fissare, to fix
fisso, fixed
flagrante, flagrant
flagranza, *f.* flagrancy
fluttuare, to fluctuate
fluttuazione, *f.* fluctuation
fondamenta, *f.* foundation
fondare, to found
fondazione, *f.* foundation
fondiario, landed
fondo, *m.* fund, stock
fondo, deep
fonogramma, *m.* written telephone message
fonte, *f.* source; spring
forma, *f.* shape

formale, formal
formalità, *f.* formality
formare, to form
formattare, to format
formula, *f.* formula; wording
formulare, to formulate; to word
formulario, *m.* formulary
fornire, to supply
fornitore, *m.* contractor; purveyor
fornitura, *f.* supply
foro, *m.* forum
fortuna, *f.* fortune
forza, *f.* force
fragile, fragile
fragilità, *f.* fragility
francamente, frankly
franchigia, *f.* franchise
franco, free
francobollo, *m.* postage stamp
fraudolento, fraudulent
frazionario, fractional
frazione, *f.* fraction
frequentare, to frequent
frequenza, *f.* frequency
frode, *f.* fraud
frontiera, *f.* frontier
fruire, to enjoy
frutto, *m.* profit, income
funzionamento, *m.* functioning
funzionario bancario, *m.* bank clerk
funzione, *f.* function; office
fuoco, *m.* fire
furto, *m.* theft
futile, futile
futilità, *f.* futility
futilmente, futilely
futuramente, in the future
futuro, *m.* the future

G

gara, *f.* tender
garante, *m.* guarantor
garantire, to guarantee
garanzia, *f.* guaranty
gazzetta, *f.* gazette
generale, *m.* general
genere, *m.* kind

generi, *m.* products
gente, *f.* people
gentilezza, *f.* kindness
genuino, genuine
gerente, *m.* manager
gerenza, *f.* management
gestione, *f.* management
gestione contabile, *f.* accounting
gestore, *m.* head clerk
gettata, *f.* jetty
giacente, unclaimed
giacenza, *f.* demurrage
giocare, to speculate
giornal-mastro, *m.* journal-ledger
giornale, *m.* journal
giornale di bordo, *m.* ship's journal
giornale di navigazione, *m.* ship's log book
giornaliero, daily
giornata, *f.* day-time
giorno, *m.* day
giovamento, *m.* enjoyment
giovare, to enjoy
girabile, endorsable
girante, *m.* endorser
girare, to endorse
girata, *f.* endorsement
giratario, *m.* endorsee
giro, *m.* endorsement
giudicare, to judge
giudice, *m.* judge
giudiziale, judicial
giudizialmente, judicially
giudiziario, judicial
giudizio, *m.* decision
giungere, to arrive; to reach
giuramento, *m.* oath
giurare, to take an oath
giurato, *m.* juror
giuria, *f.* jury
giuridice, juridicial
giurisdizione, *f.* jurisdiction
giustificare, to justify
giustificazione, *f.* justification
giustizia, *f.* justice
godere, to enjoy
godimento, *m.* enjoyment
governare, to govern
governativo, pertaining to government
governo, *m.* government

gradatamente, gradually
gradimento, *m.* approbation
gradire, to accept
grado, *m.* degree
graduale, gradual
grafico, *m.* graph
grammo, *m.* gram
grande, big; great
grandezza, *f.* greatness
gratificazione, *f.* gratification
gratis, free
gratitudine, *f.* gratitude
grato, thankful
gratuitamente, gratuitously
gratuito, free
gravare, to weight on; to burden
grave, serious, heavy
gravità, *f.* gravity
gravoso, heavy
grazia, *f.* grace
graziare, to grace
grazie, thank you
grosso, big, wholesale
gruppo, *m.* group
guadagnare, to earn; to gain
guadagno, *m.* gain; profit
guardamagazzini, *m.* storekeeper
guardaporta, *m.* doorman
guardare, to guard
guardia, *f.* guard; watch
guardiano, *m.* guard; keeper
guarnire, to trim; to furnish
guarnitura, *m.* trimming, equipment
guastare, to damage
guasto, *m.* damage
guerra, *f.* war
guerriere, warlike
guida, *f.* guide; directory
guidare, to guide
guisa, *f.* mode; manner

I

iarda, yard
idea, *f.* idea
identico, identical
identificare, to identify
identificazione, *f.* identification

identità, *f.* identity
ieri, yesterday
ignoranza, ignorance
illecito, unlawful
illegale, illegal
illeggibile, illegible
illuminazione, *f.* lighting
imballaggio, *m.* packing
Imballare, to pack
imballatore, *m.* packer
imballo, *m.* packing
imbarazzante, embarrassing
imbarazzo, *m.* difficulty
imbarcare, to embark, to ship
imbarcatoio, *m.* pier, wharf
imbarcazione, *f.* boat
imbarco, *m.* embarking
imitare, to imitate
imitazione, *f.* imitation
immagazzinamento, *m.* storage
immagazzinare, to store
immatricolazione, *f.* registration
immediatamente, immediately
immediato, immediate
immischiarsi, to meddle with
immobile, immobile
immobili, *m.* real estate
immobiliare, pertaining to real estate
immobiliari, *m.* property shares
immobilizzare, to immobilize
immune, immune
impaccare, to pack
impadronirsi, to become master of
impare, uneven
impareggiabile, incomparable
imparziale, impartial
imparzialità, *f.* impartiality
imparzialmente, impartially
impaziente, impatient
impazienza, *f.* impatience
impedimento, *m.* impediment
impedire, to hinder
impegnare, to pledge
impegnativo, binding
impegno, *m.* pledge
imperdonabile, inexcusable
imperfetto, imperfect
imperfezione, *f.* imperfection
impermeabile, water-proof

impiantare, to install; to establish
impianto, *m.* installation
impiegare, to employ
impiegato, *m.* employee
impiego, *m.* employment
implicare, to implicate
implicitamente, implicity
implicito, implicit
imponibile, dutiable
imporre, to impose
importante, important
importanza, *f.* importance
importare, to import
importatore, *m.* importer
importazione, *f.* import
importo, *m.* amount
importunare, to trouble
impossibile, impossible
impossibilità, *f.* impossibility
imposta, *f.* tax, duty
impostare, to post (a letter)
impresa, *f.* enterprise
impresario, *m.* contractor
impressionante, outstanding
impressionare, to impress
impressione, *f.* impression
imprevedibile, unforeseeable
imprevisto, unforeseen
imprimere, to stamp
improduttivo, unproductive
improvviso, suddenly
impulso, *m.* impulse
impurità, *f.* impurity
imputare, to impute
imputazione, *f.* imputation, accusation
inabilità, *f.* inability
inabilitare, to disqualify
inaccettabile, unacceptable
inadatto, unfit
inatteso, unexpected
inattivo, inactive
inaugurare, to inaugurate
inaugurazione, *f.* inauguration
inavvertenza, *f.* inadvertence
incapace, incapable
incapacità, *f.* incapacity
incaricare, to charge, to entrust
incarico, *m.* appointment, task
incartare, to pack in paper

incassare, to cash
incasso, *m.* collection
incauto, imprudent
incendiare, to set on fire
incendio, *m.* fire
incertezza, *f.* uncertainty
incerto, uncertain
incessante, ceaseless
inchiesta, *f.* enquiry
incidente, *m.* incident
inclinazione, *f.* inclination
includere, to include
incommensurabile, incommensurable
incomodare, to trouble
incomodo, inconvenient
incompatibile, incompatible
incompetente, incompetent
incompetenza, *f.* incompetence
incontestabile, irrefutable
incontestato, undisputed
incontrare, to meet
inconveniente, inconvenient
inconvertibile, inconvertible
incorporare, to incorporate
indagare, to enquire
indagine, *f.* enquiry
indeciso, undecided
indenizzare, to indemnify
indenizzo, *m.* indemnity
indennità, *f.* indemnity
indeterminato, indeterminate
indicare, to indicate
indicatore, *m.* directory
indicazione, *f.* indication
indice, *m.* index
indigeno, native
indiretto, indirect
indirizzare, to address
indirizzo, *m.* address
indiscutibile, unquestionable
indispensabile, indispensable
indisponibile, unavailable
individuale, individual
individualità, *f.* individuality
indiviso, undivided
indizio, *m.* sign
indugiare, to tarry, delay
indugio, *m.* delay
indurre, to induce

industria, *f.* industry
industriale, industrial
inerente, inherent
inesatto, inaccurate; mistaken
inesistente, non-existent
inesplicabile, inexplicable
inevitabile, inevitable
inferiore, inferior
inferiorità, *f.* inferiority
influenza, *f.* influence
influenzare, to influence
influire, to affect
infondato, unfounded
informare, to inform
informazione, *f.* information
infortunio, *m.* accident
infrazione, *f.* infraction
ingannare, to deceive
ingannevolmente, deceitfully
inganno, *m.* deceit
ingegnere, *m.* engineer
ingegneria, *f.* engineering
ingerirsi, to interfere
ingiurioso, injurious
ingombrante, cumbersome
ingombrare, to encumber
ingresso, *m.* input
ingrosso, wholesale
iniziale, initial
inizializzare, to commence operation of
iniziare, to start
iniziativa, *f.* initiative
inizio, *m.* beginning
innovazione, *f.* innovation
inondazioni, *f.* floods
inscrivere, to enter; to record
inscrizione, *f.* entry, inspection
inserzione, *f.* advertisement
insoluto, unpaid
insolvente, insolvent
insolvenza, *f.* insolvency
insussistenza, *f.* write off
intatto, intact
integrato, fully paid
intendenza, *f.* superintendence
intenzione, *f.* intention
interdire, to interdict
interdizione, *f.* interdiction
interessamento, *m.* concern; interest

interesse, *m.* interest
intermediario, *m.* middle-man
intermedio, *m.* intermediary
interno, internal
intero, whole
interpellare, to question
interpellazione, *f.* question
interporre, to interpose
interpretare, to interpret
interpretazione, *f.* interpretation
interrogare, to interrogate
interrogatorio, *m.* interogatory
interrompere, to interrupt
interruzione, *f.* interruption
intervallo, *m.* interval
intervenire, to intervene
intervento, *m.* intervention
intervista, *f.* interview
intervistare, to interview
intesa, *f.* agreement
intestare, to head
intestato, headed; registered
intestazione, *f.* heading
intimare, to inform; to notify
intimazione, *f.* notification
intimità, *f.* intimacy
intimo, intimate
intollerabile, intolerable
intraprendere, to undertake
intraprenditore, *m.* entrepreneur
intrattenere, to detain; to entertain
intrinseco, intrinsic
introitare, to cash
introito, *m.* collection; receipt
inutile, useless
invendibile, unsaleable
inventare, to invent
inventariare, to inventory
inventario, *m.* inventory
inventario di bordo, *m.* inventory of the
   cargo
inventore, *m.* inventor
invenzione, *f.* invention
investimento, *m.* investment
investire, to invest
inviare, to send
invio, *m.* consignment
invitare, to invite
invito, *m.* invitation

ipoteca, *f.* mortgage
ipotecare, to mortgage
ipotesi, *f.* hypothesis
irrecuperabile, unrecoverable
irregolare, irregular
irregolarità, *f.* irregularity
irrevocabile, irrevocable
irrevocabilità, *f.* irrevocability
iscrivere, to register
ispettore, *m.* inspector
ispezione, *f.* inspection
istante, urgent
istanza, *f.* petition
istituire, to establish
istituzione, *f.* institution
istruire, to instruct
istruttore, *m.* instructor
istruttoria, *f.* judicial enquiry
istruzione, *f.* instruction
itinerario, *m.* itinerary

L

laboratorio, *m.* laboratory
laboriosamente, laboriously
laborisità, *f.* industry
laborioso, laborious
laceramento, *m.* tearing
lacerare, to tear
lacerazione, *f.* tearing
lacrima, *f.* drop; tear
lacrimare, to weep
ladreria, *f.* theft
ladro, *m.* thief
ladroneria, *f.* theft
ladronesco, thievish
lama, *f.* blade
lamentare, to lament
lamentazione, *f.* lamentation
lanciamento, *m.* floating a company
lanciare, to launch
lancio, *m.* launching
larghezza, *f.* width
largo, wide
lasciare, to leave
lato, *m.* side
latore, *m.* bearer
laureato, *m.* graduate

lavorante, m. worker
lavorare, to work
lavorativo, workable
lavoratore, m. worker
lavorazione, f. workmanship
lavori, m. works
lavoro, m. work
lecito, allowed
ledere, to harm
legale, lawful
legalità, f. legality
legalizzare, to legalize
legalizzazione, f. legalization
legalmente, legally
legare, to bind
legatario, m. legatee
legato, m. legacy
legatura, f. binding
legge, f. law
leggere, to read
leggibile, legible
legittmazione, f. legitimation
legittima defesa, f. self-defence
legittimità, f. legitimacy
legittimo, legitimate
lentamente, slowly
lentezza, f. slowness
lento, slow
lesinare, to haggle
lesione, f. injury
lesivo, injurious
lettera, f. letter
lettera di credito, f. letter of credit
lettera di vettura, f. carriage note
letterale, literal
lettura, f. reading
levata, collection (of letters)
libbra, f. pound
libera pratica, f. clearance
liberare, to free
liberazione, f. liberation
libero, free
libertà, f. freedom
libretto, m. booklet
libretto di assegni, m. cheque-book
libretto deconto, m. pass-book
libretto di lavoro, m. employment
libretto di patente, m. licence card
libro, m. book

libro copialettere, m. invoice copybook
libro degli inventari, m. inventory list
libro di cassa, m. cash book
libro di riferenza, m. letter register
libro protocollo, m. reference book
licenza, f. licence; leave
licenza di caccia, f. shooting licence
licenza di circolazione, f. car licence
licenza commerciale, f. commercial licence
licenza di pesca, f. fishing licence
licenziamento, m. dismissal
licenziare, to dismiss
licitare, to auction
licitazione, f. auction sale
lieto, glad
lieve, light
limitare, to limit
limitazione, f. limitation
limite, m. limit, confine
limitrofo, neighbouring
linea, f. line
linea di carico, f. load-line
lingua, f. language
liquidare, to liquidate
liquidatore, m. liquidator
liquidazione, f. liquidation
liquido, liquid; due; payable
lira, f. lira
lira sterlina, f. pound sterling
lista, f. note; list
listino, m. small note; list
lite, f. lawsuit
litigio, m. litigation
litro, m. litre
livellamento, m. levelling
livello, m. level
locale, local
locali, m. premises
locatario, m. tenant
locativo, for letting
locatore, m. landlord
locazione, f. tenancy
locomotiva, f. locomotive
lodare, to praise
lode, f. praise
logorio, m. wear and tear
lontano, distant
lordo, gross

lottare, to fight
lotteria, *f.* lottery
lotto, *m.* lot; batch
lucrativo, profitable
lucro, *m.* profit
lunghezza, *f.* length
lungo, long
luogotenente, *m.* deputy; lieutenant
luogotenenza, *f.* lieutenancy
lusso, *m.* luxury
lussuoso, luxurious
lustra, *f.* deception
lustro, *m.* gloss; polish
lutto, *m.* mourning
luttuoso, mournful

M

macchina, *f.* machine; car
macchina da scrivere, *f.* typewriter
macchinario, *m.* machinery
magazzinaggio, *m.* storing
magazzini, *m.* stock-in-trade
magazziniere, *m.* storekeeper
magazzino, *m.* store; warehouse
maggioranza, *f.* majority
mala fede, bad faith
malgrado, in spite of
malintendere, to misunderstand
malinteso, *m.* misunderstanding
malore, *m.* sudden illness
malversazione, *f.* embezzlement
mancanza, *f.* scarcity; lacking
mancare, to lack
mancia, *f.* tip
mandare, to send
mandatario, *m.* agent
mandato, *m.* mandate; agency
maniera, *f.* manner
manifatturieri, *m.* manufacturing shares
manifestare, to demonstrate; to show
manifestino, *m.* pamphlet
manifesto, *m.* poster
manipolare, to handle
manipolazione, *f.* handling
mano, *f.* hand
manoscritto, *m.* manuscript
manovra, *f.* manoeuvre

manovrare, to manoeuvre
mantenere, to keep
mantenimento, *m.* maintenance
manuale, *m.* handbook
marca, *f.* brand; mark
marcare, to mark
marcatura, *f.* labelling
mare, *m.* sea
marea, *f.* tide
marginale, marginal
margine, *m.* edge; margin
marina, *f.* navy
marino, naval
marittimo, maritime
maschera, *f.* mask
mass, *f.* bulk
massima, *f.* maxim
massimo, most
mastro, *m.* ledger
materia, *f.* matter; subject
materiale, *m.* material
materie, *f.* materials
matricola, *f.* register number
matricolare, to register
maturare, to mature
meccanica, *f.* engineering
meccanici, *m.* engineering shares
meccanico, *m.* engineer
meccanismo, *m.* mechanism
meccanizzare, to computerize
medesimo, same
media, *f.* average
mediano, *m.* medium
mediatore, *m.* broker
mediazione, *f.* brokerage
medio, *m.* medium
meglio, better
memoria, *f.* memory; note
memoriale, *m.* memorial
meno, less
mensile, monthly
mente, *f.* mind
menzionare, to mention
meraviglia, *f.* surprise
meravigliare, to surprise
mercante, *m.* merchant
mercanteggiare, to bargain
mercantile, mercantile
mercanzia, *f.* merchandise

mercato, *m.* market
merce, *f.* goods
merceologia, *f.* science of commerce
mercuriale, *m.* market-list
meritare, to deserve
meritevole, deserving
merito, *m.* merit
mese, *m.* month
metà, *f.* half
metallico, metallic
metallo, *m.* metal
metallurgici, *m.* metallurgical shares
metodo, *m.* method
metrico, metric
metro, *m.* metre
mezzo, *m.* means
migliaio, *m.* thousand
miglio, *m.* mile
miglioramento, improvement
migliorare, to improve
milione, *m.* million
minacciare, to menace
minerale, *m.* mineral
minerari, *m.* mining shares
minimo, lease
ministero, *m.* ministry
ministro, *m.* minister
minorenne, *m.* infant
minutamente, in detail
minuto, retail
minuzia, *f.* trifle
minuzioso, in detail
mira, *f.* aim
mirare, to aim at
missione, *f.* mission
misto, mixed
misura, *f.* measure
misurare, to measure
misurazione, *f.* measurement
mittente, *m.* sender
mobile, mobile
mobili, *m.* furniture; chattels
mobiliare, movable; personal
mobilitazione, *f.* mobilization
mobilizzare, to mobilize
moda, *f.* fashion
modalità, *f.* way, manner
modello, *m.* model
modico, cheap

modificare, to alter
modificazione, *f.* alteration
modo, *m.* mode; manner
modulo, *m.* coupon; form
molo, *m.* pier
moltiplicazione, *f.* multiplication
momentaneo, temporary
momento, *m.* moment
mondiale, world
moneta, *f.* coin
monetario, monetary
monopolio, *m.* monopoly
monopolista, *m.* monopolist
monopolistico, monopolistic
monopolizzare, to monopolize
montaggio, *m.* fitting; mounting
montante, *f.* amount
montare, to fit, to load
montatore, *m.* fitter
mora, *f.* delay
moralità, *f.* morality
moratoria, *f.* moratorium
mostra, *f.* show
motivare, to justify
motivo, *m.* motive
moto, *m.* motion
moto, *f.* motor-cycle
motore, *m.* motor
motoscafo, *m.* motor-boat
motrice, motive power
movimentazione, *f.* turnover
movimento, *m.* movement
mozione, *f.* motion
multa, *f.* fine
multare, to fine
multiple, multiple
municipale, municipal
munire, to furnish
mutamento, *m.* change
mutare, to change
mutuale, mutual
mutuo, *m.* loan
mutuo, mutual

N

narrare, to narrate
narratore, *m.* narrator

narrazione, *f.* narration
nascita, *f.* birth
nascondere, to hide
nastro, *m.* ribbon; tape
natura, *f.* nature
naturale, natural
naturalizzare, to naturalize
naturalizzazione, *f.* naturalization
naturalmente, naturally
naufragare, to shipwreck
naufragio, *m.* shipwreck
nautico, nautical
navale, naval
nave, *f.* boat; ship
nave da carico, *f.* cargo boat
navigabile, navigable
navigabilità, *f.* navigability
navigare, to navigate
navigazione, *f.* navigation
naviglio, *m.* craft
nazionale, national
nazionalità, *f.* nationality
nazionalizzazione, *f.* nationalization
necessario, necessary
necessità, *f.* necessity
negare, to deny
negativo, negative
negligente, careless
negligenza, *f.* carelessness
negoziabile, negotiable
negoziabilità, *f.* negotiability
negoziare, to negotiate
negoziazione, *f.* negotiation
negozio, *m.* shop
netto, net
netto ricavo, *m.* net proceeds
neutrale, neutral
neutralità, *f.* neutrality
neutro, neutral
nocivo, harmful
noleggiare, to charter
noleggiatore, *m.* charterer
noleggio, *m.* charter party
nolo, *m.* freight
nomina, *f.* nomination
nominale, nominal
nominare, to nominate
norma, *f.* rule, mode
normale, normal

nota, *f.* note
nota di accreditamento, *f.* credit note
nota di addebitamento, *f.* debit note
nota di pegno, *f.* dock warrant
nota di spedizione, *f.* carriage note
notare, to note
notaro, *m.* solicitor
notificare, to notify
notificazione, *f.* notification
notizia, *f.* news item
noto, known
notorietà, *f.* notoriety
notorio, known; legal
nullità, *f.* nullity
nullo, null, void
numerare, to number
numerario, *m.* cash
numeratore, *m.* numerator
numeratrice, *f.* calculating machine
numerazione, *f.* numeration
numero, *m.* number
nuocere, to harm
nuovità, *f.* novelty
nuovo, new

O

obbligare, to oblige
obbligatorio, obligatory
obbligazione, *f.* obligation; debenture; bond
obbligo, *m.* bond; engagement
obiettare, to object
obiezione, *f.* objection
obliterare, to obliterate
occasionalmente, occasionally
occasionare, to cause
occasione, *f.* opportunity
occorrente, necessary
occorrenza, *f.* occurrence
occorrere, to need
occupante, *m.* occupier
occupare, to occupy
occupato, busy
occupazione, *f.* occupation
odiernamente, at present
odierno, of today
offendere, to offend

offensiva, *f.* offensive
offensivo, offensive
offerente, *m.* bidder
offerta, *f.* offer
offesa, *f.* offence
officina, *f.* workshop
offrire, to offer
oggetti, *m.* materials
oggetto, *m.* aim; object
oggi, today
oltremare, overseas
oltremisura, beyond measure
oltrepassare, to overtake
omettere, to omit
omissione, *f.* omission
ommaggio, *m.* compliment
omogeno, homogeneous
oncia, *f.* ounce
onda, *f.* wave
ondata, *f.* wave
onere, *m.* burden
oneroso, burdensome
onestà, *f.* honesty
onestamente, honestly
onoralibilità, *f.* honourableness
onorare, to honour
onorario, *m.* fee
onorario, honorary
onore, *m.* honour
opera, *f.* work
operaio, *m.* workman
operare, to work, to act
operato, *m.* action
operatore, *m.* operator
operazione, *f.* operation, transaction
opinione, *f.* opinion
opporre, to oppose
opportunità, *f.* opportunity
opportuno, timely
opposizione, *f.* opposition
oppure, or else
opzione, *f.* option
ora, *f.* hour
ora, now
oralmente, orally
orario, *m.* schedule; time-table
ordinamento, *m.* arrangement; system
ordinanza, *f.* decree; order
ordinare, to order

ordinario, ordinary
ordinazione, *f.* order
ordine, *m.* order
ordine di consegna, *m.* delivery note
ordine di imbarco, *m.* shipping note
organico, organic
organizzare, to organize
organizzazione, *f.* organization
originale, original
originario, originating
origine, *f.* origin
orlo, *m.* border, brink
ormeggiare, to moor
ormeggio, *m.* mooring
oro, *m.* gold
orologio, *m.* clock
osare, to dare
oscillante, oscillating
oscillare, to oscillate
oscillazione, *f.* oscillation
osservanza, *f.* observance
osservare, to observe
osservazione, *f.* observation
ostacolare, to hinder
ostacolo, *m.* obstacle
otterne, to obtain
ottimismo, *m.* optimism
ottimizare, to optimize
ottimo, best
ovviare, to avoid
ovvio, obvious
ozio, *m.* idleness
ozioso, idle; uninvested

P

pachetto, *m.* packet
pacco, *m.* parcel
paccotiglia, *f.* shoddy goods
pace, *f.* peace
pacifico, peaceful
padronanza, *f.* command
padrone, *m.* master
paese, *m.* country
paga, *f.* pay
pagabile, payable
pagamento, *m.* payment
pagamento a contanti, *m.* cash payment

pagamento a rate, *m.* payment by instalments
pagare, to pay
pagatore, *m.* payer
pagherò, *m.* promissory note
pagina, *f.* page
paglia, *f.* straw
paio, *m.* couple
panico, *m.* panic
pannello, *m.* panel
paralizzare, to paralyse
parcella, *f.* bill of costs
pareggiare, to balance
pareggio, *m.* balance
parere, to appear
parere, *m.* opinion
pari, *m.* par
pari, equal
parità, *f.* parity
parlare, to speak
parola, *f.* word
prola d'ordine, *f.* slogan
parte, *f.* part
partecipante, *m.* participant
partecipare, to participate
partecipazione, *f.* participation
partenza, *f.* departure
particolare, *m.* detail
particolare, particular
partire, to leave, to sail
partita, *f.* departure; entry; lot
partita doppia, *f.* double entry
partita semplice, *f.* simple entry
partitario, *m.* ledger
parziale, partial
passabile, passable
pasaggio, *m.* passage
passaporto, *m.* passport
passare, to pass
passato, *m.* past
passato, gone by; past
passeggiero, *m.* passenger
passeggiero, transitory
passibile, liable
passibilmente, liable to
passività, *f.* liabilities
passivo, *m.* debit side
passivo, passive
passo, *m.* step

patentare, to license
patente, *f.* licence
patente, obvious
patente di guida, *f.* driving licence
patente di sanità, *f.* bill of health
patrimoniale, patrimonial
patrimonio, *m.* estate
patto, *m.* agreement; pact
pattuire, to agree; to bargain
pattuito, agreed
pecuniario, pecuniary
pegno, *m.* pledge; token
pena, *f.* penalty
penale, penal
penalità, *f.* penalty
pendente, outstanding
pendenza, *f.* pending business
pensare, to think
pensionato, *m.* pensioner
pensione, *f.* pension
penuria, *f.* scarcity
per cento, per cent
percentuale, *f.* percentage
percepire, to cash; to collect
percettore, *m.* tax collector
percorrere, to run; to cover
percorso, *m.* distance
perdere, to lose
perdita, *f.* loss
perfetto, perfect
perfezionare, to improve
pericolo, *m.* danger
periodo, *m.* period
perito, *m.* expert; surveyor
perito, skilled
perizia, *f.* survey
periziare, to estimate; to value
permanente, permanent
permanenza, *f.* duration; stay
permesso, *m.* leave; permission
permettere, to allow
perquisire, to search
perquisizione, *f.* search
perseguire, to follow up; to prosecute
persona, *f.* person
personale, *m.* personnel
personale, person
personalizzare, to personalize
persuadere, to persuade

pervenire, to reach
pesa, *f.* weights
pesante, heavy
pesare, to weigh
pesata, *f.* weighing
pesatore, *m.* weigher
pesatura, *f.* weighing
peso, *m.* weight
peso lordo, *m.* gross weight
peso netto, *m.* net weight
pessimo, worst
petroliferi, *m.* oil shares
pezzo, *m.* piece
piacere, *m.* pleasure
piacimento, *m.* pleasure
piano, *m.* plan
pianta, *f.* list; map; plant
piattaforma, *f.* platform
piatto, flat
piazza, *f.* market
piazzista, salesman
piccolo, small
piede, *m.* foot
piega, *f.* fold
piegare, to fold
piegatura, folding
pigione, *f.* rent
pilota, *m.* pilot
pilotaggio, *m.* pilotage
pilotare, to pilot
piroscafo, *m.* ship
pista, *f.* runway; track
politica, politics
polizza, *f.* policy
polizza di assicurazione, *f.* insurance policy
polizza di carico, *f.* bill of lading
polizzetta, *f.* slip of paper
ponte, *m.* bridge
porgere, to offer; to present
porta, *f.* door
portafoglio, *m.* portfolio
portare, to carry; to post
portata, *f.* capacity; reach
portatile, portable
portatore, *m.* bearer; holder
porto, *m.* port
porto affrancata, postage paid
porto assegnato, postage unpaid

porto compreso, postage included
porto franco, carriage paid
posa piano, handle with care
posare, to lay; to handle
positivo, positive
posizione, *f.* position
possedimento, *m.* possession
possesso, *m.* possession
possessore, *m.* holder
possibile, possible
possibilità, *f.* possibility
posta, *f.* post
postale, *m.* mail boat
postale, postal
posteggio, *m.* cab rank; parking
posto, *m.* place, spot
potenza, *f.* power
potenzialità, *f.* potentiality
potere, to be able
potere, *m.* power
pratica, *f.* practice
praticare, to practise
pratiche, *f.* file
pratico, practical; experienced
preambolo, *m.* preamble
preavvisare, to notify
preavviso, *m.* notice
precauzione, *f.* caution
precedente, *m.* precedent
precedente, previous
precedenza, *f.* priority
precipitare, to precipitate
precipitazione, *f.* precipitation
precisare, to clarify; to specify
precisazione, *f.* clarification
precisione, *f.* precision
preciso, accurate; precise
pedominante, predominant
preferenza, *f.* preference
preferibile, preferable
preferire, to prefer
pregare, to request
preghiera, *f.* request
pregiarsi, to have the honour to
pregiata, *f.* letter
preguidicare, to prejudice
pregiudizievole, prejudicial
pregiudizio, *m.* damage; prejudice
prelevamento, *m.* withdrawal (of money)

prelevare, to draw out (money)
premeditato, deliberate
premiare, to award prize
premio, *m.* premium; prize
premura, *f.* solicitude
prendere, to take
prenditore, *m.* payee
prenotare, to book
prenotazione, *f.* booking
preparare, to prepare
preparatorio, preparatory
preparazione, *f.* preparation
prerogativa, *f.* prerogative
presa, *f.* collection
prescritto, prescribed
prescrizione, *f.* prescription
presentare, to introduce; to present
presentatore, *m.* holder
presentazione, *f.* introduction
presente, *f.* letter
presente, *m.* present time
presenza, *f.* appearance; aspect; presence
presidente, *m.* president
presidenza, *f.* presidency
presidere, to preside
pressione, *f.* pressure
prestabilire, to arrange in advance
prestamento, *m.* loan
prestare, to lend
prestatore, *m.* lender
prestazione, *f.* tax; impost
prestito, *m.* loan
presto, soon
presuntivo, presumptive
presunzione, *f.* presumption
pretendere, to claim
pretensione, *f.* claim
pretese, *f.* salary required; wage
pretesto, *m.* pretext
pretore, *m.* magistrate
prevedere, to foresee
prevenire, to inform
preventivare, to estimate
preventivo, *m.* estimate
preventivo, estimated
previdenza, *f.* contingency; foresight
previo, previous
previsioni, *f.* forecast
previsto, foreseen

prezzo, *m.* price
prima, first
primario, first-rate
primato, *m.* primacy
primo ordine, first-rate
principale, *m.* employer
principale, main
principio, *m.* principle
privare, to deprive
privatamente, privately
privato, private
privilegiare, to privilege
privilegio, *m.* privilege
privo, deprived
probabile, probable
probabilità, *f.* probability
problema, *m.* problem
procedere, to proceed
procedimento, *m.* proceedings
procedura, *f.* procedure
processo, *m.* process; trial
processo verbale, *m.* official record
processuale, pertaining to a trial
proclama, *m.* proclamation
proclamare, to proclaim
proclamatore, *m.* proclaimer
procura, *f.* letter of attorney; proxy
procurare, to obtain
procuratore, *m.* procurator, attorney
prodotto, *m.* product
produrre, to produce
produttività, *f.* productivity
produttivo, productive
produttore, *m.* producer
produzione, *f.* production
professionale, professional
professione, *f.* profession
profittare, to profit
profittevole, profitable
profitto, *m.* profit
progettare, to plan
progetto, *m.* plan
programma, *m.* programme
programmatura, *f.* software
progredire, to progress
progressione, *f.* progression
progressivo, *m.* running total
progressivo, progressive
pregresso, *m.* progress

prolungamento, *m.* extension
prolungare, to extend
promessa, *f.* promise
promettere, to promise
promozione, *f.* promotion
promuovere, to promote
pronosticare, to forecast
pronostico, *m.* forecast
prontamente, readily
prontezza, *f.* readiness
pronto, ready
pronunciare, to pronounce
propizio, favourable
proporre, to propose
proporzionale, proportional
proporzionalmente, proportionally
proporzione, *f.* proportion
proposito, *m.* proposition
proposta, *f.* proposal
proprietà, *f.* property
proprietario, *m.* owner
proprio, own
proroga, *f.* postponement; renewal
prorogare, to postpone; to renew
proseguire, to pursue
prosperità, *f.* prosperity
prospero, prosperous
prospettiva, *f.* prospect
prospetto, *m.* prospectus; statement
prossimo, next
proteggere, to protect
protesta, *f.* protest
protestare, to protest
protesto, *m.* protest
protettore, *m.* protector
protezione, *f.* protection
protocollare, to file
protocollo, *m.* file
prova, *f.* test, mark
provare, to prove; to test
provenienza, *f.* origin
provenire, to originate
provento, *m.* income; proceeds
provvedere, to provide
provvedimento, *m.* provision
provveditore, *m.* supplier
provvigione, *m.* brokerage
provvisorio, provisional
provvista, *f.* provision; purchase

prudenza, *f.* prudence
pubblicare, to publish
pubblicazione, *f.* publication
pubblicità, *f.* publicity
pubblico, *m.* public
pulire, to clean
pulsante, *f.* switch
punibile, punishable
punire, to punish
punto, *m.* dot; point
puntuale, punctual
puntualità, *f.* punctuality
punzonare, to punch
punzonatrice, *f.* punching machine
punzonatura, *f.* punching
purificare, to purify
purificazione, *f.* purification
purità, purity
puro, pure

Q

quaderna, *f.* set of four numbers
quadernaccio, *m.* scrap book
quaderno, *m.* exercise-book; quire
quadrare, to balance
quadrato, *m.* square
quadratura, *f.* squaring
quadro, *m.* framework; list; picture
quadro, square
quadruplicare, to quadruplicate
quadruplo, *m.* quadruple
qualifica, *f.* qualification
qualificare, to qualify
qualità, *f.* quality
quantità, *f.* quantity
quantitativo, *m.* amount
quantizzare, digitize
quarantena, *f.* quarantine
quarto, *m.* quarter
querela, *f.* complaint
querelare, to summons
questionario, *m.* questionnaire
questione, *f.* question
quietanza, *f.* receipt
quietanzare, to receipt
quindicina, *f.* fortnight
quindicinale, fortnightly

quintale, *m.* quintal
quota, *f.* quota, share
quotare, to quote
quotazione, *f.* quotation
quotidianamente, every day
quotidiano, *m.* daily (newspaper)
quotizzare, to assess
quotizzazione, *f.* assessment

R

raccommandare, to recommend
raccomandata, *f.* registered letter
raccomandatario, *m.* agent
raccomandatore, *m.* recommender
raccomandazione, *f.* recommendation
rada, *f.* roadstead
raddoppiare, to redouble
raddoppio, *m.* doubling
radiogramma, radio telegram, wireless cable
radiotelefono, *m.* radio telephone
raggiungere, to attain
raggiungimento, *m.* attainment
raggrupare, to regroup
ragguardevole, considerable
ragione, *f.* reason; price; style
ragioneria, *f.* accounting
ragioniere, *m.* accountant
ramificazione, *f.* ramification
rammentare, to remind
rapidità, *f.* speed
rapido, speedy
rapporto, *m.* relation; report
rappresentante, *m.* representative
rappresentanza, *f.* agency
rappresentare, to represent
rata, *f.* instalment
rateale, partial
ratealmente, by instalments
ratifica, *f.* ratification
ratificare, to ratify
razzo, *m.* rocket
realizzare, to realize
realizzazione, *f.* realization
realtà, *f.* reality
reazione, *f.* reaction
recapitare, to deliver

recapito, *m.* delivery
recente, recent
recesso, *m.* renouncement
reciprocamente, mutually
reciprocità, *f.* reciprocity
reciproco, mutual
reclamare, to claim
reclame, *f.* advertisement
reclamo, *m.* claim; complaint
recondito, hidden
redatto, drawn up
redattore, *m.* editor
redditivo, profitable
reddito, *m.* income; revenue
reddituario, *m.* annuitant
redigere, to draft
redimere, to redeem
redimibilità, *f.* redeemability
referenza, *f.* reference
regalo, *m.* donation; gift
reggere, to bear
regime, *m.* diet; régime
registrare, to register, to enter
registratore, *m.* register
registrazione, *f.* entry; registration
registro, *m.* register book
registro di classificazione, *m.* certificate of character
regola, *f.* rule
regolamento, *m.* regulations
regolare, to settle
regolare, regular
regolarità, *f.* regularity
regolarmente, in due course
regolatore, *m.* regulator
regressione, *f.* regression
regresso, *m.* recourse
relativo, relative
relatore, *m.* maker of a report
relazione, *f.* report
remissione, *f.* remission
rendere, to render
rendiconto, *m.* statement of assets and liabilities
rendimento, *m.* yield
rendita, *f.* rent; yield
reo, guilty
reparto, *m.* department
replica, *f.* reply; retort

replicare, to reply
reputazione, *f.* reputation
requisito, *m.* requisite
resa, *f.* delivery
residenza, *f.* residence
residuo, *m.* residue
resistente, resistant
resistenza, *f.* resistance
respiro, *m.* delay
responsabile, authoritative; responsible
responsabilità, *f.* liability
restituire, to hand back
restituzione, *f.* restitution
resto, *m.* remainder
restritivo, restrictive
restrizione, *f.* restriction
rete, *f.* network
rettifica, *f.* amendment
rettificare, to amend
revoca, *f.* revocation
riacquistare, to buy back
riacquisto, *m.* repurchase
rialzare, to raise again
rialzista, *m.* bull
rialzo, *m.* rise (in prices)
riassicurare, to reinsure
riassicurazione, *f.* reinsurance
riassumere, to sum up
riassunto, *m.* summary
ribassare, to lower
ribassista, *m.* bear
ribasso, *m.* decline; fall (in prices)
ricambiare, to exchange
ricambio, exchange; replacement
ricaricare, to reload
ricaricazione, *f.* reloading
ricavare, to draw out; to obtain
ricavo, *m.* proceeds
ricchezza, *f.* wealth
ricco, wealthy
ricerca, *f.* search
ricercare, to search
ricevente, *m.* receiver
ricevere, to receive
ricevimento, *m.* reception
ricevitore, *m.* receiver
ricevuta, *f.* receipt
richiedente, *m.* applicant
richiedere, to require

richiesta, *f.* request
ricompra, *f.* repurchase
ricomprare, to repurchase
riconoscere, to recognize
riconoscimento, *m.* acknowledgement
riconsegna, *f.* redelivery
ricordare, to remember
ricordo, *m.* memory
ricorrente, *m.* petitioner
ricorrere, to have recourse to
ricorso, *m.* petition
ricuperare, to recover
ricupero, *m.* recovery
ridurre, to reduce
riduzione, *f.* reduction
riepilogo, *m.* summary
riesportare, to re-export
riesportazione, *f.* re-export
riferimento, *m.* reference
riferire, to refer
rifiutare, to refuse
rifiuto, *m.* refusal
riforma, *f.* reform
riformare, to reform
rifornimento, *m.* supply
rifornire, to supply
riga, *f.* line
rigettare, *m.* to reject
rigetto, *m.* rejection
rigore, *m.* rigour
rigorosamente, rigorously
riguardare, to regard
riguardo, *m.* regard
rilasciare, to release
rilassamento, *m.* slackness
rilevante, considerable
rilevare, to point out; to take over
rimanente, *m.* remainder
rimanenza, *f.* residue
rimborsabile, reimbursable
rimborsare, to repay
rimborso, *m.* repayment
rimediabile, remediable
rimediare, to remedy
rimedio, *m.* remedy
rimessa, *f.* remittance
rimettere, to remit
rimorchiatore, *m.* tug
rimpiegare, to re-employ

rimpiego, *m.* re-employment
rimunerare, to remunerate
rimunerativo, remunerative
rincarare, to rise
rincaro, *m.* rise
rinfusa, (in) bulk
rinnovabile, renewable
rinnovare, to renew
rinnovazione, *f.* renewal
rinuncia, *f.* renunciation
rinunciare, to renunciate
rinviare, to adjourn
rinvio, *m.* adjournment
ripartire, to distribute
ripartizione, *f.* distribution
riparto, *m.* department; division
riparto di azioni, *m.* allotment of shares
ripetere, to repeat
riportare, to carry over; to transfer
riporto, *m.* amount carried forward; contango
ripristinare, to restore
ripristino, *m.* restoration
ripulire, to clean up
risarcimento, *m.* compensation
risarcire, to compensate
riscattare, to redeem
riscatto, *m.* redemption
rischiare, to risk
rischio, *m.* risk
rischioso, risky
riscontare, to rediscount
risconto, *m.* rediscount
riscontrare, to audit
riscontro, *m.* audit; reply
riscossione, *f.* collection (of bills)
riscosso, *m.* cash collected
riserbo, *m.* discretion
riserva, *f.* reserve
reservare, to reserve
risoluzione, *f.* resolution
risolvere, to resolve
risparmiare, to save
risparmio, *m.* saving
rispedire, to forward
rispedizione, *f.* forwarding
rispettabile, respectable
rispettabilità, *f.* respectability
rispettivo, respective

rispetto, *m.* respect
rispondere, to answer
risposta, *f.* answer
ristretto, *m.* lowest price
ristretto, restricted
risultare, to result
risultato, *m.* result
ritardare, to delay
ritardo, *m.* delay
ritenere, to think; to withhold
ritirare, to withdraw
ritiro, *m.* withdrawal
ritornare, to return
ritorno, *m.* return
riunione, *f.* meeting
riuscire, to succeed
riuscita, *f.* success
rivale, *m.* rival
rivalsa, *f.* redraft
rivendicare, to claim
rivendita, *f.* resale
riversibile, reversible
rivista, *f.* review
rivolgere, to turn
rompere, to break
rotondo, round
rotta, *f.* route
rottura, *f.* breakage
rovina, *f.* ruin
rovinare, to ruin
rubrica, *f.* reference; title
ruolo, *m.* list

S

sabottagio, *m.* sabotage
sabotare, to sabotage
sabotatore, *m.* saboteur
sacco, *m.* bag
saggio, *m.* rate
saggio dello sconto, *m.* discount rate
sala, *f.* hall
salariare, to pay wages
salariato, *m.* wage earner
salario, *m.* wage
saldamento, *m.* settlement
saldare, to settle
saldo, *m.* balance (of an account)

saldo, firm; steady
salire, to climb
salita, *f.* ascent
salutare, to salute
salute, *f.* health
saluti, *m.* greetings
saluto, *m.* salutation
salvaguardare, to safeguard
salvare, to save
salvataggio, *m.* salvage; storage
salvezza, *f.* safety
salvo, safe
salvo, except
sanità, *f.* health
sanzionare, to sanction
sanzione, *f.* sanction
sapere, to know
sbagliare, to make a mistake
sbaglio, *m.* mistake
sbarcare, to land
sbarco, *m.* landing; unloading
sbarramento, *m.* crossing a cheque
sbarrare, to cross a cheque
sbilancio, *m.* balance; deficit
sblocco, *m.* unfreezing of pieces
sbocco, *m.* market; outlet
sbrigare, to expedite
scacchiere, *m.* exchequer
scadente, inferior
scadente, falling due
scadenza, *f.* maturity; renewal date
scadenzario, *m.* bill book
scadere, to expire; to mature
scaduto, expired
scafo, *m.* hull
scala, *f.* index; scale
scalare, to reduce
scaletta, *f.* interest on amortization
scalo, *m.* port of call
scambiare, to exchange
scambio, *m.* exchange
scapitare, to lose
scapito, *m.* loss
scaricamento, *m.* unloading
scaricare, to unload
scaricatore, *m.* unloader
scarico, *m.* unloading
scarseggiare, to be scarce
scarsità, *f.* scarcity

scarso, scarce
scartare, to reject
scarto, *m.* rejection
scatola, *f.* box
scegliere, to choose
scelta, *f.* choice
scheda, *f.* application form; card
schedario, *m.* card index
schedino, index
schiarimento, clarification
schiarire, to clarify
scialuppa, *f.* sloop
scialuppa da salvataggio, *f.* lifeboat
sciente, aware of
scientifico, scientific
scienza, *f.* science
scienziato, *m.* scientist
sciogliere, to loose
scioglimento, loosening; termination
scioperante, *m.* striker
scioperare, to strike
sciopero, *m.* strike
sciupare, to spoil; to waste
sciupio, *m.* waste
scommessa, *f.* bet
scommettere, to bet
sconsigliare, to dissuade
scontabile, discountable
scontare, to discount
scontista, *m.* discounter
sconto, *m.* discount
scontrino, *m.* note; ticket
scoperta, *f.* discovery
scoperto di conti, *m.* overdraft
scopo, *m.* aim; purpose
scoppiare, to explode
scoppio, *m.* explosion
scoprire, to discover
scoraggiare, to discourage
scorso, last
scorta, *f.* stock
scotto, *m.* account; bill
screditare, to discredit
scrittura, *f.* entry; writing
scritturale, *m.* book-keeper; clerk
scritturare, to enter; to post
scritturazione, *f.* posting; writing-up
scrivente, *m.* writer
scrivere, to write

scusa, *f.* excuse
scusabile, excusable
scusare, to excuse
sdaziamento, *m.* payment of duty
sdaziare, to pay duty
sdebitare, to pay off
sdoganamento, *m.* clearing through customs
sdoganare, to clear through customs
sede, *f.* office; seat
sede centrale, *f.* headquarters
sedere, to sit
seduta, sitting
segnalare, to signal
segnalazione, *f.* signalling
segnale, *m.* signal
segnare, to mark
segno, *m.* mark
segretaria, *f.* secretary
segretario, *m.* secretary
segretaria, *f.* secretary's office
segretezza, *f.* secrecy
segreto, *m.* secret
seguente, following
seguire, to follow
selezionare, to select
selezione, *f.* selection
semestre, *m.* half-year
semplice, simple
semplificare, to simplify
semplificazione, *f.* simplification
sensale, *m.* broker
senseria, *f.* brokerage
sensibile, considerable
senso, *m.* meaning
sentenza, *f.* verdict
sentimento, *m.* feeling
senza, without
separare, to separate
separazione, *f.* separation
sequestrare, to confiscate, to sequestrate
sequestro, *m.* seizure
seria, *f.* series
seriamente, seriously
serio, serious
servire, to serve
servizio, *m.* service
sessione, *f.* session
settimana, *f.* week

settimanale, weekly
sezione, *f.* section
sforzare, to force
sforzo, *m.* effort
sfruttamento, *m.* exploitation
sfruttare, to exploit
sgomberare, to clear out; to remove
sgombero, *m.* clearance; removal
sgombero, empty
sgravamento, *m.* alleviation
sgravare, to alleviate
sicuramente, certainly; safely
sicurezza, *f.* safety; confidence
sicuro, safe
sicurtà, *f.* assurance; insurance
sigillare, to seal
sigillo, *m.* seal
sigla, *f.* initials; monogram
significare, to mean
significato, *m.* meaning
silenzio, *m.* silence
silenzioso, silent
sinceramente, sincerely
sincerità, *f.* sincerity
sindacato, *m.* committee; syndicate; trade union; trust
sindacatore, *m.* controller; supervisor
sindacazione, *f.* supervision
sindaco, *m.* mayor; trustee
singolo, single
sinistro, *m.* accident; loss
sinossi, *f.* synopsis
sinotici, synoptic
sintesi, *f.* synthesis
sintetico, synthetic
sistema, *m.* method; system
sistemare, to arrange; to settle
sistemazione, *f.* arrangement
sistemista, *m.* systems expert
situazione, *f.* situation
smerciare, to sell
smercio, *m.* sale
smontare, to unload
soccorso, *m.* help; relief
sociale, pertaining to a company
società, *f.* company; partnership
società anonoma, *f.* joint-stock company
società a responsabilità limitata, *f.* limited liability company

società in accomandita per azioni, *f.* partnership limited by shares
società in accomandita semplice, *f.* limited partnership
società in nome collettivo, *f.* general partnership
socio, *m.* member; partner
sodalizio, *m.* association; guild
soddisfacente, satisfactory
soddisfare, to satisfy
soddisfazione, *f.* satisfaction
sofferenza, *f.* pain, patience
sofferenza (cambiale in), unmet (bill)
soggettivo, subjective
soggetto, *m.* subject; theme
soggiornare, to reside; to stay
soggiorno, *m.* residence; stay
sola, *f.* sole
sola di cambio, *f.* sole of exchange
soldino, *m.* small sum of money
soldo, *m.* money
solidale, joint; united
solidità, *f.* solidity
solido, solid
solito, customary
sollecitare, to solicit
sollecitazione, *f.* solicitation
sollecitudine, *f.* solicitude
soluzione, *f.* solution
somma, *f.* sum of money; total
sommare, to add up; to sum up
sommario, *m.* summary
sommario, concise
sopperire, to provide for
sopraccaricare, to overload
sopraccarico, *m.* overload
sopraluogo, *m.* delivery on the spot
sopraprofitto, *m.* excess profit
sopratassa, *f.* surtax
sopravvenienza, *f.* contingency
sormontare, to overcome; surpass
sorprendere, to surprise
sorpresa, *f.* surprise
sorta, *f.* kind
sorteggiare, to draw lots
sorteggio, *m.* draw
sorveglianza, *f.* supervision
sorvegliare, to supervise
sospendere, to suspend

sospensione, *f.* suspension
sospetto, *m.* suspicion
sospettoso, suspect
sosta, *f.* demurrage
sostanza, *f.* substance
sostegno, *m.* support
sostenere, to support
sostituire, to replace
sostituzione, *f.* replacement
sotto, under
sotto condizione, on condition
sottomano, *m.* writing pad
sottomettere, to submit
sotto notato, undermentioned
sottoscrittore, *m.* subscriber
sottoscrivere, to subscribe
sottoscrizione, *f.* subscription
sottrare, to subtract
sottrazione, *f.* subtraction
sovvenzionare, to subsidize
sovvenzione, *f.* subsidy
specialità, *f.* speciality
specializzare, to specialize
specificare, to specify
specifico, specific
speculare, to speculate
speculatore, *m.* speculator
speculazione, *f.* speculation
spedire, to dispatch
speditore, *m.* sender; shipper
spedizione, *f.* consignment
spedizioniere, *m.* forwarding agent
spendere, to spend
speranza, *f.* hope
sperare, to hope
spesa, *f.* charge; expense
spesato, paid for
spessore, *m.* thickness
spettabile, honourable
spettanza, *f.* concern; fee
spettare, to concern
spiegare, to explain
spiegazione, *f.* explanation
spostare, to remove
stabile, firm; stable
stabilemtno, *m.* establishment; factory
stabilire, to establish
stabilità, *f.* stability
stabilizzare, to stabilize

stagione, *f.* season
stampa, *f.* press; print; stamp; printout
stampabile, printable
stampante, *f.* printer
stampare, to print; to stamp
stampatello, *m.* block letters
stampato, *m.* printed matter by post
stampe, *f.* printed matter
stampiglia, *f.* rubber stamp
stampigliare, to rubber stamp
stampino, *m.* stencil
stampo, *m.* form; mould
stanziamento, *m.* appropriation; grant
stanziare, to grant
statale, *m.* civil servant
statale, pertaining to the state
statistica, *f.* statistics
statistico, statistical
stato, *m.* state
statutale, statutory
statuto, *m.* statute; constitution
statuto sociale, *m.* article of association
stazionario, stationary
stazione, *f.* station
stazza, *f.* tonnage
stazza lorda, *f.* gross tonnage
stazza netta, *f.* net tonnage
stazzare, to gauge
stazzatura, *f.* gauging
stenodattilografa, *f.* shorthand typist
stenografa, *f.* shorthand writer
stenografare, to write in shorthand
stenografia, *f.* shorthand writing
stero, *m.* one cubic metre
stilografica, *f.* fountain pen
stima, *f.* esteem; estimate; valuation
stimare, to estimate; to value
stimata, *f.* letter
stipulare, to stipulate
stipulazione, *f.* stipulation
stiva, *f.* hold (in ship)
stivaggio, stowage
stivamento, *m.* stowing
stivare, to stow
stivatore, *m.* stevedore
stivatura, *f.* stowage
stornare, to divert; to cancel; to transfer
storno, *m.* cancellation
strada, *f.* road; way

strada ferrata, *f.* railway
stradale, pertaining to roads
straniero, foreign
strettamente, strictly
stretto, *m.* straits
stretto, narrow, quick
struttura, *f.* structure
strutturare, to construct; to fabricate
suaccennato, mentioned above
subagente, *m.* sub-agent
subagenzia, *f.* sub-agency
subappaltare, to subcontract
subappaltatore, *m.* subcontractor
subire, to undergo
subnoleggiare, to subfreight
subnoleggiatore, *m.* subfreighter
succedere, to succeed
successione, *f.* succession
successivamente, successively
successivo, next
successo, *m.* success
successore, *m.* successor
suddetto, mentioned above
suggellare, to seal
suggello, *m.* seal
suggerimento, *m.* suggestion
suggerire, to suggest
superare, to overcome
superficiale, superficial
superfluo, superfluous
superiore, superior
superiorità, *f.* superiority
supplementare, additional
supplemento, *m.* supplement
supplente, *m.* deputy
supporre, to suppose
supremazia, *f.* supremacy
suscettibile, susceptible
suscettibilità, *f.* susceptibility
suscitare, to arouse
sussidiare, to subsidize
sussidio, *m.* subsidy
svalutare, to depreciate; to devalue
svantaggio, *m.* disadvantage
svantaggioso, disadvantageous
svariato, various
svendere, to sell below cost
sventura, *f.* misfortune
sviluppare, to develop; to unfold

sviluppo, *m.* development
svincolare, to redeem; to release
svincolo, *m.* clearance; release

T

tabella, *f.* list; table
tabellare, tabular
tabulato, *m.* tabulation
taccuino, *m.* diary
tacitamente, tacitly
tacitare, to satisfy
tacito, tact
tagliando, *m.* coupon
tagliare, to cut
taglio, *m.* amount
talloncino, *m.* coupon; slip
tanto, so much
tara, *f.* tare
tardi, late
tardivo, late
tariffa, *f.* tariff
tariffare, to lay tariff on
tassa, *f.* tax, duty
tassare, to tax
tasso, *m.* rate
tastiera, *f.* keyboard
tasto, *m.* key
tavola, *f.* table
tecnica, *f.* technique
tecnico, *m.* technician
tecnico, technical
telefonare, to telephone
telefonata, *f.* telephone call
telefonista, *m.* telephone operator
telefono, *m.* telephone
telegiornale, *m.* TV news
telegrafare, to telegraph
telegrafia, *f.* telegraphy
telegrafico, telegraphic
telegrafista, *m.* telegraph operator
telegrafo, *m.* telegraph
telegramma, *f.* telegram
telescrivente, *m.* teleprinter
temperatura, *f.* temperature
tempesta, *f.* storm
tempestoso, stormy
tempo, *m.* time

tempo reale, *m.* real time
temporaneamente, temporarily
temporaneo, temporary
temporeggiare, to temporize
tendenza, *f.* tendency
tendenzioso, tendentious
tenere, to keep
tenore, *m.* contents, terms
tentativo, *m.* attempt
tergo, *m.* back; reverse side
terminale, *m.* terminal
terminare, to finish
termine, *m.* date; term
terremoto, *m.* earthquake
terreno, *m.* ground, plot
terreste, terrestrial
territorialità, *f.* territoriality
terrotorio, *m.* territory
terza persona, *f.* third party
terzi, *m.* third parties
terzo, third
tesoreria, *f.* treasury
tesoriere, *m.* treasurer
tesoro, *m.* treasury
tessera, identity card
tesserare, to enrol
tessili, *m.* textile shares
testa, *f.* head
testamentario, testamentary
testamento, *m.* will
testare, to bequeath
testatore, *m.* testator
testimone, *m.* witness
testimoniale, bearing witness
testimonianza, *f.* witness
testimoniare, to witness
testo, *m.* text
testuale, textual
testualmente, textually
timbro, *m.* stamp
tipo, *m.* type
tiraggio, *m.* issue
titolare, *m.* titular; principal
titolare, titular
titoli, *m.* securities
titoli di stato, *m.* gilt-edged
titolo, *m.* instrument; title
toccare, to touch
tollerabile, permissible

tollerare, to tolerate
tollerenza, *f.* allowance; tolerance
tondo, round
tonnellagio, *m.* tonnage
tonnellata, *f.* ton
tornaconto, *m.* profit
torto, *m.* tort; wrong
totale, *m.* total amount
totale, total; whole
tradizione, *f.* tradition
tradurre, to translate
traduttore, *m.* translator
traduzione, *f.* translation
traente, *m.* drawer
trafficante, *m.* trader
trafficare, to trade
traffico, *m.* trade; traffic
traforo, *m.* tunnel
tralasciare, to omit
transazione, *f.* transaction
transitare, to pass in transit
transitario, *m.* forwarding agent
transito, *m.* transit
transitorio, transitory
trapasso, *m.* assignment
trarre, to draw
trasbordare, to tranship
trasbordo, *m.* transhipment
trascorrere, to elapse; to pass
trascrivere, to transcribe
trascrizione, *f.* transcription
trascurabile, negligible
trascurare, to neglect
trasferimento, *m.* assignment
trasferire, to assign; to transfer
trasformare, to transform
trasformazione, *f.* transformation
trasgredire, to transgress
trasgressione, *f.* transgression
traslocare, to remove
traslochi, *m.* removals
trasmettere, to transmit
trasmissibile, transferable
trasmissibilità, *f.* transferability
trasmissione, *f.* transfer
trasportare, to carry
trasportatore, *m.* carrier
trasporti, *m.* transport shares
trasporto, *m.* carriage

tratta, *f.* draft
trattabile, accommodating
trattamento, *m.* treatment; salary
trattare, to deal; to treat
trattario, *m.* drawee
trattativa, *f.* negotiation
trattato, *m.* treaty
trattenere, to hold back
treno, *m.* train
tributario, tributary
tributo, *m.* tax
trimestrale, quarterly
trimestre, *m.* quarter
triplicare, to treble
triplice, triple
trovare, to find
turno, *m.* duty; turn
tutto, all

U

ubicato, located
ubicazione, *f.* location, position
udibile, audible
udienza, *f.* audience
udire, to hear
uditore, *m.* hearer
uditorio, *m.* auditorium
udizione, *f.* audition
ufficiale, *m.* officer
ufficiale, formal; official
ufficio, *m.* office
ufficio postale, *m.* post office
ufficioso, semi-official
uguagliare, to equal
uguale, equal
ugualità, *f.* equality
ulteriore, ulterior
ulteriormente, besides; further
ultimamente, recently
ultimare, to complete; to finish
ultimatum, *m.* ultimatum
ultimazione, *f.* completion
ultimo, last
umore, *m.* humour
umorismo, *m.* humour
umorista, *m.* humourist
unanime, unanimous

unanimità, *f.* unanimity
unico, solc; unique
unificare, to consolidate; to unite
unificazione, *f.* consolidation; unification
uniforme, uniform
unionc, *f.* union
unire, to unite
unità, *f.* unity
uomo, *m.* man
uragano, *m.* hurricane
urgente, urgent
urgenza, *f.* urgency
urtare, to knock; to hit
urto, *m.* knock; shock; collision
usanza, *f.* custom
usare, to use
uscente, closing; expiring
usciere, *m.* bailiff; doorkeeper
uscire, to be published; to go out
uscita, *f.* exit; export
uscite, *f.* liabilities
uso, *m.* custom; use
usuale, usual
usufruire, to take advantage of
usufrutto, *m.* usufruct; tenancy
usufruttuario, *m.* tenant
usura, *f.* usury
usuario, *m.* usurer
utensile, *m.* tool
utente, *m.* user
utenza, *f.* use
utile, *m.* profit
utile, useful
utile lordo, *m.* gross profit
utile netto, *m.* net profit
utilità, *f.* utility
utilitario, utilitarian
utilizzabile, usable
utilizzare, to utilize
utilizzazione, *f.* utilization
utilmente, usefully
utopia, *f.* utopia
utopista, *m.* utopist
utopistico, utopian

V

vacabile, likely to be vacant

vacante, vacant
vacanza, *f.* holiday
vaglia, *m.* postal order
vaglia bancario, *m.* bank draft
vaglia cambiaro, *m.* promissory note
vaglia postale, *m.* postal order
vagliare, to select
vago, vague
vagonata, *f.* wagon load
vagone, *m.* wagon
valevole, valid
validamente, validly
validità, *f.* validity
valido, valid
valore, to be current; to be worth
valore, *m.* security; value
valori, *m.* stocks and shares
valuta, *f.* paper money; currency
valuta estera, *f.* foreign currency
valutare, to estimate; to value
valutario, of currencies
valutazione, *f.* valuation
vantaggio, *m.* advantage
vantaggiosamente, advantageously
vantaggioso, advantageous
vapore, *m.* steamboat
varare, to launch
variabile, variable
variare, to change; to vary
variazione, *f.* variation
varo, *m.* launching (of a ship)
vedere, to see
veduta, *f.* sight; view
vela, *f.* sail
veloce, fast
velocità, *f.* speed
venale, saleable
vendere, to sell
vendibile, saleable
vendita, *f.* sale
vendita a rate, *f.* hire purchase
vendita all'asta, *f.* auction
vendita all'ingrosso, *f.* wholesale
vendita al minuto, *f.* retail sale
vendita su campione, *f.* sale by sample
venditore, *m.* seller
ventilatore, *m.* ventilator
ventilazione, *f.* dispute
vento, wind

ventura, *f.* fortune; luck
venturo, next
venuta, *f.* arrival
verbale, *m.* minutes; record
verbale, verbal
verbalmente, verbally
veridicità, *f.* veracity
verifica, *f.* audit
verificare, to audit; to check
verità, *f.* truth
vero, true
versamento, *m.* payment down
versare, to pay down
vertenza, *f.* dispute
vetrina, *f.* shop window
vettore, *m.* carrier
vettura, *f.* car; railway carriage
via, *f.* way; road
via aerea, *f.* airmail
via di mare, *f.* by sea
via marittima, *f.* sea route
viaggiante, travelling
viaggiare, to travel
viaggiatore, *m.* passenger
viaggio, *m.* travel
video, *m.* display; screen
vidimare, to legalize; to stamp; to check
vidimazione, *f.* stamping
vietare, to forbid
vigente, in force
vigilanza, *f.* care; vigilance
vigilare, to be vigilant
vigore, *m.* force; vigour
vincere, to win
vincolare, to bind; to deposit (money)
vincolo, *m.* bond; tie
violare, to violate
violazione, *f.* violation
visita, *f.* visit
visitare, to visit
viso, *m.* face; visage
vista, *f.* sight

visto, *m.* visa
vita, *f.* life
viveri, *m.* provisions
vivo, alive
voce, *f.* voice; word
voga, *f.* vogue
voglia, *f.* desire
volenteroso, eager
volere, to want
volgare, to address; to turn
volontà, *f.* will
volontario, voluntary
volta, *f.* dome
volta, time; turn
voltarsi, to turn round
volume, *m.* volume
voluminoso, bulky
votare, to vote
votazione, *f.* ballot; vote
voto, *m.* vote; vow
vulnerabile, vulnerable
vuotare, to empty
vuoto, *m.* emptiness
vuoto, empty

Z

zavorra, *f.* ballast
zavorrante, *m.* ballast man
zavorrare, to ballast
zecca, *f.* mint
zecchino, *m.* old Italian coin
zelante, zealous
zelantemente, zealously
zelare, to show zeal
zelo, *m.* zeal
zero, *m.* zero
zona, *f.* area; zone
zonale, zonal
zonizzare, to zone

ENGLISH–ITALIAN

(English nouns are indicated by *n.* and verbs by *v.*; Italian masculine nouns are indicated by *m.* and feminine by *f.*)

A

abbreviation, *n.* abbreviazione, *f.*
abolish, *v.* abolire
abolition, *n.* abolizione, *f.*
abrogate, *v.* abrogare
abrogation, *n.* abrogazione, *f.*
abuse, *n.* abuso, *m.*
abuse, *v.* abusare
accede, *v.* accedere
accept, *v.* accettare; adottare
acceptable, accettabile
acceptance, *n.* accettazione, *f.*; adozione, *f.*
acceptor, *n.* accettante, *m.*
accessory, accessorio
accident, *n.* accidente, *m.*; infortunio, *m.*
accompany, *v.* accompagnare
account, *n.* conto, *m.*
account, *v.* contare; spiegare
accountancy, *n.* contabilità, *f.;* ragioneria, *f.*
accountant, *n.* contabile, *m.*; ragioniere, *m.*
accumulate, *v.* accumulare
accumulation, *n.* accumulazione, *f.*
accuracy, *n.* esatezza, *f.*
accuse, *v.* accusare
acknowledge, *v.* accusare
acquaintance, *n.* conoscenza, *f.*
act, *n.* atto, *m.;* azione, *f.*
act, *v.* agire; operare
action, *n.* azione, *f.*; operato, *m.*
actual, effetivo
adapt, *v.* adattare
adaptation, *n.* adattamento, *m.*
add, *v.* addizionare; aggiungere
addition, *n.* addizione, *f.*; agginta, *f.*
additional, addizionale; aggiuntivo; supplementare
address, *n.* indirizzo, *m.*
address, *v.* destinare; indirizzare

addressee, *n.* destinatario, *m.*
adequate, adequato
adjourn, *v.* rinviare
adjournment, *n.* rinvio, *m.*
adjudge, *v.* aggiudicare
adjudication, *n.* aggiudicazione, *f.*
adjudicator, *n.* arbitro, *m.*
adjust, *v.* aggiustare
administer, *v.* amministrare
administration, *n.* amministrazione, *f.*
administrative, amministrativo
administrator, *n.* amministratore, *m.*; gerente, *m.*
adoption, *n.* adozione, *f.*
adulterate, *v.* adulterare
adulteration, *n.* adulterazione, *f.*
advance, *n.* anticipazione, *f.*; aumento, *m.*
advance, *v.* anticipare
advent, *n.* arrivo, *m.*
adventure, *n.* avventura, *f.*
advert, *n.* annunzio, *m.;* inserzione, *f.*; reclame, *f.*
advertise, *v.* annunziare; avvisare
advertising, *n.* pubblicità, *f.*
affair, *n.* affare, *f.*
affect, *v.* colpire; influire
affidavit, *n.* affidavit, *m.*
affirm, *v.* affermare
affirmation, *n.* affermazione, *f.*
affix, *v.* apporre
affluence, *n.* affluenza, *f.*
after, appresso; dopo
agency, *n.* agenzia, *f.*; mandato, *m.*
agent, *n.* agente, *m.* mandatario, *m.*; raccomandatario, *m.*
agrarian, agrario
agree, *v.* accordarsi; concordare; convenire; pattuire
agreement, *n.* accordo, *m.;* concordato, *m.*; patto, *m.*
aid, *n.* aiuto, *m.*
aim, *n.* aspirazione, *f.*
aim, *v.* aspirare

airmail, via aerea
all, tutto
allegation, *n.* allegazione, *f.*
alleviate, *v.* sgravare
alleviation, *n.* sgravamento, *m.*
allot, *v.* assegnare
allotment, *n.* assegnazione, *f.*
allottee, *n.* assegnatario, *m.*
allow, *v.* comportare; permettere
allowance, *n.* assegno, *m.;* bonificazione, *f.*
almanac, *n.* almanacco, *m.*
alter, *v.* alterare; cambiare
alteration, *n.* alterazione, *f.*; cambiamento, *m.*
alternative, *n.* alternative, *f.*
ambiguity, *n.* ambiguità, *f.*
ambit, *n.* ambito, *m.*
amortization, *n.* ammortamento, *m.*
amortize, *v.* ammortizzare
amount, *n.* ammontare, *m.*; importo, *m.*
amount, *v.* ammontare
amplification, *n.* ampliazione, *f.*; amplificamento, *m.*
amplify, *v.* ampliare
analyse, *v.* analizzare
analysis, *n.* analisi, *f.*
anchor, *n.* àncora, *f.*
anchorage, *n.* ancoraggio, *f.*
angle, *n.* angolo
annexed, annesso
annuitant, *n.* reddituario, *m.*
annuity, *n.* annualità, *f.*; vitalizio, *m.*
anticipation, *n.* anticipo
appeal, *n.* appello, *m.*
appeal, *v.* appellare
appear, *v.* comparire; parere
appendix, *n.* appendice, *f.*
applicant, *n.* aspirante, *m.*; petente, *m.*
application, *n.* applicazione, *f.*
applications package, *n.* corredo d'applicazione, *m.*
apply, *v.* applicare
appoint, *v.* nominare
appointment, *n.* nomina, *f;* appuntamento, *m.*
appreciate, *v.* apprezzare; rincarare
apprentice, *n.* apprendista, *m.*
appropriate, *v.* appropriare

approval, *n.* approvoazione, *f.*
approve. *v.* approvare
approximate, approssimativo
approximation, *n.* approssimazione, *f.*
April, aprile
arbitrage, *n.* arbitraggio, *m.*
arbitrary, arbitrario
arbitration, *n.* arbitrato, m.
archive, *n.* archivio, *m.*
archivist, *n.* archivista, *m.*
area, *n.* area, *f.*; zona, *f.*
arm, *v.* armare
armament, *n.* armamento, *m.*
arrears, *n.* arretrati, *m.*
arrest, *n.* arresto, *m.*
arrest, *v.* arrestare
arrival, *n.* arrivo, *m.*
arrive, *v.* arrivare
arsenal, *n.* arsenale, *m.*
article, *n.* articolo, *m.*; merce, *f.*; clausola, *f.*
articles (ship's), *n.* regole d'equipaggio, *f.*
articles of association, *n.* statuto di società anonima, *m.*
ascent, *n.* salita, *f.*
aspect, *n.* aspetto, *m.*
assess, *v.* quotizzare
assessment, *n.* quotizzazione, *f.*
assets, *n.* attivo, *m.*
assign, *v.* cedere; trasferire; assegnare
assignable, cedibile
assignee, *n.* cessionario, *m.*
assigner, *n.* cedente, *m.*
assignment, *n.* cessione, *f.*; traspasso, *m.*; trasferimento, *m.*
association, sodalizio, *m.*
assurance, *n.* sicurtà, *f.* assicurazione, *f.*
attain, *v.* conseguire; raggiungere
attainment, *n.* raggiungimento, *m.*
attempt, *n.* tentativo, *m.*
attention, *n.* avvertenza, *f.*; cura, *f.*
auction, *n.* licitazione, *f.*
auction, *v.* licitare
audience, *n.* udienza, *f.*
audit, *n.* riscontro, *m.*; verifica, *f.*
audit, *v.* riscontrare; verificare
audition, *n.* udizione, *f.*
auditorium, uditorio, *m.*
August, agosto

authorize, *v.* autorizzare
authorization, *n.* autorizzazione, *f.*
authority, *n.* facoltà, *f.*; autorità, *f.*
automate, *v.* automatizzare
automatic, automatico
automation, *n.* automazione, *f.*
average, *n.* media, *f.*; avaria, *f.*
aviation, *n.* aviazione, *f.*
avoid, evitare; ovviare
award (prize), *n.* premio, *m.*
award, *v.* assegnare; premiare
axis, *n.* asse, *f.*

B

back, *n.* dorso, *m.*; tergo, *m.*
bad faith, mala fede
bag, *n.* sacco, *m.*
bail, *n.* cauzione, *f.*
bail, *v.* prestare cauzione
balance, *n.* bilancio, *m.*; saldo, *m.* sbilancio, *m.*
balance, *v.* bilanciare; saldare
balance of trade, bilancia del commercio
balance-sheet, *n.* bilancio, *m.*
ballast, *n.* zavorra, *f.*
ballast, *v.* zavorrare
ballast man, *n.* zavorrante, *m.*
ballot, *n.* votazione, *f.*
bank, *n.* banca, *f*; banco, *m.*; cassa, *f.*
bank, *v.* mettere in banca
bank clearing, *n.* bancogiro, *m.*
bank-draft, *n.* vaglia bancario, *m.*
bank-note, *n.* biglietto di banca, *m.*; banconota, *f.*
bank-rate, *n.* tasso di sconto, *m.*
bankable, bancabile
banker, *n.* banchiere, *m.*
banking, bancario
banking (shares), bancari, *m.*
bankrupt, *n.* bancorottiere, *m.*
bankrupt (to go), *v.* fallire
bankruptcy, *n.* bancarotta, *f.*
bargain, *n.* contratazione, *f.*
bargain, *v.* mercanteggiare
barratry, *n.* baratteria, *f.*
barrel, *n.* botte, *f.*
barter, *n.* baratto, *m.*

barter, *v.* barattare; scambiare
base, *n.* base, *f.*
base, *v.* basare
base coin, *n.* moneta falsa, *f.*
basic, fondamentale
basic wage, *n.* paga base, *f.*
basis, *n.* base, *f.*
batch, *n.* gruppo, *m.*; lotto, *m.*
bear, *v.* reggere
bear, *n.* ribassista, *m.*
bearer, *n.* latore, *m.*; portatore
February, febbraio
behaviour, condotta, *f.*
beneficient, benefico
benefit, *n.* vantaggio, *m.*
benefit, *v.* beneficiare
bet, *n.* scommessa, *f.*
bet, *v.* scommettere
better, meglio
bill, *n.* bolletta, *f.*; distinta, *f.* conto, *m.*; cambiale, *f.*
bill book, *n.* scadenzario, *m.*
bill of entry, *n.* bolletta doganale, *f.*
bill of exchange, *n.* cambiale, *f.*
birth, *n.* nascita, *f.*
blade, *n.* lama, *f.*
blank, *n.* modulo, *m.*
blank, bianco; vuoto
blank-cheque, *n.* assegno in bianco, *m.*
block, *n.* blocco, *m.*
block, *v.* bloccare
blockade, *n.* blocco, *m.*
blow, *n.* colpo. *m.*
board, *n.* cassa, *f.*
boat, *n.* imbarcazione, *f.*; nave, *f.*
boat (cargo), *n.* nave da carico, *f.*
book, *n.* libro, *m.*
book, *v.* prenotare
book-keeper, *n.* computista, *m.*; scritturale, *m.*
booking, *n.* prenotazione, *f.*
booklet, *n.* libretto, *m.*
bottle, *n.* bottiglia, *f.*
box, *n.* scatola, *f.*
breakage, *n.* rottura, *f.*
brief, *n.* sommario, *m.*
brief, *v.* costituire
brief, breve; conciso
bring, *v.* portare

bring about, *v.* causare
bring forward, *v.* riportare
build, *v.* costruire
builder, *n.* costruttore, *m.*
building, *n.* costruzione, *f.*; fabbricato, *m.*
building plot, *n.* area fabbricabile, *f.*
bulk, *n.* massa, *f.*
bulk (in), rinfusa; in monte
bull, *n.* rialzista, *m.*
bulletin, *n.* bollettino, *m.*
bullion, *n.* oro in verghe, *m.*
burden, *n.* aggravio, *m.*; onere, *m.*
burdensome, oneroso
business, *n.* faccenda, *f.*
button, *n.* bottone, *m.*
buy, *v.* acquistare; comprare
buyer, *n.* compratore, *m.*
buying, *n.* acquisto, *m.*; compra, *f.*
by-product, *n.* prodotto secondario, *m.*

C

cable, *v.* telegrafare
cablegram, *n.* cablogramma, *m.*
calculate, *v.* calcolare
calculating machine, *n.* numeratrice, *f.*
calculation, *n.* calcolo, *m.*
calculator, *n.* calcolatore, *m.*; calcolatrice, *f.*
calendar, *n.* calendario, *m.*
call, *n.* domanda, *f.*; chiamata, *f.*
call, *v.* chiamare
capacity, *n.* portata, *f.*
capital, *n.* capitale, *m.*; maiuscola, *f.*
capital (fixed), *n.* beni immobili, *m.*
capital (paid up), *n.* capitale versato, *m.*
capital (working), *n.* capitale circolante, *m.*
capitalization, *n.* capitalizzazione, *f.*
capitalize, *v.* capitalizzare
car, *n.* macchina, *f.*
car park, *n.* autoparco, *m.*
carat, *n.* carato, *m.*
card, *n.* cartellino, *m.*; carta, *f.*
card index, *n.* schedario, *m.*
card (licence), *n.* libretto di patente, *m.*
cardboard, *n.* cartone, *m.*
care, *n.* cura, *f.*

careen, *v.* carenare
careless, negligente
carelessness, *n.* negligenza, *f.*
cargo, *n.* carico, *m.*
carriage, *n.* trasporto, *m.*
carriage note, *n.* nota di spedizione, *f.*
carriage paid, porto franco
carrier, *n.* trasportatore, *m.*
carry, *v.* portare; trasportare
carry out, *v.* eseguire
cash, *v.* incassare; introitare
cash payment, *n.* pagamento a contanti, *m.*
cashier, *n.* cassiere, *m.*
catalogue, *n.* catalogo, *m.*
catalogue, *v.* catalogare
cause, *n.* causa, *f.*
cause, *v.* causare
caution, *n.* cautela, *f.*
caution, *v.* cautelare
cautious, cauto
cease, *v.* cessare
ceaseless, incessante
central, centrale
central memory, *n.* memoria centrale, *f.*
centralization, *n.* centralizzazione, *f.*
centralize, *v.* centralizzare
centre, *n.* centro, *m.*
certificate, *n.* certificato, *m.*
certify, *v.* certificare
change, *n.* mutamento, *m.*; cambiamento, *m.*
change (money), *n.* spiccioli, *m.*
change, *v.* mutare; cambiare
character, *n.* carattere, *m.*
characteristic, *n.* caratteristica, *f.*
charge, *n.* carica, *f*; carico, *m.*; spesa, *f.*
charge, *v.* caricare
charter, *n.* carta, *f.*; patente, *f.*
charter, *v.* noleggiare
charterer, *n.* noleggiatore, *m.*
cheap, buon mercato
check, *n.* contromarca, *f.*; scontrino, *m.*
check, *v.* verificare; collazionare
checking, *n.* collazionamento, *m.*
cheque, *n.* assegno, *m.*; mandato, *m.*
cheque book, *n.* libretto degli assegni, *m.*
chief, *n.* capo, *m.*
chip, *n.* piastrina, *f.*

chit, *n.* nota, *f.*
choose, *v.* scegliere
cipher, *n.* cifra, *f.*
cipher, *v.* cifrare
circle, *n.* cerchio, *m.*
circular, *n.* circolare, *f.*
circular letter, *n.* circolare, *f.*
circulate, *v.* circolare
circumstance, *n.* circostanza, *f.*
civil servant, *n.* statale, *m.*
claim, n. reclamo, *m.*
claim, *v.* reclamare
clarify, *v.* precisare; schiarire
class, *n.* classe, *f.*
classification, *n.* classificazione, *f.*
classify, *v.* classificare
clause, *n.* clausola, *f.*
clean, *v.* pulire
clearance, *n.* libera pratica, *f.*
clerk, *n.* impiegato, *m.*
clerk of works, *n.* capomastro, *m.*
client, *n.* cliente, *m.*
clientele, *n.* clientela, *f.*
coin, *n.* moneta, *f.*
coin, *v.* coniare
coinage, *n.* coniazione, *f.*
collapse, *n.* crollo, *m.*
collapse, *v.* crollare
colleague, *n.* collega, *m.*
collection, *n.* colletta, *f*; collezione, *f.*; presa, *f.*; riscossione, *f.*
colour, *n.* colore, *m.*
colouring, *n.* colorazione, *f.*
command, *n.* comando, *m.*; ordine, *m.*
command panel, *n.* quadro di comando, *m.*
commandant, *n.* comandante, *m.*
commerce, *n.* commercio, *m.*
commissary, *n.* commissario, *m.*
commission, *n.* commissione, *m.*
commissioner, *n.* commissario, *m.*
committee, *n.* collegio, *n.*; comitato, *m.*
committee (select), *n.* comitato speciale, *m.*
commodity, *n.* comodità, *f.*
common, comune
communicate, *v.* comunicare
communication, *n.* comunicazione, *f.*
company, *n.* società, *f.*

company (joint stock), *n.* società anonima, *f.*
compel, *v.* costringere
compensation, *n.* compenso, *m.*; compensazione, *f.*; corrispettivo, *m.*
compete, *v.* competere; concorre
competition, *n.* concorrenza, *f*; concorso, *m.*
competitor, *n.* competitore, *m.*
compilation, *n.* compilazione, *f.*
compile, *v.* compilare
complete, *v.* completare
complex, *n.* complesso, *m.*
compound, composto
compromise, *n.* compromesso, *m.*
computation, *n.* computazione, *f.*
compute, *v.* computare
computer, *n.* calcolatore elletronico, *m.*
computerization, *n.* meccanografia, *f.*
computerize, *v.* meccanizare
computerized, meccanizzato; meccanografico
concept, *n.* concetto, *m.*
concern, *n.* spettanza, *f.*
concern, *v.* concernare; spettare
concession, *n.* concessione, *f.*
conciliate, *v.* conciliare
conclude, *v.* conchiudere
condition, *n.* condizione, *f.*
condition, *v.* condizionare
conditional, condizionale
confidence, *n.* confidenza, *f.*
confidential, confidenziale
confine, *n.* limite, *m.*
confirm, *v.* confermare
confirmation, *n.* conferma, *f.*
confiscate, *v.* confiscare; sequestrare
confiscation, *n.* confisca, *f.*
conform, *v.* conformare
conformity, *n.* conformità, *f.*
conformity (in), conforme
congratulate, *v.* congratulare
congratulations, *n.* congratulazioni, *f.*
conjecture, *n.* congettura, *f.*
conjunctural, congiunturale
conjuncture, *n.* congiuntura, *f.*
consecutive, consecutive
consent, *n.* consenso, *m.*
consent, *v.* consentire

consequence, *n.* consequenza, *f.*
consequential, conseguente
consider, *v.* considerare
considerable, rilevante
consideration, *n.* considerazione, *f.*; compenso, *m.*
consignee, *n.* consegnatario, *m.*; destinatario, *m.*
consignment, *n.* spedizione, *f.*
consignor, *n.* committente, *m.*; mittente, *m.*
consist, *v.* consistere
consolidate, *v.* consolidare
consolidation, *n.* consolidazione, *f.*
consul, *n.* console, *m.*
contact, *n.* contatto, *m.*
contents, *n.* contenuto, *m.*
contingency, *n.* contingenza, *f.*
contract, *n.* contratto, *m.*
contract, *v.* contrattare
contracting, contraente
contractor, *n.* impresario, *m.*
contractual, contrattuale
contradictory, contradittorio
contribute, *v.* contribuire
contribution, *n.* contributo, *m.*
control, *n.* controllo, *m.*
controller, *n.* controllore, *m.*
controversy, *n.* controversia, *f.*
controvert, *v.* controvertere
convene, *v.* convocare
conversation, *n.* conversazione, *f.*
conversion, *n.* conversione, *f.*
convert, *v.* convertire
convertibility, *n.* convertibilità, *f.*
convertible, convertible
convocation, *n.* convocazione, *f.*
convoy, *n.* convoglio, *m.*
co-operation, *n.* cooperazione, *f.*
co-operative, *n.* cooperativa, *f.*
copy, *n.* copia, *f.*
copy, *v.* copiare
cordial, cordiale
corporation, *n.* corporazione, *f.*
correct, *v.* correggere
correction, *n.* correzione, *f.*
correspond, *v.* corrispondere
correspondence, *n.* corrispondenza, *f.*
correspondent, *n.* corrispondente, *m.*

corrupt, *v.* corrompere
corruption, *n.* corruzione, *f.*
cost, *n.* costo, *m.*
cost, *v.* costare
costing, *n.* costo, *m.*
costly, costoso; caro
count, *n.* conto, *m.*
count, *v.* contare
counter, *n.* contatore, *m.*
counterpart, *n.* controparte, *m.*
coupon, *n.* modulo, *m*; tagliando, *m.*
course, *n.* corso, *m.*
courtesy, *n.* cortesia, *f.*
craft, (boat), *n.* naviglio
craft, *n.* mestiere, *m.*
crash, *n.* fallimento, *m.*
credit, *n.* credito, *m.*
credit, *v.* accreditare
credit note, *n.* nota di accreditamento, *f.*
credit side, *n.* avere, *m.*
creditor, *n.* creditore, *m.*
crew, *n.* equipaggio, *m.*
crisis, *n.* crisi, *f.*
critical, critico
cursor, *n.* cursore, *m.*
custodian, *n.* custode, *m.*
custom, *n.* costume, *m.*; consuetudine, *f.*
customary, consueto
customs, *n.* dogana, *f.*
customs officer, *n.* doganiere, *m.*
cut, *n.* taglio, *m.*
cut, *v.* tagliare
cycle, *n.* ciclo, *m.*

D

daily, quotidiano
damage, *n.* danno, *m.*; guasto, *m.*; pregiudizio, *m.*
damage, *v.* danneggiare; guastare
data, *n.* dati, *m.*
database, *n.* base dati, *f.*
data processing, *n.* elaborazione dei dati, *f.*
date, *n.* data, *f.*
date, *v.* datare
datum, *n.* dato, *m.*
day, *n.* giorno, *m.*

day-book, *n.* giornale, *m.*
day-time, *n.* giornata, *f.*
de-activate, *v.* disattivare
dead, morto; estinto
dead-loss, *n.* perdita totale, *f.*
dead-reckoning, *n.* calcolo della rotta, *m.*
dead-weight, *n.* peso morto, *m.*
deal, *n.* patto, *m.*; affare, *m.*
deal, *v.* trattare
dealer, *n.* mercante
dear, caro; costoso
debit, *n.* addebito, *m.*
debit, *v.* addebitare
debit side, *n.* dare, *m.*
debiting, *n.* addebitamento, *m.*
debt, *n.* debito, *m.*
debtor, *n.* debitore, *m.*
decay, *n.* deperimento, *m.*
decay, *v.* deperire
December, dicembre
deception, *n.* lustra, *f.*
decide, *v.* decidere
decimal, decimale
decipher, *v.* decifrare
decision, *n.* decisione, *f.*; giudizio, *m.*
decisive, decisivo
declare, *v.* dichiarare
declaration, *n.* dichiarazione, *f.*
decline, *n.* ribasso, *m.*
decline, *v.* discendere
decree, *n.* decreto, *m.*
decree, *v.* decretare
deduction, *n.* deduzione, *f.*
deed, *n.* documento, *m.*
defaulter, *n.* debitore, *m.*
defect, *n.* difetto, *m.*
defer, *v.* deferire
deficiency, *n.* deficienza, *f.*
deficient, deficiente
deficit, *n.* deficit, *m.*; disavanzo, *m.*
define, *v.* definire
definition, *n.* definizione, *f.*
degree, *n.* grado, *m.*
delay, *n.* dilazione, *f.*; indugio, *m.*
delay, *v.* dilazionare; indugiare
delegate, *v.* delegare
delegation, *n.* delega, *f.*; delegazione, *f.*
deliberate, premeditato
deliver, *v.* consegnare

deliverable, consegnabile
delivery, *n.* consegna, *f.*; resa, *f.*
demand, *n.* domanda, *f.*
demand, *v.* domandare
demand note, *f.* intimazione, *f.*
demurrage, *n.* giacenza, *f.*; sosta, *f.*
denominate, *v.* denominare
denomination, *n.* denominazione, *f.*
denominator, *n.* denominatore, *m.*
denounce, *v.* denunziare
denunciation, *n.* denunzia, *f.*
deny, *v.* negare
department, *n.* dipartimento, *m.*
department store, *m.* grande magazzino, *m.*
departmental, dipartimentale
depend, *v.* dipendere
deposit, *n.* deposito, *m.*; caparra, *f.*
deposit, *v.* depositare
depositary, *n.* depositario, *m.*
depot, *n.* deposito, *m.*
depreciate, *v.* svalutare
depreciation, *n.* deprezzamento, *m.*; svalutazione, *f.*
depression, *n.* depressione, *f.*
depth, *n.* fondo, *m.*
deputy, *n.* deputato, *m.*
derogate, *v.* derogare
derogation, *n.* deroga, *f.*
deserve, *v.* meritare
deserving, meritevole
desire, *n.* voglia, *f.*
destination, *n.* destinazione, *f.*
develop, *v.* sviluppare
development, *n.* sviluppo, *m.*
deviate, *v.* deviare
deviation, *n.* deviazione, *f.*
diagram, *n.* diagramma, *f.*
dial, *n.* quadrante, *m.*; disco, *m.*
diary, *n.* diario, *m.*
dictaphone, *n.* dittafono, *m.*
dictate, *v.* dettare
dictation, *n.* dettatura, *f.*
difference, *n.* differenza, *f.*
differential, differenziale
digit, *n.* cifra, *f.*
digital, digitale
digitize, *v.* digitalizzare
dilute, *v.* diluire

diminish, *v.* diminuire
diminution, *n.* diminuzione, *f.*
direct, diretto
directive, *n.* direttivo, *m.*
directly, direttamente
director, *n.* amministratore, *m.*
directorate, *n.* direttorio, *m.*
directory, *n.* directory, *f.*; guida, *f.*
disagreement, *n.* disaccordo, *m.*
disapproval, *n.* disapprovazione, *f.*
disapprove, *v.* disapprovare
disconnect, *v.* dissociare
discount, *n.* sconto, *m.*
discount, *v.* scontare
discountable, scontabile
discounter, *n.* scontista, *m.*
discourage, *v.* scoraggiare
discover, *v.* scoprire
discovery, *n.* scoperta, *f.*
discretion, *n.* discrezione, *f.*; riserbo, *m.*
discuss, *v.* discutere
discussion, *n.* discussione, *f.*
dishonour, *m.* disonore, *m.*
disk, *n.* disco, *m.*
disk (floppy), *n.* disco mobile, *m.*
disk (hard), *n.* disco fisso, *m.*
dismiss, *v.* licenziare
dismissal, *n.* licenziamento, *m.*
display, *n.* video, *m.*
display, *n.* mostra, *f.*; esposizione, *f.*
display, *v.* mostrare
displease, *v.* dispiacere
disposal, *n.* disposizione, *f.*
dispose, *v.* disporre
dispute, *n.* disputa, *f.*; vertenza, *f.*; ventilazione, *f.*
dissuade, *v.* sconsigliare
distance, *n.* distanza, *f.*
distant, lontano
distinguished, distinto
distribute, *v.* distribuire; ripartire
distribution, *n.* distribuzione, *f.*
divide, *v.* dividere
dividend, *n.* dividendo, *m.*
dock, *n.* darsena, *f.*
dock warrant, *n.* nota di pegno, *f.*
document, *n.* documento, *m.*
documents, *n.* documentazione, *f.*
dose, *n.* dose, *f.*

double, *v.* doppiare
double, doppio
doubt, *n.* dubbio
doubt, *v.* dubitare
doubtful, dubbioso
drawback, *n.* rimborso d'esportazione, *m.*; svantaggio, *m.*
drawee, *n.* trattario, *m.*
drawer, *n.* traente, *m.*
due, debito; liquido
dull, fiacco
dullness, *n.* fiacchezza, *f.*
duly, debitamente
dump, *v.* vendere sottoprezzo
duplicate, *v.* duplicare
duration, *n.* durata, *f.*
dutiable, daziabile; imponibile
duty, *n.* dazio, *m.*; diritto, *m.*; imposta, *f.*
duty free, franco di dazio
duty paid, sdoganato

E

earn, *v.* guadagnare
earnest, *n.* caparra, *f.*; pegno, *m.*
economic, economico
economize, *v.* economizzare
economist, *n.* economista, *m.*
economy, *n.* economia, *f.*
edge, *n.* margine, *f.*
editor, *n.* redattore, *m.*
effect, *n.* effetto, *m.*
effect, *v.* effettuare
effective, efficace
effects, *n.* effeti, *m.*
elaborate, *v.* elaborare
elastic, elastico
elasticity, *n.* elasticità, *m.*
electrical (shares), *n.* elettrici, *m.*
electronic, elettronico
eliminate, *v.* eliminare
elimination, *n.* eliminazione, *f.*
elude, *v.* eludere
embargo, *n.* embargo, *m.*
embark, *v.* imbarcare
embarking, *n.* imbarco, *m.*
emigrate, *v.* emigrare
emigration, *n.* emigrazione, *f.*

emission, *n.* emissione, *f.*
employee, *n.* addetto, m.; dipendente, *m.*; impiegato, *m.*
employer, *n.* principale, *m.*; padrone, *m.*
employment, *n.* impiego, *m.*
emporium, *n.* emporio, *m.*
enclose, *v.* accludere; allegare
end, *n.* fine, *f.*
endorse, *v.* girare
endorsee, *n.* giratario, *m.*
endorsement, *n.* girata, *f.*; giro, *m.*
endorser, *n.* girante, *m.*
energy, *n.* energia, *f.*
enjoy, *v.* giovare; fruire
enjoyment, *n.* giovamento, *m.*
engineer, *n.* ingegnere, *m.*; meccanico, *m.*
engineering, *n.* ingigneria, *f.*; meccanica, *f.*
enquiry, *n.* inchiesta, *f.*
enter, *v.* entrare
entity, *v.* entità, *f.*
entrust, *v.* confidare
envelope, *n.* busta, *f.*
equal, equale; pari
equation, *n.* equazione, *f.*
equilibrium, *n.* equilibrio, *m.*
equip, *v.* equippaggiare
equitable, equo
equivalent, equivalente
erroneous, erroneo
erroneously, erroneamente
error, *n.* errore, *m.*
essential, essenziale
establish, *v.* stabilire; istituire
establishment, *n.* stabilimento, *m.*
estimate, *n.* preventivo, *m.*
estimate, *v.* preventivare; periziare; valutare
evade, *v.* evadere
evasion, *n.* evasione, *f.*
evasive, evasivo, *m.*
eventual, eventuale
eventuality, *n.* eventualità, *f.*
evidence, *n.* evidenza, *f.*
exact, esatto
exactly, esattamente
exacting, esigente
exaggerate, *v.* esagerare
exaggeration, *n.* esagerazione, *f.*

examination, *n.* esame, *m.*
examine, *v.* esaminare
example, *n.* esempio, *m.*
exchange, *v.* scambiare
exchange, *n.* borsa, *f*
exchange, (money), *n.* cambio, m.; scambio, *m.*
exchange (stock), *n.* borsa valori, *f.*
exclude, *v.* escludere
exclusion, *n.* esclusione, *f.*
exclusive, esclusivo
exclusively, esclusivamente
execution, *n.* esecuzione, *f.*
executive, *n.* dirigente, *m.*
executive, esecutivo
executor, *n.* esecutore, *m.*
exemplary, esemplare
exempt, esente
exemption, *n.* esenzione, *f.*
except, salvo
exercise, *v.* esercitare
exhibit, *v.* esibire
exhibition, *n.* esposizione, *f.*; mostra, *f.*
exhibitor, *n.* espositore, *m.*
exigency, *n.* esigenza, *f.*
exist, *v.* esistere
existence, *n.* esistenza, *f.*
exonerate, *v.* esonerare
exorbitant, esorbitente
expedient, espediente
expense, *n.* spesa, *f.*
expensive, caro; costoso
experience, *n.* esperienza, *f.*
experiment, *n.* esperimento, *m.*
experiment, *v.* esperimentare
expert, *n.* esperto, *m.*; perito, *m.*
expiration, *n.* scadenza, *f.*
expire, *v.* scadere
exploit, *v.* sfruttare
exploitation, *n.* sfruttamento, *m.*
exponent, *n.* esponente, *m.*
export, *n.* esportazione, *f.*
export, *v.* esportare
exporter, *n.* esportatore, *m.*
express, espresso
expression, *n.* espressione, *f.*
extend, *v.* estendere
extension, *n.* estensione, *f.*
extensive, esteso

extract, *n.* estratto, *m.*
extract, *v.* estrarre
extreme, estremo
eyewitness, *n.* testimone occulare, *m.*

F

face, *n.* viso, *m.*
face value, valore nominale
facilitate, *v.* agevolare; facilitare
facility, *n.* agevolezza, *f.*
facsimile, *n.* facsimile, *m.*
fact, *n.* fatto, *m.*
factor, *n.* fattore, *m.*; agente, *m.*
factory, *n.* fabbrica, *f.*
fail, *v.* fallire; far fallimento
failure, *n.* fallimento, *m.*
fair, *n.* fiera, *f.*
false, falso
fame, *n.* fama, *f.*
fashion, *n.* moda, *f.*
favour, *v.* favorire
favourable, favorevole
fee, *n.* onorario, *m.*; tassa, *f.*
figure, *n.* figura, *f.*; cifra, *f.*
file, *n.* pratiche, *f.*; protocollo, *m.*; file, *m.*; archivio, *m.*
file, *v.* schedare
finance, *n.* finanza, *f.*
finance, *v.* finanziare
financial, finanziario
financial (shares), *n.* finanziari, *m.*
financier, *n.* finanziere, *m.*
fine, *n.* multa, *f.*
fine, *v.* multare
fine, fino
finish, *v.* terminare; finire
firm, *n.* azienda, *f.*
fisc, *n.* fisco, *m.*
fiscal, fiscale
fit, *v.* montare
fitter, *n.* montatore, *m.*
fitting, *n.* montaggio, *m.*
fix, *v.* fissare
fixed, fisso
flagrant, flagrante
flagrancy, *n.* flagranza, *f.*
fluctuate, *v.* fluttuare

fluctuation, *n.* fluttuazione, *f.*
force, *n.* forza, *f.*; vigore, *m.*
force, *v.* forzare; sforzare; obbligare
foreign, estero
forfeiture, *n.* decadenza, *f.*
form, *n.* forma, *f.*; modulo, *m.*
form, *v.* formare
format, *v.* formattare
formula, *n.* formula, *f.*
formulary, *n.* formulario, *m.*
formulate, *v.* formulare
forum, *n.* foro, *m.*
fortune, *n.* fortuna, *f.*
found, *v.* fondare
foundation, *n.* fondazione, *f*; fondamenta, *f.*
forward, *v.* spedire
forwarder, *n.* speditore, *m.*
forwarding, *n.* spedizione, *f.*
forwarding agent, *n.* spedizioniere, *m.*
fraction, *n.* frazione, *f.*
fractional, frazionario
fragile, fragile
fragility, *n.* fragilità, *f.*
franchise, *n.* franchigia, *f.*
frank, *v.* affrancare
fraud, *n.* frode, *f.*
fraudulent, frodolento; doloso
free, *v.* liberare
free on board, franco a bordo
free trade, *n.* libero scambio, *m.*
freedom, *n.* libertà, *f.*
freight, *n.* nolo, *m.*
freight, *v.* noleggiare; caricare
freighter, *n.* noleggiatore, *m.*
freighter (boat), *n.* nave da carico, *f.*
freighting, *n.* noleggiamento, *m.*
frequency, *n.* frequenza, *f.*
frequent, *v.* frequentare
frontier, *n.* frontiera, *f.*; confine, *m.*
fulfil, *v.* adempire; eseguire
function, *n.* funzione, *f.*
function, *v.* funzionare
functioning, *n.* funzionamento, *m.*
fund, *n.* fondo, *m.*
funded, consolidato
funds, *n.* denaro, *m.*
furnish, *v.* munire; arredare
furniture, *n.* mobili, *m.*

futile, futile
futility, *n.* futilità, *f.*
future, *n.* futuro, *m.*
futures, *n.* operazioni a termine, *f.*

G

gain, *n.* guadagno, *m.*; profitto, *m.*
gain, *v.* guadagnare
gauge, *v.* stazzare
gauging, *n.* stazzatura, *f.*
gazette, *n.* gazetta, *f.*
general, generale
general average, *n.* avaria generale, *f.*
genuine, autentico
gilt, dorato
gloss, *n.* lustro, *m.*
gold, *n.* oro, *m.*
gold-field, *n.* terreno aurifero, *m.*
goods, *n.* beni, *m.*; merci, *m.*
goods-train, *n.* treno merci, *m.*
govern, *v.* governare
government, *n.* governo, *m.*
grace, *n.* grazia, *f.*
grace, *v.* graziare
grace (days of), *n.* giorni di grazia, *m.*
gradual, graduale
gradually, gradualmente
graduate, *n.* laureato, *m.*
gram, *n.* grammo, *m.*
grant, *v.* accordare; concedere
grantee, *n.* concessionario, *m.*
grantor, *n.* concedente, *m.*
graph, *n.* grafico, *m.*
gratification, *n.* gratificazione, *f.*
gratitude, *n.* gratitudine, *f.*
gratuitously, gratuitamente
gravity, *n.* gravità, *f.*
ground, *n.* terreno, *m.*
ground-rent, *n.* rendita fondiaria, *f.*
group, *n.* gruppo, *m.*
guarantee, *n.* garanzia, *f.*
guarantee, *v.* avallare; garantire
guarantor, *n.* avallante, *m.*; garante, *m.*
guaranty, *n.* avallo, *m.* ; garanzia, *f.*
guard, *n.* guardia, *f.*; guardiano, *m.*
guard, *v.* guardare; custodire
guide, *n.* guida, *f.*

guide, *n.* guidare
guild, *n.* maestranza, *f.*

H

haggle, *v.* mercanteggiare
half, *n.* metà, *f.*
half-pay, *n.* mezza paga, *f.*
half-year, *n.* semestre, *m.*
happen, *v.* avvenire
hard, duro
hardness, *n.* durezza, *f.*
hardware, *n.* componenti di macchina, *m.*
harm, *v.* ledere; nuocere
harmful, dannoso
harvest, *n.* raccolta, *f.*
hatchway, *n.* boccaporto, *m.*
head, *n.* capo, *m.*
head office, *n.* centrale, *f.*
health, *n.* sanità, *f.*
health (bill of), *n.* patente di sanità, *f.*
heritage, *n.* eredità, *f.*
hidden, recondito
hide, *v.* nascondere
hire, *m.* nolo, *m.*; affitto, *m.*
hire, *v.* noleggiare; affittare
hire purchase, *n.* vendita a rate, *f.*
holder, *n.* detentore, *m.*; presentatore, *m.*
holiday, *n.* vacanza, *f.*
homogeneous, omogeno
honestly, onestamente
honesty, *n.* honestà, *f.*
honorary, *n.* onorario, *m.*
honour, *n.* onore, *m.*
honour, *v.* onorare
hope, *n.* speranza, *f.*
hope, *v.* sperare
house, *n.* casa, *f.*; abitazione, *f.*
house-agent, *n.* agente d'immobili, *m.*
house-rent, *n.* pigione, *f.*
humour, *n.* umore, *m.*; umorismo, *m.*
hurricane, *n.* uragano, *m.*
husbandry, *n.* agricoltura, *f.*

I

idea, *n.* idea, *f.*
identical, identico

identification, *n.* identificazione, *f.*
identify, *v.* identificare
identity, *n.* identità, *f.*
idle, ozioso
idleness, *n.* ozio, *m.*
ignorance, *n.* ignoranza, *f.*
illegal, illegale
illegible, illeggibile
imitate, *v.* imitare
imitation, *n.* imitazione, *f.*
immediate, immediato
immediately, immediatamente
immobile, immobile
immune, immune
impartial, imparziale
impartiality, *n.* imparzialità, *f.*
impartially, imparzialmente
impatience, *n.* impazienza, *f.*
impatient, impaziente
impediment, *n.* impedimento, *m.*
implicate, *v.* implicare
implicit, implicito
implicitly, implicitamente
import, *v.* importare
importance, *n.* importanza, *f.*
important, importante
importation, *n.* importazione, *f.*
importer, *n.* importatore, *m.*
impose, *v.* imporre
impossible, impossibile
impossibility, *n.* impossibilità, *f.*
impress, *v.* impressionare
impression, *n.* impressione, *f.*
imprudent, incauto
imputation, *n.* imputazione, *f.*
impute, *v.* imputare
inability, *n.* inabilità, *f.*
inaccurate, inesatto
inactive, inattivo
inadvertence, *n.* inadvertenza, *f.*
inaugurate, *v.* inaugurare
inauguration, *n.* inaugurazione, *f.*
incapable, incapabile
incapacity, *n.* incapacità, *f.*
incident, *n.* incidente
inclination, *n.* inclinazione, *f.*
include, *v.* includere
incommensurable, incommensurabile
incompatible, incomodo

incompetence, *n.* incompetenza, *f.*
incompetent, incompetente
inconvenient, inconveniente; incomodo
inconvertible, inconvertibile
incorporate, *v.* incorporare
indemnify, *v.* indenizzare
indemnity, *n.* indenizzo, *m.*; indennità, *f.*
indent, *n.* acquisto, *n.*; intaccatura, *f.*
indent, *v.* intaccare
indeterminate, indeterminato
index, *n.* indice, *m.*; schedino, *m.*
indicate, *v.* indicare
indication, *n.* indicazione, *f.*
indirect, indiretto
indispensable, indispensabile
individual, individuale
individuality, *n.* individualità, *f.*
induce, *v.* indurre
industrial, industriale
industry, *n.* industria, *f.*
inevitable, inevitabile
inexcplicable, inesplicabile
inferior, inferiore; scadente
inferiority, *n.* inferiorità, *f.*
influence, *n.* influenza, *f.*
influence, *v.* influenzare
inform, *v.* informare; intimare
information, *n.* informazione, *f.*
inherent, inerente
initial, iniziale
initiative, *n.* iniziativa, *f.*
injurious, lesivo
innovation, *n.* innovazione, *f.*
input, *n.* ingresso, *m.*; entrata, *f.*
input, *v.* fare entrare dati
insolvency, *n.* insolvenza, *f.*
insolvent, insolvente
inspection, *n.* ispezione, *f.*
inspector, *n.* ispettore, *m*
institution, *n.* istituzione, *f.*
instruct, *v.* istruire
instruction, *n.* istruzione, *f.*
instructor, istruttore, *m.*
instrument, *n.* titolo, *m.*; istrumento, *m.*
insurance, *m.* assicurazione, *f.*
insurance (fire), *n.* assicurazione contro gli incendi, *f.*
insurance (life), *n.* assicurazione sulla vita, *f.*

insurance (third party), assicurazione di responsabilità civile
insure, *v.* assicurare
insurer, *n.* assicuratore, *m.*
intact, intatto
intention, *n.* intenzione, *f.*
interdict, *v.* interdire
interdiction, *n.* interdizione, *f.*
interest, *n.* interesse, *m.*
interest (compound), *n.* interesse composto, *m.*
intermediary, *n.* intermedio, *m.*
internal, interno
interpose, *v.* interporre
interpret, *v.* interpretare
interpretation, *n.* interpretazione, *f.*
interpreter, *n.* interprete, *m.*
interrogate, *v.* interrogare
interrogatory, *n.* interrogatorio, *m.*
interrupt, *v.* interrompere
interruption, *n.* interruzione, *f.*
interval, *n.* intervallo, *m.*
intervene, *v.* intervenire
intervention, *n.* intervento, *m.*
interview, *n.* intervista, *f.*
interview, *v.* intervistare
intimacy, *n.* intimità, *f.*
intolerable, intolerabile
intrinsic, intrinseco
invent, *v.* inventare
invention, *n.* invenzione, *f.*
inventor, *n.* inventore, *m.*
inventory, *n.* inventario, *m.*
inventory, *v.* inventariare
inventory (of cargo), *n.* inventario di bordo, *m.*
invest, *v.* investire
investment, *n.* investimento, *m.*
invitation, *n.* invito, *m.*
invite, *v.* invitare
invoice, *n.* fattura, *f.*
invoice, *v.* fatturare
invoicing, *n.* fatturazione, *f.*
irregularity, *n.* irregolarità, *f.*
irrevocability, *n.* irrevocabilità, *f.*
irrevocable, irrevocabile
item, *n.* articolo, *m.*
itemize, *v.* dettagliare
itinerary, *n.* itinerario, *m.*

J

jetty, *n.* gettata, *f.*; molo, *m.*
job, *n.* lavoro, *m.*; opera, *f.*; impiego, *m.*
jobber, *n.* cottimista, *m.*
join, *v.* associare
joint, commune; unito
journal, *n.* giornale, *m.*
journalist, *n.* giornalista, *m.*
journal-ledger, *n.* giornal-mastro, *m.*
journal (ship's), *n.* giornale di bordo, *m.*
journey, *n.* viaggio, *m.*
judge, *n.* giudice, *m.*
judge, *v.* giudicare
judicial, giudiziale
judicial enquiry, *n.* istruttoria, *f.*
judicially, giudizialmente
July, luglio
June, giugno
juridicial, giuridice
jurisdiction, *n.* giurisdizione, *f.*
juror, *n.* giurato, *m.*
jury, *n.* giuria, *f.*
justice, *n.* giustizia, *f*
justification, *n.* giustificazione, *f.*
justify, *v.* giustificare; motivare

K

keel, *n.* chiglia, *f.*
keep, *v.* tenere
keep, *n.* guardiano, *m.*
key, *n.* chiave, *f*; tasto, *m.*
keyboard, *n.* tastiera
key industry, *n.* industria chiave, *f.*
knock, *n.* urto, *m.*
knock, *v.* urtare
kind, *n.* genere, *m.*; sorta, *f.*
kind, gentile
kindness, *n.* gentilezza, *f.*
know, *v.* conoscere; sapere
knowledge, *n.* conoscenza, *f.*; sapere, *m.*
known, noto; notorio

L

laboratory, *n.* laboratorio, *m.*
laboriously, laborioso

lack, *v.* mancare
lacking, *n.* mancanza, *f.*
lament, *v.* lamentare
lamentation, *n.* lamentazione, *f.*
land, *v.* approdare; sbarcare
landing place, *n.* approdo
landlord, *n.* locatore, *m.*
launch, *n.* lancio, *m.*
launch, *v.* lanciare
law, *n.* legge, *f.*
lawful, legale
lawsuit, *n.* lite, *f.*
lay, *v.* posare
layout, *n.* disegno, *m.*; piano, *m.*
leaflet, *n.* volantino, *m.*
lease, *n.* affitto, *m.*; appalto, *m.*
leave, *v.* partire
lecture, *n.* conferenza, *f.*
lecturer, *n.* conferenziere, *m.*
legacy, *n.* legato, *m.*
legal, legale
legal tender, *n.* corso legale, *m.*
legality, *n.* legalità, *f.*
legalization, *n.* legalizzazione, *f.*
legalize, *v.* legalizzare
legally, legalmente
legatee, *n.* legatario, *m.*
legible, leggibile
legitimacy, *n.* legittimità, *f.*
legitimate, legittimo
legitimation, *n.* legittimazione, *f.*
lend, *v.* prestare
lender, *n.* prestatore, *m.*
lending, *n.* prestito, *m.*
letter, *n.* lettera, *f.*
letter of advice, *n.* lettera di notificazione, *f.*
letter of credit, *n.* lettera di credito, *f.*
level, *n.* livello, *m.*
levelling, *n.* livellamento, *m.*
liabilities, *n.* uscite, *f.*
liberation, *n.* liberazione, *f.*
licence, *n.* licenza, *f.*
licence card, *n.* libretto di patente, *m.*
lifeboat, *n.* scialuppa di salvataggio, *f.*
lighter, *n.* chiatta, *f.*
light, lieve
lighting, *n.* illuminazione, *f.*
line, *n.* riga, *f*; tratto, *m.*

line, *v.* allineare
line printer, *n.* stampante in parallelo, *f.*
line up, *v.* accodare
liquid, *n.* liquido, *m.*
liquidation, *n.* liquidazione, *f.*
liquidator, *n.* liquidatore, *m.*
lira, *n.* lira, *f.*
list, *n.* elenco, *m.*; pianta, *f.*; ruolo, *m.*; lista, *f.*
list, *v.* elencare
litigation, *n.* litigio, *m.*
litre, *n.* litro, *m.*
load, *v.* montare
loan, *n.* mutuo, *m.*; prestito, *m.*
local, locale
locate, *v.* individuare; collocare
location, *n.* ubicazione, *f.*
locomotive, *n.* locomotiva, *f.*
lot, *n.* lotto, *m.*; quantità, *f.*
lottery, *n.* lotteria, *f.*
lower, *v.* ribassare
lowest price, *n.* ristretto, *m.*
luggage, *n.* bagaglio, *m.*
luxurious, lussuoso
luxury, *n.* lusso, *m.*

M

machine, *n.* macchina, *f.*
machinery, *n.* macchinario, *m.*
magistrate, *n.* pretore, *m.*
maid servant, *n.* domestica, *f.*
main, principale
maintenance, *n.* mantenimento, *m.*
majority, *n.* maggioranza, *f.*
maker, *n.* fabbricante, *m.*
manage, *v.* dirigere
management, *n.* dirigenza, *f.*; gerenza, *f.*
manager, *n.* direttore, *m.*; gerente, *m.*
managing director, *n.* amministratore delegato, *m.*
mandate, *n.* mandato, *m.*
manner, *n.* guisa, *f.*; maniera, *f.*; modalità, *f.*
manoeuvre, *n.* manovra, *f.*
manoeuvre, *v.* manovrare
manufacture, *v.* confezionare; fabbricare
manufactured article, *n.* confezione, *f.*

manufacturer, *n.* fabbricante, *m.*
map, *n.* carta, *f.*
March, marzo
marginal, marginale
maritime, marittimo
mark, *n.* marca, *f.*; prova, *f.*
mark, *v.* marcare
market, *n.* mercato, *m.*; piazza, *f.*; sbocco, *m.*
market list, *n.* mercuriale, *m.*
mask, *n.* maschera, *f.*
material, *n.* materiale, *m.*
materials, *n.* materie, *f.*
matter, *n.* materia, *f.*
mature, *v.* maturare; scadere
maxim, *n.* massima, *f.*
May, maggio
measure, *n.* misura, *f.*
measure, *v.* misurare
measurement, *n.* misurazione, *f.*
mechanism, *n.* meccanismo, *m.*
mechanize, *v.* meccanizzare
medium, *n.* mediano, *m.*
meeting, *n.* riunione, *f.*
member, *n.* socio, *m.*
memorial, *n.* memoriale, *m.*
menace, *v.* minacciare
mention, *v.* menzionare
mercantile, mercantile
merchandise, *n.* mercanzia, *f.*
merchant, *n.* mercante, *m.*
merit, *n.* merito, *m.*
messenger, *n.* corriere, *n.*
metal, *n.* metallo, *m.*
metallic, metallico
metallurgical shares, *n.* metallici, *m.*
method, *n.* metodo, *m.*
metre, *n.* metro, *m.*
metric, metrico,
mind, *n.* mente, *f.*
mineral, *n.* minerale, *m.*
mining shares, *n.* minerari, *m.*
minister, *n.* ministro, *m.*
ministry, *n.* ministero, *m.*
mission, *n.* missione, *f.*
misunderstand, *v.* malintendere
mode, *n.* modo, *m.*
model, *n.* modello, *m.*
module, *n.* modulo, **m.**

monetary, monetario
money, *n.* denaro, *m.*; soldo, *m.*
money-changer, *n.* cambiavalute, *m.*
money-market, *n.* mercato del danaro, *m.*
money-order, *n.* vaglia, *m.*
monogram, *n.* siglia, *f.*
monopolist, *n.* monopolista, *m.*
monopolistic, monpolistico
monopolize, *v.* monopolizzare
month, *n.* mese, *m.*
monthly, mensile
mooring, n. ormeggio, *m.*
morality, *n.* moralità, *f.*
moratorium, *n.* moratoria, *f.*
mortgage, *n.* ipoteca, *f.*
mortgage, *v.* ipotecare
mortgagee, *n.* creditore ipotecario, *m.*
mortgagor, *n.* debitore ipotecario, *m.*
most, massimo
motion, moto, *m.*; mozione, *f.*
motive, *n.* motivo, *m.*
motor, *n.* motore, *m.*
motor-boat, *n.* motoscafo, *m.*
motor-cycle, *n.* motocicletta, *f.*
mould, *n.* stampo, *m.*
movable, mobiliare
movement, *n.* movimento, *m.*
multiple, multiple
municipal, municipale
mutual, mutuale; mutuo; reciproco
mutual association, *n.* mutualità, *f.*

N

narrate, *v.* narrare
narration, *n.* narratura, *f.*
narrator, *n.* narratore, *m.*
narrow, stretto
national, nazionale
nationality, *n.* nazionalità, *f.*
nationalization, *n.* nazionalizzazione, *f.*
natural, naturale
naturalize, naturalizzare
nature, *n.* natura, *f.*
nautical, nautico
naval, navale
navigability, *n.* navigabilità, *f.*
navigable, navigabile

navigate, *v.* navigare
navigation, *n.* navigazione, *f.*
navy, *n.* marina, *f.*
necessary, necessario
necessity, *n.* necessità, *f.*
need, *n.* bisogno, *m.*
need, *v.* bisognare; occorrere
negotiability, *n.* negoziabilità, *f.*
negotiable, negoziabile
negotiate, *v.* negoziare; contrattare
negotiation, *n.* negoziazione, *f.*
negative, negativo
neighbouring, limitrofo
net, netto
net proceeds, *n.* netto ricavo, *m.*
neutral, neutrale; neutro
neutrality, *n.* neutralità, *f.*
new, nuovo
news, *n.* notizie, *f.*
newspaper, *n.* giornale, *m.*
next, prossimo
nominal, nominale
nominate, *v.* nominare
nomination, nomina, *f.*
normal, normale
notary, *n.* notario, *m.*
notation, *n.* numerazione, *f.*
note, *n.* nota, *f.*
note, *v.* notare
note-book, *n.* taccuino, *m.*
notice, *n.* avviso, m.; notifica, *f.*
notice, *v.* osservare
notification, *n.* notificazione, *f.*
notify, *v.* notificare
November, novembre
null, nullo
nullity, *n.* nullità, *f.*
number, *n.* numero, *m.*
number, *v.* numerare
numeral, *n.* numero, m.; cifra, *f.*
numeration, *n.* numerazione, *f.*
numerator, *n.* numeratore, *m.*
numerous, numeroso

O

oath, *n.* giuramento, *m.*
obligatory, obbligatorio

oblige, *v.* obbligare
object, *n.* oggetto, *m.*
object, *v.* obiettare
objection, *n.* obiezione, *f.*
obliterate, *v.* obliterare
observation, *n.* osservazione, *f.*
observe, *v.* osservare
obstacle, *n.* ostacolo, *m.*
obtain, *v.* ottenere
obvious, ovvio; patente
occasion, *n.* occasione, *f.*
occupation, *n.* occupazione, *f.*
occupy, *v.* occupare
occurrence, *n.* occorenza, *f.*
October, ottobre
offence, *n.* offesa, *f.*
offend, *v.* offendere
offensive, *n.* offensiva, *f.*
offensive, offensivo
offer, *n.* offerta, *f.*
offer, *v.* offrire
offer (on), in vendita
office, *n.* ufficio, m.; sede, *f.*
office (post), *n.* ufficio postale, *m.*
officer, *n.* ufficiale, *m.*
official, ufficiale
oil, *n.* olio, m.; petrolio, *m.*
oil well, *n.* pozzo d'olio, *m.*
omission, *n.* omissione, *f.*
omit, *v.* omettere
open, aperto
opening, *n.* apertura, f.; sbocco, *m.*
operation, *n.* operazione, *f.*
operator, *n.* operatore, *m.*
opinion, *n.* opinione, f.; parere, *m.*
opportunity, *n.* opportunità, *f.*
oppose, *v.* opporre
opposition, *n.* opposizione, *f.*
optimism, *n.* ottimismo
optimize, *v.* ottimizzare
option, *n.* opzione, f.; contratto a premio, *m.*
orally, oralmente
order, *n.* ordinazione, f.; comando, *m.*
order, *v.* ordinare
ordinary, ordinario
organic, organico
organization, *n.* organizzazione, *f.*
organize, *v.* organizzare

origin, *n.* origine, *f.*
original, originale
originating, originario
oscillate, *v.* oscillare
oscillating, oscillante
oscillation, *n.* oscillazione, *f.*
output, *n.* gettito, *m.*; produzione, *f.*; uscita, *f.*
outstanding, pendente; impressionante
overcome, *v.* superare
overdraw, *v.* eccedere
overseas, oltremare
owe, *v.* dovere
own, *v.* possedere
owner, *n.* possessore, *m.*
ownership, *n.* possesso, *m.*; proprietà, *f.*

P

package, *n.* corredo, *n.*
packer, *n.* imballatore
packet, *n.* pacchetto, *m.*
packing paper, *n.* carta da imballagio, *f.*
page, *n.* pagina, *f.*
paid, pagato; versato
paid-up capital, *n.* capitale versato, *m.*
pair, *n.* paio, *m.*
pamphlet, *n.* manifestino, *m.*
panic, *n.* panico, *m.*
paper, *n.* carta, *f.*
par, *n.* pari, *m.*
paralize, *v.* paralizzare
parcel, *n.* collo, *m.*; pacco, *m.*
parity, *n.* parità, *f.*
part, *n.* parte, *f.*
partial, parziale
participant, *n.* partecipante, *m.*
participate, *v.* partecipare
participation, *n.* partecipazione, *f.*
particular, particolare
passable, passibile
passage, *n.* passaggio, *m.*
passenger, *n.* passeggiero, *m.*
passive, passivo
passport, *n.* passaporto, *m.*
patent, *n.* brevetto, *m.*
patent, *v.* brevettare
patrimonial, patrimoniale

pay, *n.* paga, *f.*
pay, *v.* pagare
pay duty, *v.* sdaziare
pay off, *v.* sdebitare
pay packet, *n.* busta-paga, *f.*
payable, pagabile
payee, *n.* beneficiario, *m.*
payer, *n.* pagatore, *m.*
payment, *n.* pagamento, *m.*
payment by instalments, *n.* pagamento a rate, *m.*
payroll, *n.* foglio paga, *m.*
peace, *n.* pace, *f.*
peaceful, pacifico
pecuniary, pecuniario
penal, penale
penalty, *n.* penalità, *f.*
pending business, *n.* pendenza, *f.*
pension, n. pensione, *f.*
pensioner, *n.* pensionato, *m.*
per cent, per cento
percentage, *n.* percentuale, *f.*
perfect, perfetto
period, *n.* periodo, *m.*
perishable, deperibile
permanent, permanente
permission, *n.* permesso, *m.*
person, *n.* persona, *f.*
personalize, *v.* personalizzare
personnel, *n.* personale, *m.*
persuade, *v.* persuadere
petition, *n.* istanza, *f.*; ricorso, *m.*
petitioner, *n.* ricorrente, *m.*
piece, *n.* pezzo, *m.*
pilot, *n.* pilota, *m.*
pilot light, *n.* spia, *f.*
pilotage, *n.* pilotaggio, *m.*
place, *n.* posto, *m.*
place, *v.* collocare
plan, *n.* piano, *m.*; progetto, *m.*
plan, *v.* progettare
plant, *n.* pianta, *f.*; impianto, *m.*
pleasure, *n.* piacere, *m.*; piacimento, *m.*
pledge, *n.* impegno, *m.*; pegno, *m.*
pledge, *v.* impegnare
point, *n.* punto, *m.*
point out, *v.* rilevare
policy, *n.* politica, *f.*; polizza, *f.*
politics, *n.* politica, *f.*

port, *n.* porto, *m.*
portable, portabile
portfolio, *m.* portafoglio, *m.*
positive, positivo
possession, *n.* possedimento, *m.*
possible, possibile
possibility, *n.* possibilità, *f.*
post, *n.* posta, *f.*; situazione, *f.*
post, *v.* impostare; registrare a mastro
postage, *n.* porto, *m.*; affrancatura, *f.*
postage paid, porto affrancato
postage unpaid, porto assegnato
postal, postale
poster, *n.* avviso, *m.*; manifesto, *m.*
postman, *n.* postino, *m.*
postpone, *v.* prorogare
postponement, *n.* proroga, *f.*
postscript, *n.* poscritto, *m.*
potentiality, *n.* potenzialità, *f.*
pound, *n.* lira sterlina, *f.*
power, *n.* potere, *m.*; potenza, *f.*
practical, pratico
practice, *n.* pratica, *f.*
practise, *v.* praticare
preamble, *n.* preambolo, *m.*
precedent, *n.* precedente, *m.*
precipitation, *n.* precipitazione, *f.*
precipitate, *v.* precipitare
precise, preciso
precision, *n.* precisione, *f.*
predominant, predominante
prefer, *v.* preferire
preferable, preferibile
preference, *n.* preferenza, *f.*
prejudice, *n.* pregiudizio, *m.*
prejudice, *v.* pregiudicare
prejudicial, pregiudizievole
premium, *n.* premio, *m.*
preparation, *n.* preparazione, *f.*
preparatory, preparatorio
prepare, *v.* preparare
prerogative, *n.* prerogativa, *f.*
prescribed, prescritto
prescription, *n.* prescrizione, *f.*
presence, *n.* presenza, *f.*
present, *v.* presentare
present letter, *n.* presente, *f.*
present time, *n.* presente, *m.*
preside, *v.* presidere
presidency, *n.* presidenza, *f.*

president, *n.* presidente, *m.*
pressure, *n.* pressione, *f.*
presumption, *n.* presunzione, *f.*
presumptive, presuntivo
pretext, *n.* pretesto, *m.*
previous, precedente
price, *n.* prezzo, *m.*
primacy, *n.* primato, *m.*
principle, *n.* principio
print, *v.* stampare
print out, *m.* stampa, *f.*
printer, *n.* stampante, *f.*; tipografo, *m.*
private, privato
privately, privatamente
privilege, *n.* privilegio, *m.*
privilege, *v.* privilegiare
probable, probabile
probability, *n.* probabilità, *f.*
problem, *n.* problema, *m.*
proceed, *v.* procedere
proceedings, *n.* procedimento, *m.*
proceeds, *n.* provento, *m.*
process, *n.* processo, *m.*
proclaim, *v.* proclamare
proclaimer, *n.* proclamatore, *m.*
proclamation, *n.* proclama, *m.*
procurator, *n.* procuratore, *m.*
produce, *n.* prodotto, *m.*
produce, *v.* produrre
producer, *n.* produttore, *m.*
product, *n.* prodotto, *m.*
production, *n.* produzione, *f.*
profession, *n.* professione, *f.*
professional, professionale
profit, *n.* profitto, *m.*
profit, *v.* profittare
profitable, profittevole
programme, *n.* programma, *m.*
programme, *v.* programmare; progettare
programmer, *n.* programmatore, *n.*
programming, *n.* programmazione, *f.*
progress, *n.* progresso, *m.*
progress, *v.* progredire
progression, *n.* progressione, *f.*
progressive, progressivo
promise, *n.* promessa, *f.*
promise, *v.* promettere
promote, *v.* promuovere
promotion, *n.* promozione, *f.*
pronounce, *v.* pronunziare

property, *n.* proprietà, *f.*
proportion, *n.* proporzione, *f.*
proportional, proporzionale
proportionally, proporzionalmente
proposal, *n.* proposta, *f.*
propose, *v.* proporre
prospect, *n.* prospettiva, *f.*
prospectus, *n.* prospetto, *m.*
prosperity, *n.* prosperità, *f.*
prosperous, prospero
protect, *v.* proteggere
protection, *n.* protezione, *f.*
protector, *n.* protettore, *m.*
protest, *n.* protesto, *m.*; protesta, *f.*
protest, *v.* protestare
prove, *v.* provare
provide, *v.* provvedere
provision, *n.* provvedimento, *m.*; provvista, *f.*
provisional, provvisorio
proxy, *n.* procura, *f.*
prudence, *n.* prudenza, *f.*
public, *n.* pubblico, *m.*
publication, *n.* pubblicazione, *f.*
publicity, *n.* pubblicità, *f.*
publish, *v.* pubblicare
punch, *v.* punzonare
punch-card, *n.* scheda perforata, *f.*
punching, *n.* punzonatura, *f.*
punching machine, *n.* punzonatrice, *f.*
punctual, puntuale
punctuality, *n.* puntualità, *f.*
punish, *v.* punire
punishable, punibile
purification, *n.* purificatione, *f.*
purify, *v.* purificare
pure, puro
purity, *n.* purità, *f.*
purse, *n.* borsa, *f.*
pursuant to, facendo seguito
pursue, *v.* proseguire
pursuit, *n.* ricerca, *f.*
push-button, *n.* pulsante, *f.*
put, *v.* mettere
put option, *n.* opzione di vendita, *f.*

Q

quadruple, quadruplo

quadruplicate, *v.* quadruplicare
qualification, *n.* qualifica, *f.*
qualify, *v.* qualificare
quality, *n.* qualità, *f.*
quantity, *n.* quantità, *f.*
quarantine, *n.* quarantina, *f.*
quarrel, *n.* bisticcio, *m.*
quarrel, *v.* bisticciare
quarter, *n.* quarto, *m.*; trimestre, *m.*
quarterly, trimestriale
query, *n.* quesito, *m.*
question, *n.* interpellazione, *f.*; questione, *f.*
question, *v.* interpellare
questionable, discutibile
questionnaire, *n.* questionario, *m.*
quick, stretto; celere; veloce
quintal, *n.* quintale
quire, *n.* quaderno, *m.*
quota, *n.* quota, *f.*
quotation, *n.* quotazione, *f.*
quote, *v.* citare; quotare

R

radio telegram, *n.* radiogramma, *m.*
radio telephone, *n.* radiotelefono
railway, *n.* ferrovia, *f.*
raise again, *v.* rialzare
ramification, *n.* ramificazione, *f.*
rate, *n.* saggio, *m.*; tasso, *m.*
rate (discount), *n.* saggio dello sconto, *m.*
ratify, *v.* ratificare
reaction, *n.* reazione, *f.*
read, *v.* leggere
ready, pronto
ready money, *n.* contanti, *m.*
real, reale; attuale
real estate, *n.* beni immobili, *m.*
real time, *n.* tempo reale, *m.*
realization, *n.* realizzazione, *f.*; realizzo, *m.*
realize, *v.* realizzare
reality, *n.* realtà, *f.*
reason, *n.* ragione, *f.*
receipt, *n.* ricevuta, *f.*
receive, *v.* ricevere
receiver, *n.* ricevente, *m.*; ricevitore, *m.*

reception, *n.* ricevimento, *m.*
reciprocity, *n.* reciprocità, *f.*
recommend, *v.* raccommandare
recommendation, *n.* raccomandazione, *f.*
recommender, *n.* raccomandatore, *m.*
recover, *v.* ricuperare
recovery, *n.* ricupero, *m.*
redeem, *v.* redimere
redeemability, *n.* redimibilità, *f.*
redemption, *n.* ammortamento, *m.*
rediscount, *n.* risconto, *m.*
rediscount, *v.* riscontare
redraft, *n.* rivalsa, *f.*
reduce, *v.* ridurre
reduction, *n.* riduzione, *f.*
re-employ, *v.* rimpiegare
re-employment, *n.* rimpiego, *m.*
refer, *v.* riferire
reference, *n.* riferimento, *m.*
reform, *n.* riforma, *f.*
reform, *v.* riformare
refusal, *n.* rifiuto
refuse, *v.* rifiutare
regard, *n.* riguardo, *m.*
register, *n.* registro, *m.*; matricola, *f.*
register, *v.* registrare; raccomandare
regulation, *n.* regolamento, *m.*; regola, *f.*
reject, *v.* rigettare
rejection, *n.* rigetto, *m.*
release, *v.* rilasciare
remainder, *n.* rimanente, *m.*
remediable, rimediabile
remedy, *n.* rimedio, *m.*
remedy, *v.* rimediare
remember, *v.* ricordare
remit, *v.* rimettere
remittance, *n.* rimessa, *f.*
remitter, *n.* mittente, *m.*
remunerate, *v.* rimunerare
remuneration, *n.* rimunerazione, *f.*
remunerative, rimunerativo
render, *v.* rendere
renew, *v.* rinnovare
renewal, *n.* rinnovazione, *f.*
rent, *n.* affitto, *m.*; nolo, *m.*; rendita, *f.*
rent, *v.* affittare
rental, *n.* affitto, *m.*
renunciate, *v.* rinunciare
renunciation, *n.* rinuncia, *f.*

repay, *v.* rimborsare
repayment, *n.* rimborso, *m.*
repeat, *v.* ripetere
repetition, *n.* ripetizione, *f.*; replica, *f.*
reply, *n.* riscontro, *m.*; risposta, *f.*
reply, *v.* rispondere; replicare
reputation, *n.* riputazione, *f.*
request, *n.* richiesta, *f.*; domanda, *f.*
resale, *n.* rivendita, *f.*
reserve, *n.* riserva, *f.*
reserve, *v.* riservare
resolution, *n.* risoluzione, *f.*
resolve, *v.* risolvere
respectability, rispettabilità, *f.*
respectable, rispettabile
respective, rispettivo
rest, *n.* residuo, *m.*
restoration, *n.* ripristino, *m.*
restore, *v.* ripristinare; ristabilire
restricted, ristretto
restriction, *n.* restrizione, *f.*
result, *n.* risultato, *m.*
result, *v.* risultare
resume, *v.* riprendere
resumption, *n.* ripresa, *f.*
return, *n.* ritorno
return, *v.* ritornare
reversibile, riversibile
review, *n.* rivista, *f*; revisione, *f.*
risk, *n.* richio, *m.*
risk, *v.* rischiare
rival, *n.* rivale
round, rotondo
route, *n.* rotta, *f.*
routine, *n.* usanza, *f.*
rubber stamp, *n.* stampino di gomma, *m.*
ruin, *n.* rovina, *f.*
ruin, *v.* rovinare
rule, *n.* regola, *f.*
run, *n.* durata; domanda, *f.*
runner, *n.* messaggero, *m.*; piazzista, *m.*
running total, *n.* progressivo, *m.*

S

sabotage, *n.* sabotaggio, *m.*
sabotage, *v.* sabotare
saboteur, *n.* sabotatore, *m.*

safe, *n.* cassaforte, *f.*
safe, salvo; sicuro
safeguard, *v.* salvaguardare
safety, *n.* salvezza, *f.*
salary, *n.* salario, *m.*; paga, *f.*
sale, *n.* vendita, *f.*; smercio, *m.*
sale by auction, *n.* vendita all'asta, *f.*
sale (retail), *n.* vendita al minuto, *f.*
sale (ready) pronta vendita
sale room, *n.* sala di vendita, *f.*
saleable, vendibile
salesman, *n.* commesso, *m.*; venditore, *m.*
salutation, *n.* saluto, *m.*
salvage, *n.* salvataggio, *m.*
salvage, *v.* salvare
sample, *n.* campione, *m.*; saggio, *m.*
sample book, *n.* campionario, *m.*
sanction, *n.* sanzione, *f.*
sanction, *v.* sanzionare
satisfy, *v.* soddisfare
save, *v.* risparmiare
saving, *n.* risparmio, *m.*
scale, *n.* scala, *f.*
scales, *n.* bilancia, *f.*
scan, *v.* analizzare
scarce, scarso
scarcity, *n.* scarsità, *f.*; carestia, *f.*; mancanza, *f.*
schedule, *n.* orario, *m.*; lita, *f.*; scheda, *f.*
scheme, *n.* schema, *m.*
screen, *n.* schermo, *n.*; video, *m.*
scrip, *n.* certificato provvisorio, *m.*
sea, *n.* mare, *m.*
seal, *n.* bollo, *m.*; sigillo, *m.*
seal, *v.* sigillare
search, *n.* ricerca, *f.*
search, *v.* ricercare
seat, *n.* sede, *f.*
secrecy, *n.* segretezza, *f.*
secret, *n.* segreto, *m.*
secretary, *n.* segretario
secretary's office, *n.* segreteria, *f.*
section, *n.* sezione, *f.*
seize, *v.* confiscare; sequestrare
seizure, *n.* confisca, *f.*; sequestro, *m.*
select, *v.* selezionare; vagliare
selection, *n.* selezione, *f.*
sell, *v.* vendere; smerciare
sell below cost, *v.* vendere

sell off, *v.* liquidare
seller, *n.* venditore
selling price, *n.* prezzo di vendita, *m.*
send, *v.* mandare
sender, *n.* speditore, *m.*
separate, *v.* separare
separation, *n.* separazione, *f.*
September, settembre
sequestrate, *v.* sequestrare
serious, serio
seriously, seriamente
serve, *v.* servire
service, *n.* servizio, *m.*
session, *n.* sessione, *f.*
set, *n.* serie, *f.*
settle, *v.* saldare
settlement, *n.* saldamento, *m.*; definizione, *f.*
share, *n.* azione, *f.*; titolo, *m.*; valore, *m.*
share, *v.* dividere
shareholder, *n.* azionista, *m.*
sheet, *n.* foglio, *m.*
ship, *n.* nave, *f.*
shipowner, *n.* armatore, *m.*
shipwreck, *n.* naufragio, *m.*
shipwreck, *v.* naufragare
shipyard, *n.* cantiere, *m.*
shop, *n.* bottega, *f.*; negozio, *m.*
shop, *v.* fare le spese
shop window, *n.* vetrina, *f.*
shopkeeper, *n.* bottegaio, *m.*
short, corte; breve
shortage, *n.* mancanza, *f.*
short weight, *n.* calo, *m.*
sign, *n.* segno, *m.*
sign, *v.* firmare
signal, *n.* segnale, *m.*
solicitor, *n.* avvocato, *m.*
sorter, *n.* distributore, *m.*
sponsor, *v.* garantire
spread, *n.* estensione, *f.*
spread, *v.* stendere; propagare
stamp, *n.* stampa, *f.*; bollo, *m.*; francobollo, *m.*
stamp, *v.* imprimere; affrancare
standard, *n.* tenore, *m.*
stay, *n.* soggiorno, *m.*
steady, saldo
stipulation, *n.* stipulazione, *f.*

stock, *n.* valore, *m.*; titolo, *m.*; fondo, *m.*
stockbroker, *n.* agente di cambio, *m.*
stock exchange, *n.* borsa valori, *f.*
stock-in-trade, *n.* magazzini, *m.*
stockpile, *n.* arsenale, *m.*
storage, *n.* salvataggio, *m.*
store, *n.* magazzino, *m.*; negozio, *m.*
store, *v.* fornire; salvare
storekeeper, *n.* magazziniere, *m.*
storing, *n.* magazzinaggio
stow, *v.* stivare
stowage, *n.* stivaggio, *m.*
stowing, *n.* stivamento, *m.*
straits, *n.* stretto, *m.*
strictly, strettamente
strike, *n.* sciopero, *m.*
strike, *v.* scioperare
striker, *n.* scioperante, *m.*
structure, *n.* struttura, *f.*
sub-agent, *n.* subagente, *m.*
sub-agency, *n.* subagenzia, *f.*
subcontract, *v.* subappaltare
success, *n.* successo, *m.*
succession, *n.* successione, *f.*
successively, successivamente
successor, *n.* successore, *m.*
suggest, *v.* suggerire
suggestion, *n.* suggerimento, *m.*
subject, *n.* argomento, *m.*
summarize, *v.* riassumere
summary, *n.* riassunto, *m.*; ripielogo, *m.*
superficial, superficiale
superfluous, superfluo
superior, superiore
superiority, *n.* superiorità, *f.*
supplement, *v.* supplemento, *m.*
suppose, supporre
supremacy, *n.* supremazia, *f.*
surname, *n.* cognome, *m.*
susceptibility, *n.* suscettibilità, *f.*
susceptible, suscettibile
switch, *n.* pulsante, *f.*
switch, *v.* deviare
synopsis, *n.* sinossi, *f.*
synoptic, sinottico
synthesis, *n.* sintesi, *f.*
synthetic, sintentico
system, *n.* sistema, *m.*
systematic, sistematico

systematize, *v.* sistemare
systems expert, *n.* sistemista, *m.*

T

tab, *n.* segna-libro, *m.*
table, *n.* tabella, *f.*; tavola, *f.*
tabular, tabellare
tabulate, *v.* catalogare
tabulation, *n.* tabulato, *m.*
tacitly, tacitamente
tact, *n.* tatto, *m.*
tape, *n.* nastro, *m.*; nastrino, *m.*
tape, *v.* registrare su nastro
tare, *n.* tara, *f.*
tariff, *n.* tariffa, *f.*
tarry, *v.* indugiare
tax, *n.* prestazione, *f.*; tassa, *f.*
tax, *v.* tassare
tax payer, *n.* contribuente, *m.*
technical, tecnico
technician, *n.* tecnico, *m.*
technique, *n.* tecnica, *f.*
telegram, *n.* telegramma, *f.*
telegraph, *n.* telegrafo, *m.*
telegraph, *v.* telegrafare
telegraph operator, *n.* telegrafista, *m.*
telegraphic, telegrafico
telegraphy, *n.* telegrafia, *f.*
telephone, *n.* telefono, *m.*
telephone, *v.* telefonare
telephone call, *n.* telefonata, *f.*
telephone operator, *n.* telefonista, *m.*
teleprinter, *n.* telescrivente, *f.*
teletype, *v.* telescrivere
teller, *n.* cassiere, *m.*
temperature, *n.* temperatura, *f.*
temporary, temporaneo
temporize, *v.* temporeggiare
tenancy, *n.* affitto, *m.*
tenant, *n.* inquilino, *m.*
tendency, *n.* tendenza, *f.*
tendentious, tendenzioso
tender, *n.* offerta, *f.*
tender, *v.* offrire
tenor, *n.* scadenza, *f.*
tenth part, *n.* decimo, *m.*
term, *n.* termine, *m.*

terms, *n.* condizioni, *f.*; tenore, *m.*
terrestrial, terrestre
territoriality, *n.* territorialità, *f.*
territory, *n.* territorio, *m.*
test, *n.* prova, *f.*
test, *v.* provare
testament, *n.* testamento, *m.*
testamentary, testamentario
testator, *n.* testatore, *m.*
testify, *v.* testificare
text, *n.* testo, *m.*
textbook, *n.* manuale, *m.*
textual, testuale
third, terzo
third parties, *n.* terzi, *n.*
tide, *n.* marea, *f.*
till, *n.* cassetto, *m.*
title, *n.* titolo, *m.*; rubrica, *f.*
titular, *n.* titolare, *m.*
titular, titolare
tolerance, *n.* tolleranza, *f.*
tolerate, *v.* tollerare
tonnage, *n.* tonnellaggio, *m.*; stazza, *f.*
tonne, *n.* tonnellata, *f.*
tort, *n.* torto, *m.*
total, *n.* totale
totality, *n.* totalità, *f.*
touch, *v.* toccare
trade, *n.* traffico, *m.*; commercio, m.
trade, *v.* trafficare; commerciare
trader, *n.* trafficante, *m.*; mercante, *m.*
trading, *n.* commercio, *m.*
tradition, *n.* tradizione, *f.*
traffic, *n.* traffico, *m.*
trafficker, *n.* commerciante, *m.*
transact, *v.* trattare
transaction, *n.* transazione, *f.*
transcribe, *v.* trascrivere
transcription, *n.* trascrizione, *f.*
transfer, *v.* trasferire
transit, *n.* transito, *m.*
transitory, transitorio
translate, *v.* tradurre
translation, *n.* traduzione, *f.*
translator, *n.* traduttore, *m.*
transmit, *v.* trasmettere
transport, *n.* trasporto, *m.*
transport, *v.* transportare
transport shares, *n.* trasporti, *m.*

travel, *v.* viaggiare
traveller, *n.* piazzista, *m.*
treasurer, *n.* tesoriere, *m.*
treasury, *n.* erario, *m.*
treat, *v.* trattare
treatment, *n.* trattamento, *m.*
treaty, *n.* trattato, *m.*
treble, triplicare
trim, *v.* guarnire
trust, *n.* consorzio, *m.*
turn, *n.* turno, *m.*
turn, *v.* rivolgere; girare
turnover, *n.* movimentazione, *f.*
twofold, doppio
type, *n.* tipo, *m.*; carattere, *m.*
type, *v.* dattiloscrivere
typewriter, *n.* macchina da scrivere, *f.*
typewriting, *n.* dattilografia, *f.*
typewritten, dattilografato
typical, tipico

U

ulterior, ulteriore
unaccepted, respinto
unanimity, *n.* unanimità, *f.*
unanimous, unanimo
understand, *v.* capire
underwrite, *v.* sottoscrivere; assicurare
underwriter, *n* assicuratore, *m.*
undo, *v.* disfare; sciogliere
uniform, uniforme
union, *n.* unione, *f.*
unionist, *n.* unionista, *m.*
unique, unico
unite, *v.* unire
unity, *n.* unità
upkeep, *n.* manutenzione, *f.*
usable, utilizzabile
use, *n.* uso, *m.*
use, *v.* usare
useful, utile
usefully, utilmente
useless, inutile
user, *n.* utente, *m.*
usual, usuale
usurer, *n.* usuario, *m.*
usury, *n.* usura, *f.*

utilitarian, utilitario
utility, utilità, *f.*
utilization, *n.* utilizzazione, *f.*
utilize, *v.* utilizzare
utopia, *n.* utopia, *f.*
utopian, utopistico
utopist, *n.* utopista, *m.*

V

vacancy, *n.* lacuna, *f.*
vacant, vacante
vague, vago
valid, valevole
validity, *n.* validità, *f.*
validly, validamente
valuation, *n.* valutazione, *f.*
value, *n.* valore, *m.; valuta, *f.*
value, *v.* valutare; stimare
valuer, *n.* valutatore, *m.*
variable, variabile
variation, *n.* variazione, *f.*
vend, *v.* vendere
vender, *n.* mercante, *m.*
vendor, *n.* venditore, *m.*
ventilation, *n.* ventilazione, *f.*
veracity, *n.* veridicità, *f.*
verbal, verbale
verbally, verbalmente
verdict, *n.* sentenza, *f.*
verify, *n.* controllare; verificare
video, *n.* video, *m.*
video cassette, *n.* video cassetta, *f.*
video recorder, *n.* registratore video, *m.*
videotape, *n.* video nastro, *m.*
view, *n.* veduta, *f.*
viewing, *n.* esame, *m.*
violate, *v.* violare
violation, *n.* violazione, *f.*
visa, *n.* visto, *m.*
visage, *n.* viso, *m.*
visit, *n.* visita, *f.*
visit, *v.* visitare
visitor, *n.* visitatore, *m.*
voice, *n.* voce, *f.*
void, vuoto; invalido
volume, *n.* volume, *m.*
voluntary, volontario

vote, *n.* votazione, *f.*
vote, *v.* votare
voucher, *n.* buono, *m.*; ricevuta, *f.*
vulnerable, vulnerabile

W

wage, *n.* salario, *m.*; paga, *f.*
wage earner, *n.* salariato, *m.*
wagon, *n.* vagone, *m.*
wagon load, *n.* vagonata, *f.*
want, *n.* bisogno, *m.*
want, *v.* desiderare
wanted (in adv.) cercasi
ware, *n.* articolo, *m.*
warehouse, *n.* magazzino, *m.*
warehousing, *n.* magazzinaggio, *m.*; deposito, *m.*
wares, *n.* mercanzia, *f.*
warn, *v.* avvertire
warning, *n.* avvertimento, *m.*
warrant, *n.* mandato, *m.*
warrant, *v.* garantire
waste, *n.* scarto, *m.*
water, *n.* acqua, *f.*
water, *v.* diluire
watermark, *n.* filigrana, *f.*
water-proof, impermeabile
wave, *n.* onda, *f.*; ondata, *f.*
wealth, *n.* ricchezza, *f.*
wealthy, ricco
wear (& tear), *n.* logorio, *m.*
weigh, *v.* pesare
weigher, *n.* pesatore, *m.*
weighing, *n.* pesata, *f.*; pesatura, *f.*
weight, *n.* peso, *m.*
weight (gross), *n.* peso lordo, *m.*
weight (net), *n.* peso netto, *m.*
weights, *n.* pesa, *f.*
wharf, *n.* imbarcazione, *f.*; molo, *m.*
wharfage, *n.* diritto di sosta, *m.*
wide, largo
width, *n.* larghezza, *f.*
wish, *n.* augurio, *m.*
wish, *v.* augurare
withdraw, *v.* ritirare
withdrawal, *n.* ritiro, *m.*
withdrawal (of money), prelevamento, *m.*

word, *n.* parola, *f.*
word processor, *n.* elaboratore di testi, *m.*
wording, *n.* dicitura, *f.*
wordy, verboso
work, *n.* lavoro, *m.*; opera, *f.*
work, *v.* lavorare; operare
workable, lavorativo
worker, *n.* lavoratore, *m.*; operaio, *m.*
working, *n.* operazione, *f.*
working capital, *n.* capitale circolante, *m.*
workless, disoccupato
works, *n.* fabbrica, *f.*
workshop, *n.* officina, *f.*
worst, pessimo
worth, *n.* valore, *m.*
worthless, senza valore
wreck, *n.* naufragio, *m.*
wreck, *n.* naufragare
writ, *n.* citazione, *f.*; ordine, *m.*
write, *v.* scrivere
writer, *n.* scrittore, *m.*; scrivente, *m.*
writing, *n.* scrittura, *f.*
wrong, sbagliato

Y

yacht, *n.* canotto, *m.*
yard, *n.* iarda, *f*

yard, *n.* cortile, *m.*
yard (goods), *n.* scalo merci, *m.*
year, *n.* anno, *m.*; esercizio, *m.*
year-book, *n.* annuario, *m.*
year (financial), *n.* esercizio finanziario, *m.*
yearly, annuale
yield, *n.* rendita, *f.*; frutto, *m.*
yield, *v.* rendere; produrre
yours, il vostro
yours faithfully, vostro devotissimo

Z

zap, *v.* cancellare
zeal, *n.* zelo, *m.*
zeal (to show), *v.* zelare
zealous, zelante
zealously, zelantemente
zero, *n.* zero, *m.*
zeroize, *v.* azzerare
zonal, zonale
zone, *n.* zona, *f.*
zone, *v.* zonizzare

Index

Abetone xiv
Abruzzi xviii
Adriatic xi, xii
Aeolus xii
Africa xi, 85
Agrigento xvi
Alassio xii
Alps xii, xiii, xiv
Alto-Adige xviii
Amalfi xii
Ancona xviii
Anzio xvii
Aosta xviii
Apennines xiii, xiv, xv, xvii
Aquila xviii
Arno xiv
Atlantic Ocean xi
Augusta xviii
Austria xii
Autostrada del Sole (*see also* Sun
  Motorway) 42

Banca Commerciale Italiana 30
Banca d'Italia 29
Banca Nazionale di Lavoro 30
Banco di Napoli 30
Banco di Roma 29, 30
Banco di Santo Spirito 29
Banco di Sicilia 30
Bari xviii, 42
Basilicata xviii
Bologna xiii, xviii, 42, 67
Brescia xviii
Brindisi xviii
Britain 42

Byzantium xvii

Calabria xvi
Cagliari xvi, xviii
Campania xvi, xviii
Campobasso xviii
Capri xii
Catania xvi, xviii
Cattaneo, Carlo 8
Cervino xii
Ceuta xi
Civitàvecchia xviii
Como, Lake xii
Credito Italiano 29, 30, 53, 62
Cremona xiii

Dante xvii

Elba xii
Emilia xiii
Emilia-Romagna xviii
Emilian Apennines xiv
Eridanus xiii
Europe xii, xv, xviii, 85

Fiat 13
Firenze 65
Florence xiii, xiv, xvii, xviii, 29, 42, 67
Flotta Lauro 52
France xii, 86
Friuli xviii
Futa xiv

165

Garda, Lake   xii
Genoa   xiv, xvii, xviii, 29, 37, 49, 67
Genova   55
Gibraltar   xi
Gran Sasso   xiv
Guerrazzi, Francesco D.   65

Herculanum   xv

Imperia   xviii
Ionian Sea   xi
Ischia   xii
Iseo, Lake   xii
Isola Tiberina   xv
Istituto Mobiliare Italiano   29, 30

La Spezia   xviii
Latin   xviii
Latium   xiv, xvi, xviii
Leghorn   xiv, xv, xvii, xviii
Levant   49
Liguria   xiv, xviii
Ligurian Sea   xi, xiv
Lipari   xii
Livorno   xv
Lombard Street   29
Lombardy   xiii, xviii
London   29
Londra   79, 80
Lucca   xviii, 29
Lugano, Lake   xii

Maggiore, Lake   xii
Mantua   xiii
Marche   xviii
Marsala   xvi
Matterhorn   xii
Mediterranean Sea   xi, xv, xvii, 29, 85
Messina   xvi, xviii, 47
Messina Straits   xii
Middle Ages   xv, xvii, 16, 49
Milan   xiii, xvii, xviii, 42, 67, 78, 81
Milano   59, 67, 68, 69, 81
Modena   60
Molise   xviii

Monaco   86
Monte Bianco   xii
Monte dei Paschi Bank   29
Montereale   xiv
Monte Rosa   xii
Mount Etna   xvi
Murano   xiii, xvii

Naples   xii, xiii, xv, xvi, xviii, 42, 67
Napolean   xii

Ostia   xiv

Padua   xviii
Palatine Hill   xv
Palermo   xvi, xviii, 67, 76, 77
Paris   86
Perugia   xviii
Pescara   xviii
Piacenza   xiii, 29
Piedmont   xii, xviii
Pisa   xiv, xvi, 27, 49
Po   xii, xiii, xvii
Pompeii   xv, 47
Ponte Vecchio   65
Pope   xi
Pope Gregory   4
Portofino   xii
Positano   xii
Potenza   xviii
Provenzal, Dino   40
Puglia   xviii

Ragusa   xvi
Rapallo   xii
Reggio   xviii
Riccione   xii
Rimini   xi
Rio Nero   xiv
Risorgimento   xi
Riviera di Levante   xii
Riviera di Ponente   xii
Roma   xv, 6, 12, 27, 78, 79, 80
Rome   xi, xiii, xiv, xv, xviii, 12, 14, 29,
   42, 67, 79

Romulus xv

Sacchetti, Franco 40
Salerno xii
San Giovanni 47
San Marino xi
Sardinia xii, xvi, xviii, 86
Savona xviii
Sicilia 47
Sicily xii, xvi, xviii
SICIT Spa 95
Siena 29, 82
Simplon xiii
St. Gotthard xiii
Stromboli xii
Sun Motorway (*see also* Autostrada del
    Sole) xiii
Switzerland xii

Taranto xviii
Tevere xiv
Tiber xi, xiv, xv
Torino 12, 30, 31, 60

Trentino xviii
Trento xviii
Trieste xviii, 67
Tripoli 49
Turin xii, xiv, xviii, 12, 39, 67
Tuscany xiv, xv, xviii
Tyrrhenian Sea xii, xiv

Ulysses xii
Umbria xviii

Val d'Aosta xviii
Vatican State xi, xv
Veneto xiii, xviii
Venezia-Giulia xviii
Venice xi, xvii, xviii, 29, 49, 67
Verona xviii
Vesuvius xvi
Via Emilia xii
Vulcano xii

Yugoslavia xii